# Governing Maya Communities
# and Lands in Belize

# Governing Maya Communities and Lands in Belize

*Indigenous Rights, Markets, and Sovereignties*

LAURIE KROSHUS MEDINA

RUTGERS UNIVERSITY PRESS
NEW BRUNSWICK, CAMDEN, AND NEWARK, NEW JERSEY
LONDON AND OXFORD

Rutgers University Press is a department of Rutgers, The State University of New Jersey, one of the leading public research universities in the nation. By publishing worldwide, it furthers the University's mission of dedication to excellence in teaching, scholarship, research, and clinical care.

Library of Congress Cataloging-in-Publication Data

Names: Medina, Laurie Kroshus, 1962– author.
Title: Governing Maya communities and lands in Belize : indigenous rights, markets, and sovereignties / Laurie Kroshus Medina.
Description: New Brunswick, NJ : Rutgers University, 2024. | Includes bibliographical references and index.
Identifiers: LCCN 2023041284 | ISBN 9781978837744 (paperback) | ISBN 9781978837751 (hardback) | ISBN 9781978837768 (epub) | ISBN 9781978837775 (pdf)
Subjects: LCSH: Indians of Central America—Government policy—Belize. | Indians of Central America—Land tenure—Belize. | Indians of Central America—Legal status, laws, etc.—Belize. | Ecotourism—Belize. | Land tenure—Government policy—Belize. | BISAC: SOCIAL SCIENCE / Anthropology / Cultural & Social | POLITICAL SCIENCE / World / Caribbean & Latin American
Classification: LCC F1445 .M54 2024 | DDC 333.2097282—dc23/eng/20231025
LC record available at https://lccn.loc.gov/2023041284

A British Cataloging-in-Publication record for this book is available from the British Library.

Copyright © 2024 by Laurie Kroshus Medina

All rights reserved

No part of this book may be reproduced or utilized in any form or by any means, electronic or mechanical, or by any information storage and retrieval system, without written permission from the publisher. Please contact Rutgers University Press, 106 Somerset Street, New Brunswick, NJ 08901. The only exception to this prohibition is "fair use" as defined by U.S. copyright law.

Maps 5 through 8 from *Maya Atlas: The Struggle to Preserve Maya Land in Southern Belize* by the Toledo Maya Cultural Council and The Toledo Alcades Association, published by North Atlantic Books, copyright © 1997 by the Toledo Maya Cultural Council and The Toledo Alcades Association. Used by permission of the publisher.

References to internet websites (URLs) were accurate at the time of writing. Neither the author nor Rutgers University Press is responsible for URLs that may have expired or changed since the manuscript was prepared.

♾ The paper used in this publication meets the requirements of the American National Standard for Information Sciences—Permanence of Paper for Printed Library Materials, ANSI Z39.48-1992.

rutgersuniversitypress.org

# Contents

List of Illustrations   vii
Preface   ix
Acronyms   xiii

1. Competing Rationalities of Rule: Sovereignty, Markets, and Indigenous Rights   1
2. Histories of Belize: Sovereignties Claimed, Sovereignties Performed   22
3. NGO Government of the State: Conducting the Conduct of State Officials   42
4. Governing through the Market: Managing Tropical Nature and Maya Communities   64
5. Contested Histories and Histories of Contestation in Southern Belize   83
6. The Production of Indigenous Rights: Indigenous Advocacy in the United Nations and the Inter-American Human Rights System   101
7. Advancing the Maya Claim through the Belizean Judicial System   121
8. Negotiating the Interface of Maya Customary Tenure and Belizean Law   141

Conclusion   159

Glossary of Non-English Terms   165
Notes   167
Bibliography   179
Index   193

# Illustrations

### Maps

| | | |
|---|---|---|
| 1 | Sixteenth-century Spanish colonial centers in relation to lowland Maya settlements and languages mentioned in the text | 24 |
| 2 | Contemporary Belize | 28 |
| 3 | Expanse of protected areas in Belize (all categories of protection included) | 56 |
| 4 | Cockscomb Basin Wildlife Sanctuary and surrounding Maya communities | 65 |
| 5 | Maya communities in the Toledo District | 88 |
| 6 | Extent and overlap of reservations, logging concessions, and lands used and claimed by Maya communities in Toledo District | 93 |

### Photos

| | | |
|---|---|---|
| 1 | The Cockscomb Basin; formation for which basin is named at left | 55 |
| 2 | Members of Maya Centre Women's Group | 73 |
| 3 | Maya Centre Women's Group Gift Shop | 74 |
| 4 | San Jose Village, Toledo District | 86 |
| 5 | Village map of Santa Cruz Village from *Maya Atlas* | 96 |
| 6 | Map of Aggregate Maya land use/land claim from *Maya Atlas* | 97 |
| 7 | Maya Leaders Alliance spokesperson Cristina Coc and alcaldes at celebration of Maya legal victory in Indian Creek, April 2015 | 142 |

8 Antoinette Moore, attorney for the Maya, addressing audience at celebration of Maya legal victory in Indian Creek, April 2015    142

9 Belize Territorial Volunteers on trip to the Sarstoon River    151

## Tables

1 Belize population by ethnicity, 1980–2010    38

# Preface

The research that informs this book has spanned more than two decades, like the legal cases it analyzes, and ranged widely across conservation, tourism, government, legal, and community sectors. I have incurred innumerable debts in the process. I am grateful for the research funding that enabled me to carry out this research. The project began with funding from a Research and Writing Grant from the John T. and Catherine D. MacArthur Foundation and has continued with support provided by the Dean of International Studies and Programs and the Dean of Social Science at Michigan State University (MSU) as part of compensation for administrative appointments. MSU's Center for the Advanced Study of International Development also funded one summer of research. To all, my thanks.

I am extremely grateful to be part of a vibrant community of scholars pursuing research in Belize, including senior Belizeanists Joseph Palacio, Assad Shoman, Nigel Bolland, and Rick Wilk, whose scholarship has always provided a model and inspiration. It is exciting to join a new generation of scholars whose work has enriched my understandings immeasurably. Thank you to Melissa Johnson, Becky Zarger, Jim Stinson, Kristina Baines, Sean Downey, Joel Wainwright, Liza Grandia, Levi Gahman, and Odile Hoffman. I especially appreciate the insightful research of an expanding cohort of Belizean scholars, including Angel Cal, Vincent Palacio, Pio Saqui, Dylan Vernon, and Filiberto Penados.

My colleagues at MSU have also been wonderful sources of intellectual support and provocation, which I have valued in equal measure! My grateful thanks to Anne Ferguson, Bill Derman, Brandt Peterson, Najib Hourani, Lucero Radonic, and Jennifer Goett. During their time as graduate students, Keri Brondo and Rowenn Kalman also provided valuable support as research assistants and interlocutors.

I offer my appreciation to Jim Anaya and Antoinette Moore for responding to queries regarding the Maya lands cases and to Ariel Dulitzky for helping me to better understand the Inter-American Human Rights System.

At the Belize Audubon Society (BAS), I had the good fortune of speaking with presidents and board members, including Earl Green, Therese Rath, and the late Miss Jean Shaw, Miss Meg Craig, and Carlos Santos. I am also grateful to a long line of BAS executive directors, beginning with the first executive director, Mickey Craig, and continuing through Osmany Salas, Valdemar Andrade, Anna Hoare, and Amanda Acosta.

I appreciate the generosity of the many leaders and members of the Belize Tourism Industry Association and the Belize Ecotourism Association, as well as staff of the Belize Tourism Board, who were all generous with their time and expertise. Weiszman Pat, in the former Ministry of Tourism and the Environment, was also extremely helpful with documents and policies; thank you!

I am deeply grateful and much indebted to the individuals and families in Maya Centre who engaged with me through interviews and conversations, and shared their perspectives and insights. B'otik te'ex! I want to express my warmest thanks to Ernesto and Aurora Saqui and their sons Rigoberto, Gabriel, and Marroquin, whose lodge always offered a home away from home, and whose many kindnesses have been much appreciated across the years. Liberato Saqui accepted the challenge of teaching me Mopan, and I am very grateful for his efforts and his patience. I am also indebted to Federica Saqui, who assisted with focus groups; I could not have carried these out without her able support. In Punta Gorda, I offer my deepest thanks to Pablo Mis and Cristina Coc, from whom I learned much about the daily work of supporting community self-governance, and to the alcaldes and other Maya leaders, who allowed me to participate in meetings in which self-governance flourished.

For the excellent maps that contribute so much to this book, I thank Mike Siegel at Rutgers Geography for working patiently with me to make them perfect. I am also extremely grateful to Tony Rath of Naturalight Productions, Dirk Francisco/BAS, Judy Lumb of Producciones de la Hamaca, Wil Maheia of PGTV, and North Atlantic Press for granting permission to use their images to illustrate the stories presented in the pages that follow.

The *American Anthropologist* and the *Political and Legal Anthropology Review* kindly granted permission to use portions of articles previously published in their pages. Portions of the data and analysis from chapter 3 were published in Laurie Kroshus Medina (2010), "When Government Targets 'The State': Transnational NGO Government and the State in Belize," *Political and Legal Anthropology Review* 33, no. 2: 245–263. Data and analysis from chapter 4 were published in Laurie Kroshus Medina (2015), "Governing through the Market: Neoliberal Environmental Government in Belize," *American Anthropologist* 117, no. 2: 272–284. And part of chapters 6 and 7 were published in Laurie Kroshus Medina (2016), "The Production of Indigenous Land Rights: Judicial Decisions across National, Regional, and Global Scales," *Political and Legal Anthropology Review* 39, no. S1: 139–153.

Finally, I want to express my deep gratitude to my family for their love and support and their ongoing engagement with this project. My son, Alejandro, and my daughter, Amalia, each began ethnographic field research in southern Belize at the

PREFACE

age of six months, with my husband, Chema, caring for them while I was interviewing, taking notes, attending meetings, and transcribing. All of them have continued their engagement with good cheer over the two decades that followed, and that has meant so much to me. Thank you to Alejandro for helping to prepare the census table and to Amalia for critical assistance with illustrations and the bibliography! I am so grateful to you all for accompanying me on this journey!

# Acronyms

| | |
|---|---|
| ADRIP | American Declaration on the Rights of Indigenous Peoples |
| BAS | Belize Audubon Society |
| BDF | Belize Defense Force |
| BTB | Belize Tourism Board |
| BTIA | Belize Tourism Industry Association |
| BTV | Belize Territorial Volunteers |
| CBWS | Cockscomb Basin Wildlife Sanctuary |
| CCJ | Caribbean Court of Justice |
| CERD | Committee on the Elimination of Racial Discrimination |
| CORPI | Coordinadora Regional de Pueblos Indigenas |
| FCD | Friends of Conservation and Development |
| HRC | Human Rights Committee |
| IACHR | Inter-American Commission on Human Rights |
| IACtHR | Inter-American Court of Human Rights |
| ICCPR | International Convention on Civil and Political Rights |
| ICERD | International Convention on the Elimination of Racial Discrimination |
| ICESCR | International Convention on Economic, Social, and Cultural Rights |
| ILO | International Labor Organization |
| ILRC | Indian Law Resource Center |
| IWGIA | International Working Group on Indigenous Affairs |
| KCB | Kekchi Council of Belize |
| MMO | Mundo Maya Organization |
| NGO | nongovernmental organization |

| | |
|---|---|
| OAS | Organization of American States |
| PUP | Peoples United Party |
| RLC | Reservation Lands Committee |
| SATIIM | Sarstoon-Temash Institute for Indigenous Management |
| TAA | Toledo Alcaldes Association |
| TCGA | Toledo Cacao Growers Association |
| TMCC | Toledo Maya Cultural Council |
| UDHR | Universal Declaration of Human Rights |
| UDP | United Democratic Party |
| UN | United Nations |
| UNDRIP | United Nations Declaration on the Right of Indigenous Peoples |
| WCS | Wildlife Conservation Society |
| WWF | World Wildlife Foundation |
| WGIP | Working Group on Indigenous Populations |
| WCIP | World Council of Indigenous Peoples |

# Governing Maya Communities and Lands in Belize

CHAPTER 1

# Competing Rationalities of Rule

SOVEREIGNTY, MARKETS, AND INDIGENOUS RIGHTS

A van carrying tourists turned off the red gravel "highway" in southern Belize onto the rutted road that wound its way into the Cockscomb Basin Wildlife Sanctuary, the world's first jaguar reserve and the rainforest portion of their "reef and rainforest" vacation. Dense foliage loomed on the left; the thatched-roof houses of the Mopan Maya village of Maya Centre dotted the cleared space to the right. Past the village, as the forest began to press in on them from both sides, the van suddenly ground to a halt. A fallen tree blocked the road ahead. A hand-lettered sign posted on a nearby tree read, "Park closed until further notice." The disappointed tourists were forced to turn back.

The tree blocking the access road to the jaguar sanctuary had not been felled by natural forces. Residents of Maya Centre had chopped it down.

In 1986, the Belizean government had designated the forested peaks of the Cockscomb Range and the basin to their south as a jaguar sanctuary, at the urging of Belizean and North American conservation nongovernmental organizations (NGOs). Conservation NGOs pitched ecotourism as a means to generate revenues to fund management of the sanctuary and—at the same time—expand the national economy.

After the sovereign act of establishing the sanctuary on lands designated as state property, the Minister of Natural Resources delegated most responsibility for managing the Cockscomb to a Belizean conservation NGO, the Belize Audubon Society (BAS). Audubon managed the sanctuary through an alliance with transnational conservation organizations. NGOs from the global North funded the construction of tourism infrastructure in the sanctuary, and ecotourism subsequently drew the Cockscomb and its protected nature into the sphere of market exchange. Tourist demand and tourism revenues began to drive the decisions of both state and conservation NGO actors regarding the sanctuary.

The creation of the reserve displaced the residents of Mopan and Q'eqchi' Maya communities near the Cockscomb from lands and resources upon which they had depended for livelihoods. Villagers from one community located inside the Cockscomb Basin were forced to leave their homes and fields and relocate to Maya Centre, just outside the basin. Prohibited from hunting or cultivating subsistence food crops on lands now enclosed in the wildlife sanctuary, Maya villagers were forced to seek livelihoods through market exchange. Many Maya Centre residents sought such opportunities in ecotourism, offering tours, cold drinks, or woven baskets to tourists.

Yet, a decade later, in 1997, Mopan women from Maya Centre felled a tree across the access road to the sanctuary to disrupt the operation of the ecotourism market and the production of the Cockscomb as a commodity. Maya Centre villagers had recently collaborated with other Maya communities in southern Belize to map the lands they had traditionally used, in support of a claim for Indigenous rights to those lands in Belizean and inter-American courts. The lands claimed by Maya Centre included lands within the Cockscomb Basin. Emboldened by their political mobilization, residents of Maya Centre challenged the existence and operation of the wildlife sanctuary, issuing that challenge both as bearers of Indigenous rights to lands and as market subjects seeking greater compensation for their loss of access to lands.

Although the government had ceded management of the wildlife sanctuary to the Belize Audubon Society for a decade by this time, the Forestry Department Head responded to the fallen tree with a second performance of state sovereignty: he threatened to exercise force to reopen the Cockscomb for tourism. "We will send in troops, take over, patrol!" he asserted. Forestry Department officials and leaders of the Belize Audubon Society arrived in Maya Centre accompanied by police. However, the Audubon Society executive director requested permission to negotiate with villagers, and those negotiations produced an agreement that ensured increased incomes from tourism to Maya Centre residents. This agreement allowed the Cockscomb Basin Wildlife Sanctuary to continue to operate as an international ecotourism commodity, while the Maya land claims made their way through national and inter-American judicial systems.

This book explores how people and nature—Mopan and Q'eqchi' Maya communities in southern Belize and the hills and valleys, forests and fields on which they depend—are governed through competing rationalities of rule that overlap, lean on, challenge, and struggle with one another. A neoliberal rationality of government mobilized market forces to manage both Maya communities and tropical forests. The Belizean state selectively performed sovereignty over the territory it claims through the exercise—or threat—of force. And the Maya claim to Indigenous rights to lands challenged market logics and disrupted practices of state sovereignty. I explore how these distinct rationalities of rule intersected in struggles over lands and livelihoods, tropical forests and tourism, and practices of sovereignty in southern Belize.

## Governing through the Market: The Neoliberalization of Nature

My analysis of these developments in Belize engages two key threads in the political ecology literature on neoliberalism and nature. The first thread explores how neoliberal policies that forced reductions in state budgets resulted in the devolution of responsibilities for managing the environment from the state to NGOs, corporations, or communities (Agrawal 2005; Bryant 2002; Castree 2007; Igoe and Brockington 2007; Igoe et al. 2010; Li 2005; Neumann 2001; Schroeder 2005; Tsing et al. 2005:28). The second thread asserts that the increasing commodification of nature was transforming environmental crises into opportunities for capitalist accumulation (Brockington and Duffy 2010; Brockington and Scholfield 2010; Buscher and Dressler 2012; Buscher et al. 2012:20; Igoe and Brockington 2007).[1] If trees had previously been commodified in their dead form, as timber, they were now commodified in their living form, as "biodiversity" or "rainforests" to be consumed aesthetically by ecotourists.[2]

I integrate governance and commodification strands of the literature on neoliberalism and nature by exploring the commodification of nature as part of the process of governing nature and people. In Belize, although the Minister of Natural Resources devolved responsibility for managing the Cockscomb Basin Wildlife Sanctuary and the Maya communities on its perimeter from the Forestry Department to the Belize Audubon Society, governance has devolved in even more significant ways to "the market," through the implementation of ecotourism. Approaching ecotourism as a technique of neoliberal environmental government, I demonstrate how ecotourism makes it possible for both nature and people to be governed through the market for tropical nature.

## Performing the Sovereign State

Even as they became enmeshed in decentralized forms of neoliberal government, Belizean state officials sometimes prioritized performances of sovereignty. Belligerent incursions by the Guatemalan military to advance Guatemala's claim to the territory of Belize prompted some Belizeans to demand an equally dramatic response from the Belize Defense Force. Instead, the prime minister and the Minister of Foreign Affairs sent notes of protest to their counterparts in the Guatemalan government. Although the notes of protest satisfied the procedures of international law, this response frustrated many Belizeans. Belizean citizens thus mobilized to perform Belizean territorial sovereignty themselves, traveling to the country's western and southern borders to plant Belizean flags.

To consider such performances of Belizean sovereignty, I adopt Michel Foucault's approach to "the state" as a theoretical starting point. Instead of "deducing concrete phenomena from universals," such as the idea of "the state," Foucault urged us to examine concrete practices. Rather than accepting a priori the existence of "the state" as an object, Foucault sought to locate—in *practices*—a "type of rationality that would enable the way of governing to be modeled on something called the state which ... plays the role both of a given ... but also, at the same time, as an objective to be constructed" (Foucault 2008:3–4).[3] Scholars building on Foucault thus approach "the state" "not as an *actual* structure" but rather as the "*effect of practices* that make such structures *appear to exist*," which Tim Mitchell calls "state effects" (Mitchell 1991:94, emphasis added, 2002; Abrams 1988). Importantly, Judith Butler (1990) calls our attention to the possibility that such practices may fail to produce their intended objects; every attempted performance puts the object to be performed at risk.

Expanding this approach, scholars have similarly deconstructed "sovereignty" and "territory," tracing their genealogies and scrutinizing their production via concrete practices (Cañas Bottos 2015; Das and Poole 2004; Elden 2013; Hansen and Stepputat 2001, 2006; Lindner 2012; Nadasdy 2017). In these analyses, sovereignty appears as "tentative and always emergent" (Hanson and Stepputat 2006:295), the outcome of struggles that produce "sovereign effects," the *apparent* existence of a sovereign (Lindner 2012:12). Similarly, territory is understood as performative, made and remade through practices and political technologies that bound space. Producing territory involves violent acts of exclusion and inclusion, while maintaining such spaces "requires constant vigilance and the mobilization of threat" (Elden 2009:xxx; 2013:9, 17, 326). The production of territory, Stuart Elden contends, is critical for the production of the state: "Territory is not a mere container for state action"; rather, "the control of territory is what makes a state possible" (Elden 2009:xxx).

Recognizing that the practices that construct state, sovereignty, and territory are mutually constituting, my analysis focuses on the critical role played by the production of property in their co-construction. The practices that transform territory into property simultaneously construct or affirm the existence of the sovereign state. The ability to "entitle" people to property and establish the conditions under which they hold property is understood as constitutive of state power (Lund 2016:1199–1200). Property represents a "recognized claim" that empowers both the property holder and the authority that recognizes the claim; thus, the act of creating—authorizing—property "recursively authorizes the authorizer" (Lund 2016:1205–1206, 1221). However, property—like state, territory, and sovereignty—must be "performed into being" and stabilized through "complex assemblages" that include state practices of mapping, titling, taxing, developing, creating or enforcing property law, and granting concessions (Blomley 2014:1296; Keenan 2010:423; Barrera and Latorre 2019; Campbell 2015).

I examine how, when, and by whom the Belizean state, territory, and sovereignty are produced.

## The Production of Indigenous Rights: Implications for States and Sovereignties

Officials acting in the name of the Belizean state have performed sovereignty in southern Belize via the creation of both state and private property in lands. However, Mopan and Q'eqchi' Maya countered state property designations with claims of Indigenous rights to the lands and territories they traditionally use. Conflicts between Maya communities and state actors escalated in the last decades of the twentieth century, as elected leaders and staff from state agencies attempted to transform lands collectively held by Maya communities into individual private property, protected areas, or timber and oil concessions. In response, Q'eqchi' and Mopan Maya in southern Belize mobilized to secure tenure over the lands upon which their livelihoods depended. With the support of allies from a North American Indigenous rights advocacy organization, Maya organizations petitioned the Belize Supreme Court and the Inter-American Commission on Human Rights (IACHR) for recognition of their collective rights to the lands they traditionally used.

Land claims by the Belizean Maya formed part of a strategy by Indigenous rights advocates from across the world to build an international jurisprudence that recognizes Indigenous peoples' rights to their traditional lands and territories. More anthropological attention has focused on Indigenous peoples' pursuit of rights via dramatic public protests, such as the marches that paralyzed Ecuador and Colombia (Jackson 2019; Sawyer 2004) and the Zapatista rebellion in Mexico (Mora 2017; Speed 2008), or via Indigenous mobilization in electoral politics in Bolivia (Goodale 2019; Postero 2017). Although the Mopan and Q'eqchi' Maya of southern Belize did engage in public protests and demonstrations, they secured their most significant victories by "judicializing" their claim (Huneeus et al. 2010:3; Sieder et al. 2005), using law and legal institutions to advance their political struggles by bringing cases before the Inter-American Commission on Human Rights and Belizean courts.

From international human rights conventions, lawyers for the Maya drew on the right to culture. From the Inter-American Human Rights System, they mobilized the right to property, a right echoed in the Belize constitution. From the common-law system, in which Belize participates as a former British colony, attorneys for the Maya invoked the doctrine of "native title." Articulating rights to culture with the right to property, attorneys for the Maya argued that, as Indigenous peoples, Mopan and Q'eqchi' communities' practice of customary tenure, that is, Maya culture, created collective property in lands.

The Inter-American Commission on Human Rights and the Belizean courts recognized Indigenous customary tenure practices, in other words, Indigenous culture, as the source of Indigenous collective property in lands. Grounding Maya collective property in Maya cultural practices, rather than the property law of the Belizean state, challenged the exclusive authority of state actors to create property and the recursive authorization of the state as producer of property. The courts insisted that the state recognize and protect Maya customary tenure practices and the collective property they have generated. However, lawyers speaking in the name of the Belizean state warned that Maya collective control of lands would threaten Belizean territorial sovereignty. I explore how Maya communities and actors who represent the Belizean state negotiate the interface between Maya customary tenure and Belizean property law, between Maya collective land rights and Belizean state sovereignty.

## Belize in Relation to Latin America: Disaggregating Neoliberalism, Multicultural "Turns," and Returns to Democracy

To interrogate how neoliberal forms of government that operate through "the market" intersect with practices of sovereignty and rights, I build on Foucault's (2008) analysis, which is distinct from dominant ways of thinking about neoliberalism and rights in Latin America. Recent scholarship on Indigenous mobilization in Latin America often defines the neoliberal context in which these mobilizations occurred in terms of specific policies. A shift from import-substitution development policies, which protected domestic producers via tariffs on imports, to free market approaches permitted goods and capital to move freely across borders (Hale 2002:486; Jackson and Warren 2005:552; Speed and Leyva Solano 2008:8). Fiscal austerity measures devolved responsibility for the welfare of citizens from the state to the private sector, NGOs, or communities and individuals themselves (Hale 2002:486; Jackson and Warren 2005:552; Postero 2007; Postero and Zamosc 2004; Speed and Leyva Solano 2008:8–9). The imperative of debt servicing led to efforts to increase exports and associated foreign exchange earnings through the privatization of lands, the intensification of land use, and the expansion of resource extraction (Postero and Zamosc 2004).

Because the imposition of neoliberal policies coincided in time with transitions from military dictatorship to multiparty electoral democracy in many Latin American countries, some scholars of the region have integrated democratization into their analysis of neoliberal policy prescriptions to focus on "neoliberal democracy" (Jackson and Warren 2005; Speed and Leyva Solano 2008). In turn, democratization opened space for Indigenous mobilizations to demand rights. In response, Colombia, Mexico, Paraguay, Nicaragua, Panama, and Guatemala adopted multicultural constitutional reforms that explicitly accorded rights to Indigenous peoples, including rights to practice their customary forms of law and hold collective property (Alfonso 2019:411; Hilbink and Gallagher 2019:43; Jackson 2019; Sieder 2002, 2011a). Ecuador and Bolivia undertook even deeper constitutional changes, with both countries declaring themselves "plurinational states" (Gargarella 2019:31–32; Goodale 2019; Postero 2007, 2017). These steps opened new roles for judiciaries to defend Indigenous rights and generated increasingly complex systems of legal pluralism in these states (Picq 2018; Sieder 2002; Sieder 2011:247).

Some scholars have cast Indigenous demands for rights and recognition of the pluricultural nature of Latin American nations as oppositional to neoliberal policies, asserting that the implementation of neoliberal reforms and the rise of Indigenous movements in Latin America "developed in explicit confrontation with each other" (Martinez 2017:74; Rodriguez-Garavito and Arenas 2005). In this view, transitions to democracy opened space for mobilization at the same time that neoliberal reforms—imposed in response to the debt crisis of the 1980s—threatened Indigenous lands and livelihoods and led to Indigenous mobilization in protest (Brysk 2000; Fischer 2009:3; Jackson and Warren 2005:553; Postero and Zamosc 2004:20; Yashar 1998, 1999).

Other scholars identify ways that multicultural reforms may reinforce state power or support neoliberal political-economic strategies (Hale 2002; Postero 2007; Speed 2008:30). State recognition of Indigenous citizenship may enable ruling elites to claim that the state is addressing the interests of Indigenous citizens, despite its failure to meet their material demands through the redistribution of resources (Speed and Leyva Solano 2008:4; Van Cott 2000). Efforts to shift responsibility for governance and social service provision from the state to nongovernment entities opened opportunities for civil society participation that resonated with some demands of Indigenous peoples for expanded political participation or increased autonomy (Jackson and Warren 2005:552). Further, states' promotion of "rights," "law," and strategies of inclusiveness may legitimize state power: granting collective rights to Indigenous peoples to engage in limited forms of self-governance reinforces the state's position as "the power that can grant and take away rights" (Speed 2008:31; Speed and Leyva Solano 2008:4). In addition, the adoption of a multicultural politics of recognition may limit the force of collective Indigenous demands by enabling political elites to divide Indigenous people whose demands they deemed "acceptable" from those they cast as "too radical" (Hale 2002:507; Speed and Leyva Solano 2008:4).

Although neoliberalization, democratization, Indigenous mobilization, and multicultural recognition occurred together in time in most Latin American countries, in Belize they did not. Belize was constituted as a multicultural nation from the earliest days of the Belizean nationalist movement, which cast its largest ethnic groups—Afro-Belizean Creole and Garifuna, Mestizo, and Yucatec, Mopan and Q'eqchi' Maya—as core constituents of the nation, along with several smaller categories—East Indian, Mennonite, Lebanese/Syrian, Chinese, White. No category represented a majority of the population, and none were able to construct the nation in their own image, though Creoles have attempted to do so (Medina 1997).

However, although Belize was constituted as a multicultural nation from its beginning, its laws contained no explicit recognition or rights for Indigenous peoples as Indigenous peoples, nor did Belize engage in the kind of multicultural constitutional reforms pursued by many Latin American countries. Nonetheless, Maya communities' autonomous self-governance had been written into law during the colonial period by British governors, who lacked resources to directly govern Maya communities in the colony's interior. Maya communities have continued to govern themselves and their lands into the present with a significant degree of autonomy. Further, legal pluralism in Belize is perhaps even more complicated than in Latin American countries because Belize, a member of the Commonwealth of former British colonies, participates in the common-law system in which judicial decisions issued in other common-law jurisdictions can be imported into Belizean legal proceedings. This adds one more layer of law in Belize, beyond international, inter-American, domestic, and Indigenous legal systems. It also positions Belize at the intersection of inter-American and common-law legal systems.

Belize is also distinct from most of its Latin American neighbors insofar as it has never experienced military dictatorship. Belize has operated as a democracy from 1964, when the British granted the colony internal self-government, through independence in 1981, and up to the present. Moreover, "the state" and its sovereign power often appear more precarious in Belize than in many other countries, as the neighboring state of Guatemala claims all or part of Belizean territory as its own.

The features that distinguish Belize from much of the hemisphere have led me to elaborate a framework that disaggregates the processes associated with neoliberalism, multiculturalism, and Indigenous rights claims in Latin America and permits analysis of their specific articulation in Belize. To make sense of the Belize case, this framework must also integrate a critical analysis of sovereignty. I develop such a framework by drawing on Foucault's approaches to neoliberal government and sovereignty. Rather than defining neoliberalism as a set of policies, Foucault approaches neoliberalism as a political rationality that seeks to govern society through "the market." He calls this rationality "government" or "governmentality." Rights, he suggests, are not part of the political rationality of government; rather, rights belong to the political rationality of sovereignty, where they challenge and limit state power. Casting government and sovereignty as distinct rationalities of rule, I interrogate their intersections. How do these different forms of rule reinforce, contradict, or challenge one another? How—or to what degree—are contradictions between them resolved?

Following Foucault, I begin with *practices of rule* in order to examine the effects they produce. As noted above, many practices that generate state-effects—the apparent existence of the state as an object—also produce related objects: sovereignty, territory, and property. I attend as well to the production of "the market" and "rights," rather than taking these as givens. Further, engaging Indigenous rights advocates' invocation of the right to cultural integrity, I deconstruct "culture," anthropology's master concept.

## Sovereignties and Rights

In his critical analysis of the origins of "the state" as an object, Foucault posits that political theorists introduced distinct species of rights to enable or legitimize distinct kinds of states. During the sixteenth and seventeenth centuries, the idea of "natural rights" justified the foundation of the sovereign state.[4] Hobbes cast individuals as the possessors of natural rights, which they jealously guarded against infringement by others, recognizing no higher authority. These autarkic individuals were destined to live in a perpetual state of war of all against all, Hobbes argued, unless they empowered a state to rule over them. Thus, the premise of natural rights justified the creation and imposition of the state to stave off this violent, uncertain existence. In turn, Hobbes's assertive state bore a strong resemblance to the individuals said to have authorized it to rule, jealously guarding its prerogatives and refusing any higher authority (Foucault 2008:2–6, 76–77; Moyn 2010:22).

If political theorists of the sixteenth and seventeenth centuries sought to legitimize the sovereign state, by the late eighteenth and early nineteenth centuries, their counterparts began to consider the problem of how to limit the exercise of sovereign power (Foucault 2008:8–9). Political philosophers identified two possible solutions to this problem: one based on the idea of rights, the other on the idea of the market. In this section, I elaborate on the development of rights; the following section focuses on the market. Political theorists built on earlier discourses of natural rights to posit that, in founding the state, individuals endowed with natural rights had exchanged some of their natural rights for the rights of citizens (Foucault 2008:8–9, 40). Prior to this time, law had served as a multiplier of sovereign power: the sovereign enacted power by creating and enforcing laws at will (Foucault 1977). Now, discourse on the rights of citizens deployed law as a tool by which citizens could limit sovereign power. The eighteenth-century emergence of citizens' rights, Foucault asserted, "renewed" sovereignty by limiting the absolute power of the sovereign state (Foucault 2008:40). However, the idea of citizens' rights also created a paradox: although the rights of citizens limited the power of the sovereign, those rights were guaranteed *by* the state (Brown 2002; Moyn 2010:23, 30).

Extending Foucault's assertion that the introduction of citizens' rights renewed sovereignty at the turn of the nineteenth century by limiting the power of the sovereign, I understand the emergence of "human rights" in the twentieth century as a further challenge to sovereignty. The United Nations (UN) General Assembly adopted the Universal Declaration of Human Rights (UDHR) in 1948. The human rights covenants that gave effect to the declaration—the International Convention on Civil and Political Rights (ICCPR) and the International Convention on Economic, Social, and Cultural Rights (ICESCR)—were completed in 1966. In contrast to citizens' rights, which had positioned individual rights holders in relation to their state, making each state accountable to its citizens, the UDHR and the human rights covenants inserted individual rights–bearers into *international* law, previously the exclusive province of states (Moyn 2010). Human rights thus impinged further on state sovereignty, making each state accountable to the community of states for its treatment of individual rights–bearers. The paradox of rights persisted, however: though human rights were intended to constrain the sovereign state, the enforcement of those rights rested with the state.

As representatives of UN member states negotiated the content of the human rights covenants that would give legal effect to the declaration, colonized peoples' demands for self-determination gained increasing force. As the push toward decolonization swept across the globe, the right of peoples to self-determination became the primary focus of international politics, "capturing" human rights (Moyn 2010:99, 197). In 1960, the UN General Assembly passed a Declaration on the Granting of Independence to Colonial Countries and Peoples, which recognized that "all peoples have the right to self-determination," and this right was adopted as the first right in each of the 1966 UN human rights covenants. Despite the conceptualization of human rights as rights held by individuals, this move enshrined a single collective right in the covenants. However, to protect the territorial integrity of existing states, UN member states promoted a "salt-water thesis": only peoples in overseas colonies would be recognized as holding the right to form their own sovereign states.

The priority accorded to the collective right to self-determination throughout the 1950s and 1960s diverted attention from individual human rights for decades. However, the violent imposition of military dictatorships across most Latin American countries and the repression of dissent that followed provoked increasing activism in support of human rights in the region (Keck and Sikkink 1998). Abuses committed against Indigenous peoples during this period were denounced as violations of their human rights.

However, during the 1980s, Indigenous activists launched international efforts to define a set of rights specific to the historical trajectories and current contexts of Indigenous peoples. The right of peoples to self-determination was central to Indigenous rights claims. Indigenous advocates have attached diverse meanings to this term, ranging from forms of local or regional autonomy to independent statehood (Engle 2010); however, regardless of which definition one embraces, the collective right to self-determination represents a challenge to existing sovereignties.

## Government, Liberal and Neoliberal

In addition to the mobilization of "rights," Foucault identified a second answer to the late eighteenth-century question of how to limit the power of the sovereign. Rather than relying on law and rights, the second response focused on de facto limits for governmental practice, identifying "those things that it would be pointless for government to interfere with" (Foucault 2008:40).

Foucault labeled this response "government" or "governmentality." Earlier, he had used the phrase "rationality of government" in a general sense to refer to "a way or system of thinking about the nature of the practice of government (who can govern; what governing is; what or who is governed), capable of making some form of that activity thinkable and practicable both to its practitioners and to those upon whom it was practiced" (Gordon 1991:3). However, in his 1977–1978 lectures, Foucault used the term in a more specific sense to refer to a new form of thinking about and exercising power, which he defined by contrast with the practice of sovereignty: while "sovereignty capitalizes a territory," he suggested, government "will try to plan a milieu" (Dean 1999:19; Foucault 2007:20). While the aim of sovereignty "is internal to itself and gets its instruments from itself in the form of law," a governmental rationality involves "arranging things" in order to achieve "an end suitable for each of the things to be governed" (Foucault 2007:99). Thus, the aim of government "is internal to the things it directs"; it seeks "the perfection, maximization, or intensification of the processes it directs"—in a word, their optimization (Foucault 2007:99). I use the specific sense of the term "government" here.[5]

## Liberalism

Foucault linked the emergence of a governmental rationality to the production of two new objects of knowledge and intervention: from political economy came "the market," from statistics "the population." The development of statistics enabled "the population" to appear as an object with its own regularities, a natural phenomenon that could not be changed by decree (Foucault 2007:104). Similarly, late eighteenth-century political economists constructed "the market" as an object "that obeyed and had to obey 'natural' mechanisms" (Foucault 2008:18, 31). Most recent scholarship on biopolitics has focused on "population," but I focus on "the market."

Although early forms of "government" prioritized the compilation of detailed knowledge about these objects so as to manage them, classic liberalism emerged as a critique of efforts to direct economic processes. "If there is a nature specific to the objects and operations of governmentality," then "governmental practice can only do what it has to do by respecting this nature" (Foucault 2008:16). "Henceforth," Foucault asserted, "*the fundamental objective of governmentality will be . . . ensuring the security of the natural phenomena of economic processes or processes intrinsic to population*" (Foucault 2007:353).

Political economy thus established a regime of truth in which the market functions as a "site of veridiction": the market would generate a "true" price that would "adequately express the relationship . . . between the cost of production and the extent of demand" (Foucault 2008:31–32).[6] The idea of "the market" was deployed to "picture" all the unequal relationships that connect commodity producers to commodity consumers as "a naturally achieved balance" between supply and demand (Mitchell 2002:227). However, in order for the market to function as a "site of truth," it had to be allowed to operate "according to its nature"; interventions would "impair and distort" the "natural mechanisms" of the market (Foucault 2008:30–31, 44).

As a corollary, the "natural" processes of the market would produce the greatest welfare for "all and everyone" only if individuals freely pursued their own interests (Foucault 2007:346). Thus, liberalism also required a particular kind of subject, *homo economicus*, the "subject of interest." Whereas the sovereign had a hold on lands and subjects, governmental reason does not deal with "things in themselves," Foucault argued. It deals with the degree to which a given thing *interests* market-rational individuals (Foucault 2008:45). Referring to the "invisible hand," invoked by Adam Smith to represent the aggregate effect of individual choices through the market, Foucault asserted, although "what is usually stressed in Smith's famous theory of the invisible hand is . . . the 'hand,' . . . the existence of something like providence which would tie together all the dispersed threads," invisibility "is at least as important." Invisibility disqualifies state intervention into the market by asserting the state's inability to "see" or know enough about individuals' interests to intervene in the market without disrupting its "natural processes." Invisibility requires the state to "laisser faire," to let homo economicus alone (Foucault 2008:283).[7]

Foucault thus defined liberalism more narrowly than most scholars, casting it as a governmental strategy focused on the production of "the market" as an object that operates according to certain natural processes, an object capable of assessing the "true" value of a thing by weighing the aggregate interest people have in that thing. If allowed to operate according to these natural processes, liberalism posited that the market would maximize the welfare of "all and everyone."

## Neoliberalism

Neoliberalism emerged during the twentieth century as a more extreme manifestation of a liberal rationality of government.[8] Deepening liberalism's commitment to the truth of the market, a neoliberal rationality of government sought to extend "the rationality of the market, the schemas of analysis it offers and the decision-making criteria it suggests" to achieve "a general regulation of society by the market," such that market rationalities come to "play a regulatory role at every moment and every point in society" (Dean 1999:57; Foucault 2008:145, 323; Lemke 2001:197–198). Thus, the state was to "govern *for* the market," taking as its "main and constant concern" the conditions of existence of the market and arranging conditions to enable new domains of life to be incorporated into market exchange and made subject to market rationality (Foucault 2008:121, 140). If "government" is "a form of activity aiming to shape, guide or affect the conduct of some person or persons," what Foucault referred to as "the conduct of conduct," a neoliberal rationality of government seeks to direct conduct through "the market" (Gordon 1991:2; Foucault 1982: 220).

The operation of a neoliberal rationality of government entailed the production of a corresponding subject. In contrast to the homo economicus of eighteenth-century liberalism, "the person who must be let alone," the homo economicus posited by neoliberal theorists responds systematically to modification of the contexts in which choices are made. This homo economicus is thus "eminently governable" (Foucault 2008:270–271). "From being the intangible partner of *laissez-faire*, *homo economicus* now becomes the correlate of a governmentality which will act on the environment and systematically modify its variables" so as to alter the calculations, decisions, and actions that result (Foucault 2008:270–271). A neoliberal governmental rationality thus seeks to direct conduct *indirectly*, to "plan a milieu" in which "the market" will operate according to its "nature" (Foucault 2007:20). Homo economicus, the market-rational subject of interest, becomes "the interface of government and the individual"; governmental power "gets a hold on" the individual "to the extent, *and only to the extent*, that he is a *homo economicus*" (Foucault 2008:253; emphasis added).

Foucault's narrow, market-focused definition of neoliberal government offers a sharper, more precise tool for analysis than definitions that begin with liberty or lists of policy prescriptions. As James Ferguson complains, "neoliberalism" has been defined in too many different ways, but it has also often been used without definition as "a sloppy synonym for capitalism" (Ferguson 2009:171). Approaching neoliberalism as a way of governing through "the market" enables an analysis that explores the complex intersections across the practices of neoliberal government, sovereignty, and Indigenous rights. The intersections among these different forms of rule, I argue, structure the possibilities imagined, the strategies pursued, and the outcomes of Indigenous struggles for autonomy and self-determination in Belize and across Latin America.

## Heterogeneous Logics that Overlap, Lean on, Challenge, and Struggle with Each Other

Multiple rationalities of rule collide in the events described at the beginning of this chapter. Cabinet ministers and heads of government departments performed sovereignty, deploying law backed by the threat of violence to designate protected areas that enclosed resources upon which the livelihoods of Maya communities depended. However, the Minister of Natural Resources subsequently devolved rule over the protected areas and nearby communities, first to conservation NGOs and then to "the market" for tropical nature. Embracing ecotourism as a market-based conservation strategy, political leaders and NGO personnel deployed market rationalities to govern both nature and people.

Government ministers and heads of departments also performed sovereignty by creating private property and issuing concessions for resource exploitation on lands they designated as state property. Maya organizations confronted these actions by mobilizing under the banner of rights to limit the exercise of state power, invoking rights to property and culture to pursue collective Indigenous rights to lands. State officials countered with warnings that collective Maya land rights threatened Belizean territorial sovereignty.

I explore the interplay of practices of neoliberal government with performances of sovereignty and claims to rights in Belize. Foucault cast neoliberal government and sovereignty as "disparate," "heterogeneous" forms of rule, which operate on the basis of distinct rationalities and produce incompatible kinds of subjects (Foucault 2007:384). The "subject of interest," for whom interest appears as a form of "absolutely subjective will," "constantly overflows the subject of right" (Foucault 2008:271).[9] However, despite the "essential incompatibility" of government and sovereignty, heterogeneity "never prevents coexistence, conjunction, or connection"; these disparate governmental rationalities "overlap, lean on each other, challenge each other, and struggle with each other" (Foucault 2008:42, 313). "What is politics," Foucault asks, "if not both the interplay of these different arts of government" and the debates to which they give rise? (Foucault 2008:313). I engage this politics here, examining the intersections among the practices of state sovereignty, Indigenous rights, and neoliberal government through the market.

### Property and Culture

Property appears as a critical point of intersection across sovereignty, markets, and rights and the paradoxes they generate. Efforts to govern through the market disempower the sovereign, because "the market" must be free to function according to its "nature." However, the operation of the market depends on the existence of a sovereign state committed to protecting property and enforcing contracts through law, backed by the threat of violence (Harvey 2005:2, 21). The creation and protection of property are also a critical practice through which political actors perform the sovereign territorial state. However, Maya land claims challenged the state precisely via its protections for property: Maya communities claimed an Indigenous right to collective property in lands as the foundation for their collective right to cultural integrity.

The invocation of "culture" in the Maya land rights claim leads me to consider this foundational anthropological object critically, including how it came to be entangled with the creation of property. Noting "the increasing deployment of talk about 'culture,' including culture as an object of rights," Jane Cowan has called for investigations of specific legal claims about culture with the aim of developing "a more adequate theoretical grasp of the contingency and complexity of social struggles involving culture and rights and of the consequences, often unanticipated and sometimes surprising, when demands are recognized or accommodated" (Cowan 2006:9, 21). My analysis responds to that call.

Anthropologists have long debated how best to define culture, the master concept of our discipline (see Jackson 2019). Definitions range from expansive approaches that include whole ways of life, to narrower approaches that identify culture as knowledge or meanings, to approaches that focus on culture as contested, power laden, and emergent. But is culture an object that exists a priori in the world, such that some definitions are more accurate and others less so? Or is culture an abstraction, the product of discourse, rather than an independently existing entity? I argue the latter; thus, no definition is more accurate than another, but every definition has effects (Abu-Lughod 1991).

Reading Roy Wagner's (1975) *The Invention of Culture* through a Foucauldian lens, I recognize "culture" as a constructed object—like "the state" or "the market" or "rights." Wagner portrayed culture as a concept created by anthropologists to explain both what anthropologists did "in the field" and what "the natives" they observed were doing: "the natives" were "doing culture," while the anthropologist was "in the field" to "learn their culture." This fiction, Wagner points out, required anthropologists to "imagine a culture for people who did not imagine it for themselves." The people anthropologists study, he suggested, saw themselves as "doing life." This treatment undermines the ontological status of culture as an a priori object, repositioning culture as an abstraction that anthropologists have used to organize our understandings and our representations of the practices we observe.

The constructedness of "culture" as an object does not make it false or unreal. As an abstraction, the term "culture" objectifies some subset—larger or smaller depending on the particular definition one deploys—of the practices Wagner refers to as "doing life." The practices and meanings designated via the term "culture" do not depend for their existence or significance on the abstract concept of culture. Without such a concept, people would still engage in meaningful practices;

they would still "do life." However, the label makes it possible to objectify and aggregate those practices into a singular object and to make comparisons across different sets of practices.

However, although culture was originally an abstraction constructed by anthropologists to organize our perceptions of our own and other people's actions, the concept has come to be used by ever-larger numbers of people outside of anthropology and the academy to organize *their* understandings of their own or other people's lives and practices (Jackson 2019; Sahlins 1999; Warren 1998). People now often see themselves as "doing culture," rather than simply "doing life." Thus, rather than advocating for a particular definition of culture, I step outside the frame of culture itself to examine the implications of the particular definitions of culture advanced by different groups of actors in the struggles I analyze. I am concerned with the *effects* of the particular definitions of culture, the possibilities their deployment opens or forecloses.

As both anthropologists and philosophers acknowledge, the law creates and shapes "that which it purports merely to recognize" (Brown 2002; Butler 1997; Cowan 2006:10, 17). Thus, legal recognition of particular framings of "culture" adds weight to definitions of culture advanced via standard-setting processes or litigation. As Indigenous and non-Indigenous actors engage one another in these legal spaces, "Indigenous culture" is produced in the "sites of contact" between them (Bens 2020:21; Cowan 2006:18; Povinelli 2002).

The Maya lands cases resulted in the legal recognition that Maya collective property in lands is created through the practice of Maya customary tenure, that is, Maya culture, rather than the property system of the Belizean state. The production of property via the practices of Maya customary tenure sets up an additional contradiction or paradox. Although property is central to the operation of "the market," Maya customary tenure practices decenter the market and the atomistic subjects formed in relation to market rationalities, introducing a distinct logic that prioritizes subsistence security, socially mediated land use, mutual commitments among community members, and a broad interspecies conviviality. Thus, if grounding property in Maya culture challenges state sovereignty, it also challenges market rationality.

## Paradox and the Critical Conduct of Rights

I engage the paradoxes that emerge at the intersections of sovereignty, rights, and neoliberal government through Ben Golder's conceptualization of the "critical conduct of rights." As discussed above, scholarship on rights in Latin America often treats rights as *either* a challenge to the state *or* a trap that reinforces state power and limits the possibility of social transformation (although Rachel Sieder [2011b] and Boaventura Santos [2002] offer more nuanced analysis). In contrast to either/or approaches, Golder's "both/and" approach to rights better captures the complex realities confronted and produced by Indigenous and state actors contesting rights.

Recognizing the paradoxes entailed in claiming rights, the "critical conduct of rights" embraces "a contrary inhabiting" of rights discourse that works simultaneously "within and against it" (Golder 2015:21). Tactically oriented, a critical conduct of rights intervenes into existing formations of law, state, and power, seeking to use rights to create and hold open alternatives (Golder 2015:3). Golder acknowledges that actors who deploy this strategy do not occupy a "position of mastery" over rights; their subjectivities are unavoidably shaped and constrained by discourses of rights and the categories they constitute (Golder 2015:91). However, the critic nonetheless works from this position to try to destabilize existing relationships of rule and open "the possibility of their being otherwise" (Golder 2015:22). I elaborate on this approach in chapters 6, 7, and 8, as I explore the ways Indigenous rights—and the legal pluralism they require—challenge the conditions under which the state, sovereignty, and territoriality are produced.

## Organization of the Book

Chapter 2 outlines the history of contested sovereignty over the territory that is now Belize, focusing on competing claims to sovereignty and competing efforts to perform sovereignty. It also highlights the transformation of territory into property as a key technique for producing the sovereign state. The chapter also positions Belize in relation to the broader Latin American context, identifying ways that Belize represents an anomalous case that requires critical analysis of the articulation of sovereignty, neoliberalism, democracy, multiculturalism, and rights.

Chapter 3 focuses on the creation of the Cockscomb Basin Wildlife Sanctuary. In the context of intersecting biodiversity and debt crises, the Belize Audubon Society and its U.S. conservation NGO allies promoted the creation of protected areas to conserve biodiversity. They simultaneously promoted ecotourism as a market-based mechanism to fund protected areas, expand the national economy, and generate funds for debt servicing. Political leaders embraced ecotourism as a development strategy, and, in an act of sovereignty, the Minister of Natural Resources declared the Cockscomb a wildlife sanctuary. However, the Minister quickly devolved responsibility for managing the sanctuary to a transnational alliance of conservation NGOs. While most analyses of NGOs' roles in environmental governance focus on efforts to manage resource-dependent rural communities, this chapter explores how this NGO alliance directed the conduct of state officials.

Political leaders' embrace of ecotourism rendered them increasingly subject to the international market for tropical nature. Thus, rather than *governing* Belizean nature, state actors assumed responsibility for *marketing* Belizean nature to specific types of non-Belizeans identified by experts as "the market" for ecotourism experiences. Seeking competitive advantage over other ecotourism destinations, the Belize Tourism Board also marketed Maya culture, manifested in the ruins of ancient cities and the lives of contemporary villagers, as a "product line" complementary to reef and rainforests.

As the Belize Audubon Society took responsibility for managing the Cockscomb Basin Wildlife Sanctuary, it also became responsible for managing the communities on its perimeter. Chapter 4 explores Audubon's engagements with the Mopan community of Maya Centre, whose residents were displaced from lands and subsistence resources upon which their livelihoods had depended, with the declaration of the sanctuary. Having lost access to subsistence resources, they became increasingly subject to market exchange for their livelihoods. Audubon pursued two strategies to win villagers' support for the sanctuary. It launched an education campaign that drew on the western science concept of "ecosystem" to explain and justify the creation of protected areas; this effort did not succeed. Audubon also mobilized villagers' expanding market subjectivities to cultivate environmental commitments, deploying ecotourism to attribute economic value to protected forests and channel income to Maya Centre residents; this strategy was more successful. As villagers earned income from ecotourism, their support for the protected area—and their compliance with hunting prohibitions—increased.

However, the market-rational arguments that won villagers' support for protected areas eventually led to conflict between the community and the BAS. Maya Centre residents appropriated the logic of BAS arguments to demand greater participation and incomes from ecotourism as compensation for lost access to lands for subsistence production. Further, villagers began to assert Indigenous rights to lands, as the Maya movement in southern Belize prepared to petition the courts for Indigenous rights to collective lands. Villagers' emerging subjectivities as rights-holders led to threats to reappropriate lands in the Cockscomb.

In response to villagers' closure of the Cockscomb, state actors suddenly threatened to exercise sovereign power to ensure the continued production and sale of the Cockscomb as an ecotourism commodity, to govern *for* the market. In contrast, the BAS Executive Director adopted a governmental approach that engaged villagers' market subjectivities, negotiating compromises to expand villagers' incomes from ecotourism to the wildlife sanctuary.

Chapter 5 examines the origins of struggles over land tenure in southern Belize, which escalated in the last decades of the twentieth century. The government sought to exercise sovereignty over the south by implementing development projects that would transform lands collectively managed by Maya communities into private property. State actors also granted concessions to transnational companies for timber extraction and oil exploration and established protected areas on lands used by Maya communities but designated by the government as state property. In response, Q'eqchi' and Mopan Maya mobilized to secure the lands they traditionally used. In alliance with North American Indigenous rights advocates, Mopan and Q'eqchi' leaders launched a mapping project to demonstrate the extent of their land use as a basis for their claim. They also petitioned the Belize Supreme Court for recognition of their land rights as Indigenous people. When the Supreme Court ignored the claim, the Maya petitioned the Inter-American Commission on Human Rights for redress.

Chapter 6 places the Maya claim before the Inter-American Commission on Human Rights in the broader context of international struggles for Indigenous rights, in which it played a significant role. I trace the production of international Indigenous rights standards, beginning with the drafting of Indigenous rights declarations in the UN and the Organization of American States (OAS) and a convention in the International Labor Organization (ILO). Indigenous rights activists sought recognition of their right to self-determination as "peoples" under international law. However, UN and OAS member states that opposed Indigenous self-determination stalled the declarations.

Indigenous advocates thus deployed existing human rights instruments to advance Indigenous rights. Mobilizing the right to culture from international human rights conventions, they won recognition from UN human rights treaty bodies for a territorializing definition of Indigenous culture that grounded Indigenous practices and cosmovisions (worldviews) in the relationships Indigenous peoples sustain with their lands and territories. As a result, Indigenous peoples' control over their traditional lands and territories was defined as foundational to their ability to practice and pass on their cultures. The subject of Indigenous rights that emerged from this process was a collective, culture-bearing subject, rooted in lands. Although UN member states had rejected Indigenous demands for self-determination, they accepted Indigenous advocates' territorializing definition of Indigenous culture.

Indigenous advocates also pursued strategic litigation through the Inter-American Human Rights System to develop a jurisprudence on Indigenous rights. Inter-American human rights instruments did not recognize a right to culture, but they did protect a right to property. Indigenous legal petitions in the Inter-American System deployed this right and drew upon the territorializing approach to Indigenous culture they had elaborated in the UN context to argue that Indigenous cultural practices for managing collectively held lands (that is, culture) *create* Indigenous property, which states must recognize and protect in the same way they protect other forms of property. Inter-American judicial bodies concurred. Grounding Maya property in Belize in the practice of Indigenous culture, rather than the law of the state, the Inter-American Commission on Human Rights directed the Belizean state to demarcate and title Mayan lands, in a decision that advanced Indigenous rights jurisprudence in the Inter-American System.

Despite the importance of the IACHR decision for advancing Indigenous land rights within the hemisphere, the Belizean government did not comply with the ruling. Maya organizations thus returned to the Belize Supreme Court to secure land rights. Chapter 7 examines the arguments advanced by attorneys for the Mopan and Q'eqchi' as well as arguments presented by lawyers for the Belizean government across the decade-long process of litigating Maya Indigenous rights to lands and territories through the Belizean judicial system. Building on international standards and judicial decisions that identified Indigenous customary tenure practices as the source of Indigenous property, lawyers for the Maya demonstrated the existence of Maya customary tenure in Indigenous communities of southern Belize, positioning the Mopan and Q'eqchi' claimants as the collective culture-bearers of Indigenous rights. Attorneys for the Belizean state challenged Mopan and Q'eqchi' indigeneity and warned that Maya collective land rights threatened state sovereignty over southern Belize.

Ultimately, the courts determined that the Mopan and Q'eqchi' are Indigenous, that their customary tenure practices give rise to property in lands, and that the Belizean state is required to protect this property in accord with the constitution's guarantees for property. The judgments complicated an already complex system of legal pluralism in Belize by recognizing Maya customary tenure, rather than Belizean property law, as the source of Maya property and ordering the Belizean state to accommodate its law to Maya customary tenure practices. However, following common-law tenets, the courts left the specifics of *how* state and Maya legal systems would interface to negotiations between the Maya and the government.

Chapter 8 explores subsequent negotiations over the interface between the state legal system and the institutions of Maya customary tenure. Actors operating in the name of the Belizean state sought to discredit Maya customary tenure practices, delay implementation, and cultivate divisions among Maya. While state actors attempted to stall or thwart the implementation of Maya land rights, Maya leaders used the courts to force the government to accelerate the implementation of their land rights. Further, beyond engagements with the state or its law, Maya communities pursued a critical conduct of rights, sustaining and reinforcing their practices of customary tenure over their traditional lands, which decenter the market and prioritize subsistence security and nonmarket forms of sociality. Members of Maya communities sought to elaborate life and livelihood options that balance their priorities for subsistence security and relationships of respect, as the collective culture-bearing subjects of Indigenous rights, with their desire to participate in markets, as market-rational subjects. I argue that the ability for communities to determine for themselves how they wish to manage the interface of market rationality with nonmarket values of respect and care is a critical dimension of self-determination.

The book concludes with an assessment of the ways that the practice of neoliberal government through the market, performances of sovereignty, and the production of Indigenous rights simultaneously contradict and lean on one another in Belize. I argue that a theoretical framework that focuses on the complex and contradictory intersections of market rationalities with assertions of state sovereignty and Maya claims to Indigenous rights to lands and culture illuminates the central tensions and challenges confronting the Belizean Maya as well as other Indigenous peoples across Latin America.

## Methods and Data

Like the Maya lands cases, the research for this book has extended over more than two decades. I conducted ethnographic field research through interviews and participant observation, along with archival research, for periods ranging from two weeks to four months in most years between 1997 and 2019, with a short postpandemic trip in 2023. I engaged conservation NGOs involved in managing protected areas and the communities around their perimeters, interviewing staff and board members past and present. I interviewed current and former government officials with responsibility for economic development, forestry, protected areas, and tourism. I conducted surveys and interviews in Maya communities implementing ecotourism. In addition, I interviewed ecotourism entrepreneurs in upscale tourism enclaves and rural villages, as well as leaders of private-sector tourism associations at national and district scales. In the community of Maya Centre, I conducted a survey of every household and followed up with additional interviews and focus groups informed by the survey data.

My research on the progress of the Maya lands cases through the inter-American and Belizean judicial systems relies largely on analysis of textual data, supplemented by interviews with lawyers and Maya leaders involved in the litigation over Maya land rights. In my analysis of the textual data generated by the trials, I focused on the legal arguments and evidence put forward by attorneys for the two sides and the decisions issued by the judicial bodies that heard these arguments. The court cases themselves were conducted largely via document submission, with little live testimony. They were literally arguments conducted through written texts, rather than orally. For the Maya, the novel legal theory that backed their claim was critical to their victory and to the production of inter-American jurisprudence on Indigenous rights to lands and territories. The attorneys representing the Maya clearly articulated this theory in submissions to the courts; because of its groundbreaking status, they also published the argument in law journals and textbooks. The evidence considered by the courts was also submitted primarily in written form, via affidavits from academic experts, Maya leaders, and government personnel, accompanied by the *Maya Atlas* (TMCC and TAA 1997).

I collected all judicial decisions rendered in the Maya lands cases, analyzing them to understand both the arguments and evidence put forward by legal counsel for both parties and the judges' evaluation of these legal arguments and evidence. I was able to analyze all written arguments and affidavits filed in the Belize Supreme Court case of 2007, which were available online at the time. For the other cases, I relied on the text of the judicial decisions themselves to assess the evidence and legal arguments submitted by each side and the judges' evaluation of the two teams' submissions. For the small portion of the testimony that was presented live in court, I relied on media coverage of the trials. Although this did not provide a complete transcript, it did highlight the issues Belizean reporters believed would be of greatest interest to the Belizean public. The decisions themselves cited primarily the written submissions, rather than live testimony.

Throughout the process of claims-making and adjudication, I followed events via online television news and newspaper coverage of the trials and judgments as they occurred. I relied on the evening news programming of two Belizean television channels, Channel 5 and Channel 7, and on newspaper coverage, primarily in the *Amandala*, the newspaper with the greatest circulation in Belize.

Once the court of last resort had ruled in favor of the Maya, media coverage provided ample evidence of the government's efforts to delay implementation and discredit Maya customary tenure practices. However, interviews and participant observation became more important ways of understanding the activities that Maya communities themselves were undertaking to implement the rulings.

This ethnography does not use pseudonyms. It would be impossible to protect the confidentiality of many individuals relying only on pseudonyms. In the chapters that focus on conservation and ecotourism, my strategy has thus been to utilize titles, the positions occupied by speakers, as identifiers. These positions have been occupied by multiple people—either at the same time in the case of "warden" or "villager" or serially in the case of "Park Director" or "BAS Executive Director." In the context of the Maya lands cases, the Maya who submitted affidavits, provided interviews to media houses, or played leadership roles in advancing Maya strategies for implementing the rulings did so publicly, under their own names. Thus, I have used their actual names in this account.

The name of the Q'eqchi' people of southern Belize has been spelled in different ways in Belize, including Kekchi and Ketchi. I will use Q'eqchi' except for when using the names of formal organizations or quoting sources that use alternative spellings.

CHAPTER 2

# Histories of Belize

## SOVEREIGNTIES CLAIMED, SOVEREIGNTIES PERFORMED

The territory that is now Belize has been subject to competing claims to sovereignty both past and present. Since the initiation of European colonialism in the Americas, sovereignty over this territory has been claimed by both Spanish and British monarchs, Maya kingdoms and military leaders, the Republic of Guatemala, and the Belizean nation-state. However, these parties have had varying degrees of success in *performing* sovereignty over this territory. The transformation of territory into property has been a key technique for performing sovereignty.

If conflicting claims to sovereignty have marked Belizean history, Belizean history itself is contested in contemporary conflicts over sovereignty and rights. In this chapter, I draw on historical scholarship for evidence as well as introducing dominant national narratives that selectively and strategically engage this evidence.

### Spanish versus Maya: Colonial Claims and Their Limits in Practice

Shifting territories controlled by different rulers played across the terrain that has become Belize prior to Spanish colonial incursions in the Americas. In most accounts of Belizean history, those who inhabited these lands before the intrusion of European colonists are referred to as Maya, adopting the practice of archaeologists who have studied, analyzed, and reported on the physical remains of their spectacular ceremonial and political centers that represent the classic (250 A.D. to 1000 A.D.) and postclassic (1000 A.D. to 1521) periods of Maya civilization.

Control over this region was also shifting and contested during the colonial period; Spanish military and religious forces never exercised effective sovereignty over the territory that is now Belize. After the conquest of the Aztec capital in what is now central Mexico, Spanish forces moved south- and eastward, establishing strongholds at Merida in Mexico's Yucatan Peninsula and Santiago de Guatemala (present-day Antigua) in the highlands of western Guatemala. From these colonial capitals, Spanish forces attempted to subjugate the Maya, control their labor, and extract tribute. However, between the areas of relative control exercised by these two colonial centers, the region that would later become Belize and the Guatemalan Peten remained beyond Spanish power.

Maya who spoke related dialects of the Yucatecan language family occupied the territories that extended southward from the Spanish center of Merida: Kowojs, Kejaches, Itzajs, and Mopans (Jones 1998:3). During the sixteenth century, Itzaj ruling elites were dominant among these related groups, exercising power from their capital at Nojpeten in what is now Guatemala. Mopan settlements were dispersed to the south and east of the Itzaj heartland, across an area that included lands along the present Guatemala-Belize border, portions of the Belize River valley in central Belize, and some rivers of southern Belize (Jones 1998:5, 22), (see map 1). Mopan living nearest to the Itzaj capital formed part of the Itzaj territorial and political domain; however, fortified Mopan towns located farther from Itzaj control indicate that some Mopan lived in larger communities that served as "capitals" of smaller autonomous territories (Jones 1998:22).

Maya populations who spoke Cholan languages lived in an arc along the southern and western frontiers of the Itzaj and related groups. Manche Chols, designated according to the name of their principal town of Manche, inhabited lands south of the Mopan region, with their territory extending north and northeast from Cahabon in Verapaz, east to the Caribbean Sea, and northward along the coast of what would become Belize (Jones 1998:5, 7). The Itzajs and their neighbors remained beyond the control of either Merida or Santiago. Long after other major Mayan polities had fallen, the Itzajs sustained the "last Maya kingdom" (Jones 1998).

South and westward from the Chol lands lived Q'eqchi' speakers, who successfully repelled efforts by Spanish forces to conquer them until 1537, when Dominican priests launched a campaign to settle, convert, and control them (Wilk 1997:43). Dominican success in "pacifying" the Q'eqchi' led them to name these lands Vera Paz, true peace.

Although the designations used above—based on language, lineage, and location—may give the impression that these groups were entirely distinct from one another, historical evidence indicates otherwise. These populations spoke languages shaped by their proximity. While all dialects of Yucatecan were mutually intelligible, the southernmost of the Yucatecan dialects, Mopan, differed from the more northerly dialects in part through the influence of Chol. Some southern Chol speakers also spoke Mopan: bilingual Chols served as interpreters for Spaniards from Santiago who ventured into Mopan territories (Jones 1998:5). The populations in this region had multiple motivations for multilingualism: trade, political integration or subordination, flight, and intermarriage. Early ethnologists also pointed to the integration of Chol- and Q'eqchi'-speakers through intermarriage in the region around Cahabón and the distinctive form of Q'eqchi' that resulted at this interface (Thompson 1930:35–36). Moreover, language does not appear to have been the basis for their self-identifications; rather, political/military and lineage/kinship affiliations provided a basis for significant bonds and lines of division. Further,

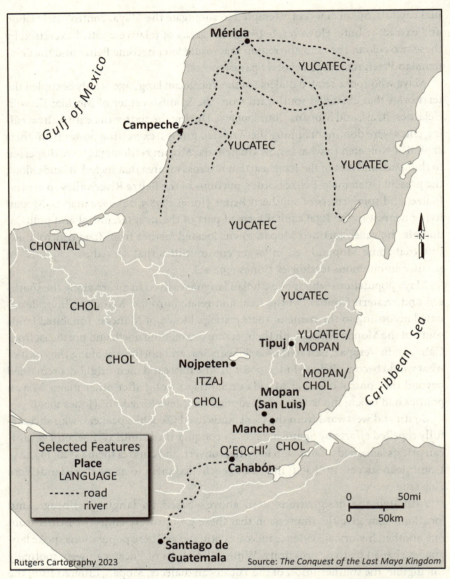

Map 1. Sixteenth-century Spanish colonial centers in relation to lowland Maya settlements and languages mentioned in the text. Credit: Michael Siegel, Rutgers Cartography 2023.

historical evidence demonstrates that communities in this region were not homogeneous: migration and intermarriage resulted in people with Itzaj, Kowoj, Kejach, and Mopan lineage names living in the same communities; the same was true for people with Q'eqchi' and Chol names (Jones 1998:22).

The year 1525 marks the first Spanish entry into the forested region that became southern Belize, when Cortés marched southward from Campeche in Mexico to the Bay of Amatique in what is now Guatemala (Dobson 1973:44–45). The account of Cortés's passage through this region provides evidence that while some Yucatec-speaking settlements sought to maintain independence from the Itzaj kingdom, others, including Mopan and Chol speakers, were subject to Itzaj military strength and trade relations. Based on his interactions with Itzaj and other native groups, Cortés determined that a large region stretching eastward from Lake Peten Itzaj into present-day south and central Belize was controlled by the principal Itzaj ruler (Jones 1998:38).[1]

Although Cortés passed through this region without attempting to conquer it, in 1544, two Spaniards set out from the colonial stronghold of Merida in northern Yucatan with aspirations to conquer, control, and extract tribute from the region drained by the Rio Hondo, the New River, and the Belize River in what is now northern and central Belize. They established a few cacao-producing *encomiendas*, a mechanism by which colonizers acquired rights to tribute from natives, collected in goods or labor. However, rebellions broke out in the region by 1547 (Jones 1998:39–40). Several subsequent attempts to establish encomiendas and missions followed; however, the towns they established included no resident Spanish and were never firmly under Spanish control (Jones 1998:40). Despite Spanish tribute requirements, Maya populations in the Hondo, New, and Belize River watersheds continued to trade in cacao, forest products, metal tools, and cotton cloth with the Itzajs and other Maya groups (Jones 1998:40). They also welcomed Maya from Yucatan, who fled southward to escape the more effective control exercised by the Spanish in that region.

A half-century later, in 1604, Dominicans from the Spanish colonial capital of Santiago in Guatemala established a mission at Manche, with the aim of converting and controlling the Chol-speaking inhabitants of southern Peten and what would become southern Belize. By 1606 they had relocated 6,000 people into nine towns, *reducciones*, concentrating the population as a means to more effectively control them (Jones 1998:57).[2] However, the Itzajs attacked the new settlements to induce the Chols to abandon the missions (Jones 1998:49). In 1631, Spanish forces from Santiago returned to reconquer the Chols, but combined Itzaj and Mopan attacks again thwarted their efforts (Jones 1998:52).

During the seventeenth century in northern Yucatan, the increased demands of illegal *repartimientos*, forced labor contracts for the production of goods that were allocated to colonial elites, pushed more Maya to flee into the southern forests, where they joined both encomienda towns and independent Maya polities (Jones 1998:40). By serving as a refuge to Maya fleeing Spanish domination and labor demands, the region that would become the Guatemalan Peten and Belize presented a serious challenge to Spanish rule over the Yucatan. The option of escape undermined Spanish control of the native population in Yucatan, and the flight of labor posed a significant economic threat to Spanish colonists. The only solution to this crisis, colonial administrators concluded, was conquest of the Itzaj kingdom (Jones 1998:41).

Plans were laid and forces assembled, and, in 1697, Spanish troops attacked and conquered the Itzaj kingdom (Jones 1998). The conquest of the Itzaj, together with Spanish efforts to construct a road to link Merida and Santiago de Guatemala, led to widespread dislocation of Maya peoples throughout the region at the turn of the seventeenth century. In the decade following the conquest of the Itzaj, Spanish troops forcibly relocated many Mopan from areas that are now in Belize and resettled them to the west in areas that are now part of the Guatemalan Peten. Even prior to the Itzaj conquest, in 1696, Spanish forces had launched renewed military efforts to capture Chol speakers from the regions that would become southern Peten and southern Belize and bring them under Spanish control by moving them into the Verapaz (Jones 1998:242). Thus, Spain's efforts to exercise sovereign power over these groups involved moving them to territory already under its control, rather than extending control over the territory of southern Belize.

### Dominant Narrative of Belizean History: Spanish Forces "Empty" Belize

The dominant narrative of Belizean history, originally elaborated by British colonial administrators and scholars, cites these Spanish raids and forced relocations to argue that the territory that would become Belize was rendered "empty"—*terra nullius*—prior to British settlement. However, this "emptiness" is subject to debate in contemporary Belize.

Archival evidence regarding the Spanish raids describes how Spanish forces entered the forests of southern Belize with lassos, and "upon discovering any Indian they lassoed him, and thus tied up they took them away, dragging them." However, the account continues, "due to the great horror and fear that they caused they succeeded in performing this cruelty on only two hundred Indians." The others "hid themselves in the innumerable, most concealed caves." Spanish soldiers "moved from one nation to another until reaching Tipu" in west central Belize, "and they left all of the lands of the Chols deserted" (Jones 1998:242–243). This account points to Chol evasion of Spanish forces, even as it suggests that Spanish troops "emptied" these territories.

Eric Thompson, an early British scholar of the Maya of this region, suggested that because the Maya "could disappear into the forest," the Spaniards were never able to "overcome them completely" in what is now Belizean territory. However, he also suggested, providing no supporting evidence, that old-world diseases introduced by the Spanish "wiped out" the Chol populations that had remained in the region (Thompson 1988:5–6). Because Spanish authorities never established a permanent presence in these territories, there is little documentation of what occurred in the region after the raids. Indeed, because southern Belize remained outside of colonial control, some archival evidence suggests that the region continued to serve as a zone of refuge where native peoples could live autonomously, even after the fall of the Itzaj kingdom.[3]

## Spain versus Britain

Because Spain did not settle or control the region that would become Belize, British privateers were able to settle on the coast in the late seventeenth and early eighteenth centuries. The privateers had previously stolen logwood from Spanish ships to sell in England, where it was used for dyeing cloth in the expanding textile industry (Bolland 1977:25). However, after a 1667 treaty outlawed piracy, privateers began to harvest logwood themselves in coastal areas where logwood grew abundantly, from Campeche down the coast of Yucatan and beyond, extending as far south as the Mosquito Coast in what is now Nicaragua (Dobson 1973:53). The earliest record of logwood cutting in what is now Belizean territory dates to 1705 (Bolland and Shoman 1977:3). When prices for logwood rose in the early eighteenth century, the woodcutters purchased enslaved Africans from Jamaica to increase production. Enslaved Africans soon outnumbered Europeans in the small coastal settlement that would later grow to become Belize City (Bolland 1977:51).

Spain protested these incursions to the British Crown, and Spanish forces attacked the woodcutters' settlement numerous times, driving them away or capturing and relocating them. However, Spain was unable to prevent the cutters from returning to the Bay of Honduras. These conflicts formed part of larger struggles between Britain and Spain over control of territory in the Americas. As Spanish naval power waned, the Spanish Crown made concessions to Britain for woodcutting. In the 1763 Paris Peace Treaty, Spain granted to Britain rights to cut logwood within territory that would become Belize (Dobson 1973:82).

However, by this time, development of a synthetic substitute for logwood had precipitated a steep drop in the value of logwood, while growing European demand for tropical hardwoods drove mahogany prices upward. The woodcutters in the Bay of Honduras turned to harvesting mahogany, and mahogany exports from the Belize settlement surpassed logwood exports by the 1770s.

In the 1783 Treaty of Versailles, Spain again accorded British settlers rights to cut logwood in the territory between the Belize and Hondo Rivers (Dobson 1973:73), (see map 2). However, the woodcutters were already extracting more mahogany than logwood and working territories that extended southward beyond these rivers. They pressed London to expand the territory in which they were granted rights.

As conflict and negotiations continued between Britain and Spain over control of territories in the Americas, Spain granted to Britain rights to cut all woods from the Hondo River to the Sibun in the 1786 Convention of London. This concession was offered in exchange for a commitment from Britain to relinquish its claim to the Mosquito Coast and relocate British woodcutters from the Mosquito Coast to the Bay of Honduras (Dobson 1973:73). These treaties accorded to the British only rights to cut wood; they prohibited the construction of fortifications or cultivation of the soil, and they provided for periodic Spanish inspections to ensure compliance with these restrictions.

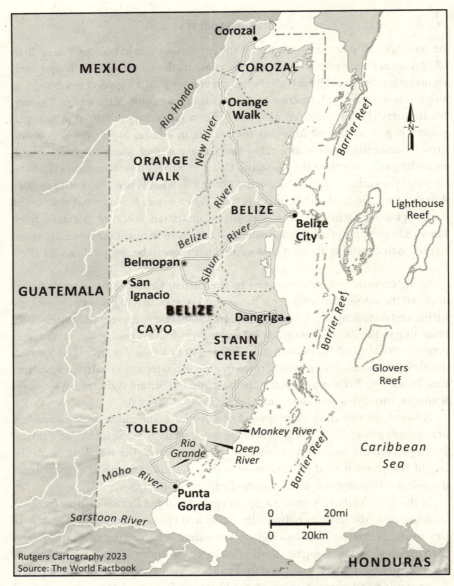

Map 2. Contemporary Belize. Credit: Michael Siegel, Rutgers Cartography 2023.

### Britain versus the Baymen: Ambivalent Relations

The first superintendent for the Belize settlement, charged with supervising the relocation of Mosquito Coast woodcutters to the Bay of Honduras, struggled to exert control over the original settlers. Directly subject to neither British nor Spanish rule, the settlers, who called themselves "Baymen," had created their own political and legal system to administer the settlement. They had established a legislature of sorts, the public meeting, to set rules for the settlement, and they had elected magistrates to enforce those rules. Through the public meeting, settlers had agreed on the rules by which they could claim logwood "works." The shift from logwood, which grew in stands in coastal swamps, to mahogany, which was scattered across inland forests, led to revised landholding practices. The settler elite parceled out among themselves large tracts of land, called "locations," along the rivers, which provided the only avenues of transport (Bolland 1977:43–45; Grant 1976:37). To claim a location, it was sufficient to "erect a hut and a grindstone" along a riverbank not already claimed (Hoffman 2021:45). Although Spain had extended cutting rights from the Belize River south to the Sibun River to accommodate woodcutters evicted from the Mosquito Coast, the established settlers had appropriated this territory for themselves long ago, without seeking permission from London or Spain (Bolland and Shoman 1977:14; Dobson 1973:90). Settlers were cutting wood far south of the Sibun River by the late 1700s: in Deep River and Stann Creek by 1799, along the Moho River in 1814, and, shortly after, all the way to the Sarstoon River (Bolland 1977:31). However, neither the Baymen nor the British superintendent had much interest in—or knowledge of—the southern region. The mountainous terrain made the rivers difficult to navigate and limited timber extraction to the lower reaches of rivers. Lands upriver were largely unknown to either the Baymen or colonial superintendents.

Because mahogany extraction required a larger labor force than logwood, cutters purchased increasing numbers of enslaved Africans to provide the additional labor. As slaveholders became an ever-smaller minority, they became more apprehensive about slave revolts. Three slave rebellions occurred during the lean years between 1765 and 1773, as logwood prices fell, and mahogany operations were just beginning; the longest of these rebellions lasted five months (Bolland 1988:21). In addition, as the mahogany cutters moved inland, traveling farther upriver to locate and extract mahogany, attacks by the Maya became more frequent (Bolland 1977:21–23).

The year 1796 marked the last time that Spanish colonial authorities inspected the settlement to ensure its compliance with the treaties. In 1798, Spanish naval forces attacked the settlement for the last time and were repelled. Subsequently, Spain ceased any pretense of exercising control over the territory. However, even as Spanish power waned, struggles continued for decades between London and its colonial administrators on the one side and the settlers in the Bay of Honduras on the other. Both parties were ambivalent about formalizing their relationship. Britain took steps to perform sovereignty over this territory, without actually claiming the Belize settlement as a British colony. However, colonial administrators sent to manage this territory encountered stiff resistance from the settlers.

In 1817, the British Crown sought to vest in itself sole authority to accord titles to landed property in the settlement. The settlers countered by proclaiming that their system of "locations" also accorded valid land titles. This claim found support in British common law, which recognizes tenure practices established prior to the exercise of British sovereignty. The settlers successfully asserted the primacy of the tenurial system they had developed; the resulting compromise designated as property of the British Crown all lands not already claimed by the settlers as "locations" (Bolland and Shoman 1977:36). Subsequently, an 1855 law converted these "locations" into titled property, uniting the location system with the law of the British sovereign (Bolland and Shoman 1977:73). Because settlers had long ago parceled out among themselves almost all lands between the Hondo and Sibun Rivers, the territories declared Crown lands lay almost entirely south of the Sibun, which formed the southern boundary of the territory in which Spain had granted British settlers rights to cut wood.

Although the Baymen jealously guarded the power they had accorded to themselves to create property and to make and enforce laws, they also pleaded for British military protection against attacks by Spain, the "predations" of "wild Indians," and slave uprisings. In response to slave rebellions in the late 1700s, settlers in the Bay of Honduras relayed urgent requests for Britain to send troops to the settlement, and revolts continued until troops from the West Indian Regiment were stationed in the settlement in the late eighteenth century (Bolland 1988:24). The Baymen also sent urgent pleas to British colonial officials for protection from Spanish attacks throughout the eighteenth century, and they demanded military retribution against the Maya, who attacked mahogany cutters with increasing frequency during the nineteenth century. The settlers were unable to effectively control either the lands they claimed as "locations" or their enslaved labor force. Many slaves escaped into the forest, and slaveowners expressed fear that escaped slaves might ally themselves with the Maya to drive the Baymen out of the territory.

Questions of sovereignty over the Belize settlement became more complex after 1821, when Mexico declared independence for the lands formerly held by Spain in North and Central America, and after 1823, when the United Provinces of Central America broke away from Mexico. Britain recognized Mexico in an 1826 treaty, but that treaty did not settle the boundary between Mexico and British Honduras (Dobson 1973:184). Britain sought to resolve the territory's status and boundaries through talks with Spain, whose sovereignty Britain had recognized in earlier treaties. In 1827, the legislature of the settlement claimed the territory south of the Sibun River all the way to the Sarstoon, with support from the Colonial Office in London (Wilk 1997:55). In 1835, as Britain attempted to settle the boundaries of British Honduras through negotiations with Spain, the colonial superintendent claimed all land between the Hondo and Sarstoon Rivers, with the western boundary formed by an imaginary line running due north and south from Garbutt's Falls on the Belize River (Dobson 1973:184). However, negotiations with Spain produced no agreement, and by 1848, the British colonial secretary abandoned these efforts.

Even though the settlement was not a formal British colony, Britain imposed its 1833 Abolition Act on the settlement, over the opposition of slaveholders. However, to ensure woodcutters a ready source of labor, Britain simultaneously raised the price of state-held land to prevent freed slaves from acquiring land on which to pursue independent livelihoods, and employers used debt peonage to secure labor (Bolland 1988:119–120, 159; Grant 1976:51–52). However, despite the measures taken to ensure that freed slaves would provide an adequate and pliant postemancipation labor supply for the forestry industry, employers complained of labor scarcity. As early as 1802, Garifuna migrating northward from Honduras had settled the southern coast of the territory claimed by Britain. Some mahogany cutters had hired them to labor in their mahogany works alongside slaves. The Garifuna were descendants of Africans integrated into Indigenous communities on St. Vincent in the eastern Caribbean. They had repelled British incursions into their territory until 1797, when British forces defeated them and exiled many to the island of Roatan in present-day Honduras. From Roatan, Garifuna groups expanded north and south along the coast of Central America (Gonzalez 1988). After emancipation, forestry barons increasingly sought out Garifuna labor. In addition, in 1865, Britain brought a small number of indentured workers from China, Barbados, and Jamaica to the Belize settlement; those from Jamaica included people of African descent as well as East Indians (Shoman 1994:87).

### Britain versus the Maya versus Mexico

In response to rising demand for mahogany during the 1830s and 1840s, British woodcutters extended their mahogany harvesting farther upriver and deeper into the forests of central and northwestern British Honduras (Bolland 1988:93). They also extended timber extraction to rivers in the south, though here they worked closer to the coast. The expansion of woodcutting activities provoked attacks by the Maya groups who occupied these areas (Bolland 1988:101). The Baymen requested military support from Britain, reporting to London that "Wild Indians" were committing "depredations" on their mahogany works (Bolland 1988:93).

Conflicts between woodcutters and Maya intensified as the Maya of Yucatan revolted against Spanish Mexicans in 1847, in a rebellion that came to be called the Caste War (Reed 1964). Merchants from the British settlement in the Bay of Honduras sold arms and ammunition to the rebels, who became known as the Santa Cruz Maya (Bricker 1981). In return, the Santa Cruz Maya refrained from attacking the territory claimed by Britain. Representatives of the Mexican government pressured the British to halt this trade. However, British colonial officials allowed the trade to continue, reluctant to antagonize the Santa Cruz Maya, who ruled the territory adjacent to the British settlement (Bolland 1988:95).

In 1853, several groups of Maya pledged support for the Mexican government against the Santa Cruz Maya (Bolland 1988:96). This alliance provoked repeated Santa Cruz attacks against these groups, which pushed many southward into territories claimed by Guatemala and Britain. In British Honduras, the superintendent complained that one of the groups, the Chichanhas, were "burning and otherwise destroying bush and mahogany trees with a view to the cultivation of the soil" (Bolland 1988:97). As British woodcutters extended their operations upriver, the woodcutters came into conflict with them. In 1856 and 1857, the Chichanha Maya raided mahogany works in northern British Honduras, demanding rent for cutting wood in Chichanha territory and ransom for prisoners they had taken (Bolland 1988:96). In 1858, after another Santa Cruz attack, the Chichanha Maya dispersed farther southward, joining existing communities or founding new villages at several locations in what is now northwestern and west-central Belize (Bolland 1988:97). One of the northernmost communities, Icaiche, continued to attack mahogany camps, demanding rent for the lands from which the cutters were harvesting timber; they also took prisoners, for whom they demanded ransom (Bolland 1988:98).

As conflicts with Maya groups in the north and west continued, Britain concluded a treaty with Guatemala in 1859 that recognized the western and southern boundaries of the Belize settlement. The treaty recognized British sovereignty over the territory from the River Hondo in the north to the Sarstoon River in the south, with a western boundary running north from Gracias a Dios Falls on the Sarstoon to Garbutt's Falls on a branch of the Belize River, then due north to the Mexican border (see map 2). Article 7 of this treaty provided for the two parties to jointly construct a road to link Guatemala City to a port on the Caribbean (Dobson 1973:202–211). After the 1859 treaty settled the western and southern boundaries of British territory, Britain finally declared British Honduras an official colony in 1862, with a lieutenant-governor under the authority of the governor of Jamaica. However, as Britain began to demarcate the northern portions of the western border on the ground, colonial officials feared the Icaiche Maya would attack the surveyors. They expressed concern that when the border survey was completed, "many Indians will be dispossessed of land 'which heretofore they have considered as belonging to them'" (Hoffman 2014:63).

In response to Maya attacks on woodcutters, British troops were dispatched upriver in 1866 to defeat and punish the Icaiche Maya. However, this force was routed by an alliance between the Icaiche and Maya from villages farther south, throwing the new colony into crisis (Bolland 1988:98). To confront this threat, the British colonial government sent a force of over 300 soldiers into the forests in 1867 to "avenge the rout of the preceding year" (Bolland 1988:110). British forces burned the houses, food stores, and fields of Maya villages in northwestern British Honduras, driving the Maya out of the area. However, though British forces declared victory, they were not able to prevent the displaced Maya population from returning to rebuild their villages (Bolland 1988:99). The British had succeeded in controlling neither the territory nor the Maya.

Maya attacks soon led to a dramatic change in governance for the new colony of British Honduras. During the crisis of 1866–1867, when mahogany camps in the west and northwest were under constant threat from Maya forces who claimed the territories they were logging, the large landowners pressed for military action to enforce British control over these lands. However, members of the colony's Legislative Assembly were unable to agree on how to pay for military expeditions against the Maya. The Legislative Assembly was dominated by great landowners and urban merchants. The landowners sought to raise revenues for the colony's defense by increasing import duties, while the merchants pushed to increase land taxes. With the two factions of elites unable to agree on a strategy to raise revenues from within the colony, the Legislative Assembly voted to request Crown colony status. British Honduras thus became a Crown colony in 1871, ceding control of the colony's finances to London but forcing London to shoulder the cost of defending the colony (Bolland 1988:111).

The Icaiche Maya continued to assert their claim to territory. In 1870 and 1872, they attacked the two major towns of northern British Honduras, although their leader was fatally wounded in the latter attack (Bolland 1988:99). In 1875, the Icaiche joined forces with other Maya groups to lay claim to the entire north bank of the Belize River, one of two main arteries for transporting timber in the settlement; however, their strength had been diminished (Bolland 1988:99). Finally, in negotiations between the British governor of British Honduras and the Icaiche in 1882, the governor threatened a trade blockade; in response, the Icaiche agreed to respect the territorial boundaries claimed by Britain (Bolland 1988:99).

Following the agreement with the Icaiche, Great Britain's relationships with the two sides in Mexico's decades-long Caste War shifted. Under intense diplomatic pressure from the Mexican government, Britain finally severed relations with the Santa Cruz Maya. This paved the way for an 1893 treaty between Mexico and Britain that set the border between British Honduras and Mexico at the Rio Hondo. The treaty also prohibited Britain from supplying arms to the Santa Cruz Maya (Bolland 1988:99).

In addition to Maya groups who fled southward from the Yucatan during the Caste War, a smaller number of Mexican Spanish elites and members of the intermediate "Mestizo" strata, a term that designated mixed Indigenous and Spanish descent, also fled into territory claimed by Britain south of the River Hondo (Cal 1991:217). Spanish or Mestizo immigrants with capital were allowed to purchase land and establish the first sugar plantations in British Honduras (Judd 1989). After the agricultural efforts of the Yucatecan elites proved successful, colonial officials began to promote the cultivation of sugar in British Honduras. As mahogany prices and production declined sharply after a peak in 1847, timber barons began to establish sugar plantations on some of their northern holdings, where mahogany stocks had been cut (Bolland 1988:105).

During the 1860s and 1870s, the British colonial government sought to "secure the extremities of the colony" for agricultural production (Bolland 1988:110). In their racialized construction of the proper roles for distinct categories of people, British administrators sought to attract white immigrants to establish sugar plantations, by making land available for them to purchase as private property. To secure Maya and Garifuna labor for the plantations they envisioned, colonial administrators prohibited Maya and Garifuna from owning land in the colony.

In 1867, the lieutenant governor issued a regulation declaring, "No Indian will be at liberty to reside upon or occupy or cultivate any land without previous payment or engagement to pay rent whether to the Crown or the owner of the land," a restriction that applied to both Maya and Garifuna (Bolland 1988:110). The following year, the subsequent lieutenant governor recommended the creation of reservations for Maya communities located on lands claimed as state property, that is, Crown lands. The Crown Lands Ordinance of 1872 formalized both prohibitions against Maya and Garifuna land ownership and provisions for establishing reservations for them (Bolland 1988:110; Van Ausdal 2000:16). Colonial officials saw the creation of reservations for Maya and Garifuna as a means to attract Maya and Garifuna to British Honduras, while charging rent for the use of reservation lands would compel them to seek wage labor. Rents might also serve as a token of recognition for British sovereignty and the property in lands claimed by colonial authorities (Bolland 1988:134; Wainwright 2007:59).

However, as O. Nigel Bolland observed, "Though the intent of the colonial policy was to make the Maya more dependent upon the government and more available as a wage-labour force, it was not too effective because . . . it was easier to pass a law in Belize Town than it was to implement it in the remote parts of the colony" (Bolland 1988:136). Maya groups in the north were engaged in warfare against the British as these regulations were issued. Even after the British won Maya submission to British rule in the north, they were unable to implement the reservation policy in that region, because the Crown did not hold lands adequate for agriculture. The policy was only partially implemented in the west, where Maya were reported to make their *milpas* (rainy-season corn plots) wherever they pleased. The colonial administration had greater success implementing its reservation policy in the south, where the government claimed vast tracts as Crown lands (Bolland 1988:138–139).[4]

Though efforts to facilitate plantation agriculture in British Honduras focused primarily on the north, colonial officials did recruit a group of ex-Confederates to establish a plantation in the far south in the late 1860s, after their defeat in the U.S. Civil War. Although British administrators secured indentured laborers from India to provide labor for this endeavor, the plantation failed; its demise was blamed on insufficient labor (Dobson 1973:248; Wilk 1997:56). In the 1880s, a wealthy landowner established a coffee and cacao plantation in the southwestern corner of British Honduras and arranged for Q'eqchi' Maya workers from the Guatemalan Verapaz to work on his estate. This effort prospered until World War I curtailed access to European markets for its products (Wilk 1997:60). After a large Q'eqchi' settlement became established on this plantation, other Q'eqchi' followed, forming independent settlements in the region.

Seeking to secure a labor supply in the south, in 1886 the government welcomed a group of Mopan-speakers from the town of San Luis in the Guatemalan Peten, who were escaping forced labor and taxation by the Guatemalan state (Gregory 1984:1; Thompson 1988:23). They petitioned the British colonial government for lands and received permission to settle and land to cultivate (Wilk 1997:57). Three years later, the community, concerned that its location might not be far enough east to be inside British Honduras, moved farther eastward to the current location of San Antonio village. The state allocated to them a reservation area of two square miles in which the one hundred or so families could live and farm upon payment of land occupancy fees of one dollar per year each (Van Ausdal 2000:15).

Thus, in their earliest efforts to develop agriculture in British Honduras, colonial officials cast the Maya as labor for plantations that would be owned by elites of European descent. The reservations afforded Maya communities the opportunity to self-provision through the practice of milpa cultivation, a form of swidden agriculture based on the rotational clearing, cultivation, and fallowing of plots over a cycle of years. Milpa livelihoods could thus sustain households and communities when wage labor was not available, or wages were insufficient. Communities managed their lands collectively, selecting their own leaders to govern relationships among members and to manage their access to lands.

As discussed above, the first part of the dominant narrative of Belizean history relies on the supposed "emptying" of Belizean territory by the Spanish at the turn of the seventeenth century, leading to claims that British woodcutters had encountered an unoccupied land. The second half of that narrative rests on accounts of the nineteenth-century arrival to Belize of Yucatec-speaking Maya and Spanish-speaking Mestizos in the north and Q'eqchi'- and Mopan-speaking Maya and Garifuna-speakers in the south. Maya groups are thus cast as immigrants, like all other groups in Belizean territory.[5]

## Britain versus Guatemala

In the late 1800s, the British government engaged in negotiations over several options to connect Guatemala's interior to the Caribbean Sea to fulfill the agreement set out in Article 7 of the 1859 treaty, but these came to naught (Dobson 1973:231–232). In 1933, Britain completed a survey of the southern half of the colony's western boundary, and the Guatemalan government agreed that the boundary had been correctly marked (Dobson 1973:235). However, later that year the Guatemalan president reminded Britain of the agreement contained in Article 7 of the 1859 treaty. By this time, the Guatemalan government had built a railway connecting Guatemala City to Puerto Barrios on the Caribbean coast. Britain asserted that this railway fulfilled the requirements of Article 7 and offered to pay 50,000 pounds to defray the expenses incurred by Guatemala in constructing the railway. Guatemala rejected this offer, instead issuing an ultimatum: Britain must either pay Guatemala 400,000 pounds or cede the whole territory of British Honduras to Guatemala upon payment of 400,000 pounds by Guatemala to Britain (Dobson 1973:235). Britain refused this demand. In response, in 1939, Guatemala repudiated the 1859 treaty (Dobson 1973:236).

Subsequently, a new Guatemalan constitution, written in 1945, declared "Belice" part of Guatemalan national territory (Dobson 1973:237). In 1948, Guatemala threatened to invade and "recover" British Honduras, although Guatemala had never controlled it. Britain sent battleships to British Honduras to repel this threat, and the colony's Legislative Council passed a resolution of loyalty to the British Crown to strengthen Britain's claim to British Honduras.

## British Performance of Sovereignty: Colonial Development

During the early decades of colonial rule, Britain had focused on securing the colony's territory. In the twentieth century, Britain sought to develop the territory, sending teams of experts in successive waves to assess the resources of the colony and make recommendations for their use. After a report filed by one team of forestry experts revealed that uncontrolled exploitation of timber resources in British Honduras had destroyed forest stocks, the colonial government established a Forestry Department in 1923 to scientifically manage forests via the establishment of timber plantations (Dobson 1973:261; Van Ausdal 2000:17).

However, colonial administrators also sought more rapid returns on investment than timber plantations offered. Trade deficits caused by declining timber exports and the rising costs of importing food had made the colony of British Honduras uneconomic for Great Britain (Wilk 1997:68). Prioritizing agricultural production, colonial officials created an Agriculture Department in 1928 (Dobson 1973:269). Beginning in the late nineteenth century and continuing across the twentieth century, a series of commissions and study teams published report after report on the agricultural potential of British Honduras, issuing recommendations for land use and crop choices across the colony (Wilk 2006). The colonial government supported sugar production in Orange Walk and Corozal Districts in the north and citrus production in the Stann Creek District in the south. During the 1930s, the government began construction of two roads to connect the northern towns of Orange Walk and Corozal and the western Cayo District to the colony's largest urban center at Belize City.

In 1959, combined sugar and citrus exports surpassed the value of timber exports for the first time. During the same year, another expert report recommended a massive redirection of the economy from forestry to agriculture (Dobson 1973:265; Downie 1959). The Forestry Department's budget was cut by half, and the department concentrated its activities in a few areas with high productive potential, designated "principal forest lands" (Hartshorn et al. 1984:94).

## Britain versus Belizean Nationalists versus Guatemala

Despite the Legislative Council's resolution of loyalty to Britain when Guatemala threatened to invade, the working-class population of British Honduras had been mobilizing against the colonial government for decades, protesting low wages, low standards of living, and high unemployment. In the 1930s, after a major hurricane exacerbated conditions, unemployed workers mobilized the Laborers and Unemployed Association to demand relief work and a minimum wage, uniting the poor across several regions of the colony (Bolland 1988:172). A union movement built on these solidarities during the 1940s, organizing the work forces of the colony's largest employers. In 1950, a currency devaluation by the colonial government sparked the formation of a political party that demanded independence, the Peoples United Party (PUP). Building on the foundation created via union organizing, the

PUP sought to construct and mobilize a nation out of the colony's diverse population, in whose name the nationalists would claim independence.

PUP demands for independence on behalf of this emerging Belizean nation provoked more belligerent declarations and actions from Guatemala, with the Guatemalan president asserting, "*Belice* will be ours by right or might," "by reason or force" (Dobson 1973:239). In 1960 the British government and delegates from British Honduras reached agreement on the steps that would bring the colony to independence, and in 1963 a constitutional conference prepared the framework for British Honduran self-government. Guatemala ruptured diplomatic relations with Britain in response (Dobson 1973:239).

In 1964, British Honduras achieved internal self-government. However, because of the Guatemalan claim, Britain maintained responsibility for defense and foreign relations. The PUP won all elections from 1964 onward, and the party continued to push toward full independence, changing the country's name to Belize in 1973. Guatemala threatened to invade Belize in 1972, 1975, and 1977, rumbling tanks up to the border. In response, the United Kingdom reinforced its military presence in Belize (Shoman 1994:220). Repeated efforts to achieve a negotiated settlement with Guatemala failed. Belizean political leaders thus began to pursue an alternative route to independence: internationalization. PUP leaders lobbied the leaders of postcolonial states to support Belizean independence, beginning with Caribbean and Commonwealth states, expanding to the Non-Aligned Movement, and finally winning support from Latin American countries (Shoman 2010). Beginning in 1975, resolutions calling for Belizean independence were submitted to the United Nations General Assembly each year. In 1977, 110 states voted in favor, with nine against and sixteen abstentions, including the United States. In 1978, 127 states voted in favor. In 1979, 134 states voted in favor. In 1980, the resolution called for Belizean independence with territorial integrity before the end of the next session of the UN General Assembly. The vote was 139 in favor, including, for the first time, the United States. With overwhelming international support, Belize claimed full independence on September 21, 1981, though this step relied on a British defense guarantee in the face of the Guatemalan claim.

## Belizean Nationalists Perform Sovereignty
### *Constructing a Belizean Nation*

As they pushed for independence, Belizean nationalists had worked to forge a Belizean nation in whose name they could demand an independent state. In an effort to dismantle the racial hierarchies instituted by colonial labor regimes, nationalist leaders adopted ethnolinguistic labels to define the emerging nation's constituent groups in less hierarchical terms (Medina 1997), (see table 1). Each language-based category was understood to index a distinct ethnic culture. However, these categories were also depicted as indicators of ancestry; as a result, the categories sustained assumptions associated with the older, explicitly racializing labels. As nationalist leaders promoted this shift in categories, the content of the ethnic

## TABLE 1
### BELIZE POPULATION BY ETHNICITY, 1980–2010

| Category | 1980 | | 1991 | 2000 | | 2010 |
|---|---|---|---|---|---|---|
| Creole | 40.0 | | 29.8 | 24.9 | | 25.9 |
| Mestizo | 33.4 | | 43.6 | 48.7 | | 52.9 |
| Garifuna | 7.6 | | 6.6 | 6.1 | | 6.1 |
| Maya Ketchi [Q'eqchi'] | 2.8 | | 4.3 | 5.3 | | 6.3 |
| Maya | 6.8 | Mopan | 3.7 | 3.9 | | 4.0 |
| | | Yucatec | 3.1 | 1.4 | | 0.9 |
| White | 4.2 | | 0.8 | 0.8 | | 1.2 |
| | | Mennonite | 3.1 | 3.6 | | 3.6 |
| East Indian | 2.1 | | 3.5 | 3.0 | | 3.9 |
| Chinese | 0.2 | | 0.4 | 0.7 | | 1.0 |
| Black/African | | | | 0.3 | | 0.5 |
| Other | 0.6 | | 1.0 | | | 0.4 |
| | | Syrian | 0.1 | 1.1 | Lebanese | 0.1 |

Sources: 1980 Census; 1991 Census; 2000 Census; 2010 Census.

cultures they identified was limited to expressive forms: in addition to having its own language, each group was understood to have its own traditional foods, folktales, dress, music, and dance.

Creoles, described as the mixed descendants of African and European ancestors, spoke Creole. They were concentrated in Belize City, the colony's commercial capital, seat of government, and largest population center. They were associated with genres of music and folktales that combined European, African, and local elements. The census label "Mestizo" designated people understood to be of mixed Maya and Spanish ancestry; this group was colloquially called "Spanish," the language that defined membership in the category. Mestizos were concentrated in the northern districts of Corozal and Orange Walk as well as western Cayo District. The content of Mestizo culture was defined by distinctive dances, dishes, and folktales with roots in the Yucatan Peninsula of Mexico. Garifuna, defined as the mixed descendants of Carib Indian and African ancestors, spoke Garifuna and predominantly lived in towns and villages along the southern coast. They practiced a distinctive religious and healing tradition, had their own form of traditional dress, and were known for dishes that reflected livelihoods based on fishing and the cultivation of cassava and other root crops, plantains, and coconuts. People previously lumped into the racial category "Indian" were redefined as Yucatec, Mopan, and Q'eqchi', based on their respective languages. Yucatecs lived primarily in the northern districts, while Mopan and Q'eqchi' were concentrated in the inland regions of southern Belize.[6] Yucatec identity was associated with much of the same food culture and dance that characterized Mestizos, while Mopan and Q'eqchi' identities were associated with rurality and the cultivation and consumption of corn, as well as distinctive forms of women's dress and music that distinguished Mopan from Q'eqchi'. Although one color designation—"White"—remained, people previously lumped together in this category were divided into two separate categories: Mennonites were accorded their own designation as German-speakers who lived in rural farming communities, primarily in the north and west, practicing their own religion and dressing in distinctive ways, while the label "White" was applied to non-Mennonite, largely English-speaking, light-skinned elites, whose expressive forms manifested the class status that marked them as different from other Belizeans.

The linguistic determination of this approach assumed that each language identified a group that shared common descent and its own distinct culture. These assumptions ignored multilingualism and "mixing" across official categories, despite the prevalence of both in Belize. Though Creole, Mestizo, and Garifuna categories were all defined by "mixture," they effectively relegated mixing to the distant past. Contemporary mixing across ethnolinguistic categories was not recognized through the creation of additional classifications. If the new ethnolinguistic categories do not account for current mixing across groups, neither do they account for group affiliations in the distant past. As this chapter has shown, during the colonial period, Maya groups who spoke the same language but identified with different communities waged war against one another, while political alliances or trade relations bound together members of Maya groups that spoke different languages. Some Maya fled colonial rule, moving into territories beyond Spanish control that were inhabited by speakers of different languages, while other Maya were forcibly dislocated from their home regions and taken to regions where different languages predominated. Further, the assumption that speakers of distinct languages practice distinct cultures also precludes the possibility of any shared Maya cultural beliefs or practices that would cross language boundaries, despite evidence of such shared cultural features (Carlsen 1997; Fischer 1999).

Citing the "colonial policy of divide and rule," which "ensured that our various cultures remained largely isolated from, and suspicious of each other," nationalists declared the elimination of "all colonially inherited prejudices about each other's cultures" an "essential part of the decolonization process" (Medina 1997:757). The cultural forms associated with each ethnic category could be recognized and celebrated by all Belizeans as equal in value. Nationalist leaders thus cast the Belizean nation as multiethnic from its beginning.

However, to avert potential ethnic competition or conflict, Belizean political leaders also promoted an overarching national culture, which, they asserted, all Belizeans shared across ethnolinguistic categories. They defined Belizean national culture as a set of shared values—democracy, peace, and the valorization of ethnic diversity itself—that oriented social and civic life in Belize and united all members of the Belizean nation. Casting Belize as an exemplary nation—peaceful, democratic, and multicultural—legitimized its very existence as an independent country, as Guatemala continued to assert its claim to Belize (Medina 1997). While a series of military dictatorships in Guatemala prosecuted a brutal counterinsurgency war targeting Guatemala's Indigenous Maya population, Belizean political leaders constructed Belize as an anti-Guatemala.

Belizean leaders thus constructed a nation that was quite distinct from its Central American neighbors or broader Latin American patterns, in which nationalist leaders had sought to produce homogeneous nations by assimilating Indigenous peoples into European or Mestizo populations and norms (de la Peña 2005). Indeed, as Belize approached independence, Creoles represented the largest ethnic category, and Belize was often defined as a "Black country." Postindependence, new school textbooks described Belize as "a Caribbean nation in Central America." The numeric and cultural dominance of Creoles meant that Belizean Mestizos could not occupy the mythological space the Mestizo category occupies in other Central American countries.

Of course, the creation of Belize as a plural nation did not erase class hierarchies of power and status; while a few White, Creole, and Mestizo families comprised a small economic elite, the vast majority, across ethnic categories, were poor and powerless (Wilk 1986:75).

## *Property and Development*

In addition to efforts to mobilize a Belizean nation around a set of core values, Belizean nationalists pursued economic development as a complementary territorializing strategy to materialize and extend state power across the entire national space (Medina 2004; Wainwright 2007). Development policies aimed to perform and legitimize the Belizean state, justify its inheritance of the prerogatives of the colonial state that preceded it, and materialize its control over the territory claimed on behalf of the Belizean nation. When Belizean nationalists attained self-government in 1964, they appropriated from the colonial power control over lands the British had declared "Crown lands." At the time, only 5 percent of the lands in Belize with high agricultural potential were under cultivation; the remainder was forested (Dobson 1973:273). Casting the forests that covered most of Belize as "idle lands" that contributed nothing to national development, nationalists confined timber harvesting to areas with high concentrations of commercially valuable species. They distributed national lands—the former Crown lands—to small and large farmers, who were required to clear their forest cover to cultivate export crops. The government acquired additional forested lands from absentee owners for distribution to farmers and conversion to agriculture (Bolland and Shoman 1977:113). The creation and distribution of private property in lands constituted the Belizean state as a sovereign territorial force; property creation also anchored national development, which further substantiated the existence of a sovereign Belizean state.

Sugar became the country's dominant export and foreign exchange earner. As sugar production expanded in northern Belize, so did Belizean GDP, the incomes of large and small farmers, and job opportunities for wage laborers. The PUP also encouraged the cultivation of citrus and bananas for export in the Stann Creek District of southern Belize.

## Analysis
### *Performing State, Sovereignty, and Territory*

In addition to providing the historical context required to understand the events that play out in subsequent chapters, this chapter has also demonstrated why it is necessary to interrogate—rather than take for granted—the existence of the sovereign territorial state. Though many political actors have claimed sovereignty over the lands and territories represented on contemporary Belizean maps, most have struggled to *perform* sovereignty or consolidate state control over this territory. This chapter also illustrated the intertwined production of state, sovereignty, and territory and the central role played by the production of property in their co-construction. As subsequent chapters explore how Indigenous communities and tropical nature are governed in the present, they will attend to how and to what degree contemporary Belizean political leaders perform state presence, assert sovereignty, and materialize Belizean territory, all in the shadow of the Guatemalan threat.

This chapter also demonstrates ways that Belize represents an anomaly in relation to regional patterns. As a British colony, whose economy relied overwhelmingly on the labor of enslaved Africans, it followed a trajectory distinct from Latin American historical patterns and more similar to Caribbean countries. However, its Indigenous and Mestizo populations, which now represent nearly two thirds of its total population, reflect its location on the mainland of Central America. Further, although Belizean independence came very late relative to Latin American countries, the Belizean nation was defined as multicultural from the earliest days of the nationalist movement. The Guatemalan claim, which delayed Belizean independence, continues to threaten its territorial sovereignty. Finally, Belize has been a formal democracy since it attained self-government in 1964. Unlike most Latin American countries, including its Central American neighbors, Belize has never experienced military dictatorship. The distinct trajectory of Belize requires an approach that disentangles neoliberalism from the context of democratic and multicultural reforms that accompanied neoliberal policies in much of the region. I also distinguish *Indigenous* rights, which have been the focus in Belize, from the human rights concerns that were prominent in opposition to Latin American dictatorships, because the two have distinct implications for the content and practice of sovereignty.

CHAPTER 3

# NGO Government of the State

## CONDUCTING THE CONDUCT OF STATE OFFICIALS

This chapter explores the devolution of governmental power from "the state" to an alliance of nongovernmental organizations (NGOs), as Belize confronted a debt crisis by implementing neoliberal reforms. Although literature on neoliberalism focuses primarily on the impact of neoliberal policies on the least powerful, here I examine how NGO leaders sought to direct the conduct of elected officials and senior civil servants who perform "the Belizean state." To avoid casting the state as a monolithic or self-evident object, I focus on the actions and interactions of specific actors who occupy specific positions within the cabinet, ministries, or government departments. I avoid the suggestion of a neat divide between "state" and "nonstate" by exploring relationships that cross this supposed divide.

The chapter also explores how the implementation of ecotourism further devolved the governance of Belizean nature from conservation NGOs to "the market" for tropical nature. I approach ecotourism as a mechanism of neoliberal government, through which the commodification of "tropical rainforests" and the conjuring of a "market" that desires to consume such commodities enables nature to be governed through the application of market rationalities. In the process, both conservation NGO personnel and Belizean state officials also come to be governed through the market, their decisions shaped by their perceptions of northern tourists' desire to experience tropical nature.

### Intersecting Debt and Biodiversity Crises
#### *The Debt Crisis*

From the beginning of self-government, Belizean nationalists pursued a development strategy based on the conversion of Belizean forests, which they described as "idle lands," to agricultural production for export. Sugar production in the northern districts of Corozal and Orange Walk accounted for more than half the total value of Belizean exports. When world sugar prices dropped by 60 percent between 1980 and 1981, government leaders responded to the shortfall in sugar revenues by contracting additional loans (Hartshorn et al. 1984:15, 17). This plunged the country into a debt crisis shortly after it achieved independence. As loans came due, officials from the Ministry of Finance turned to the International Monetary Fund (IMF) for a Compensatory Financing loan (World Bank 1984:xv). As a condition for assistance, the IMF required "structural adjustments," including reductions in state budgets and the diversification and expansion of the nation's export base. The former would redirect state funds from government programs to debt servicing; the latter would increase foreign exchange earnings, required to repay the nation's debts and cover its import bill. As a first step to diversify the national economy, the Ministry of Agriculture and Natural Resources moved to expand nonsugar agricultural exports, privatizing state-owned banana farms (Moberg 1997), and distributing state lands to both small- and large-scale farmers who would clear their forest cover to plant citrus (Medina 2004). Forest clearance in Belize doubled or tripled during the 1980s, especially in the heavily forested south (King et al. 1993:54–55). Belize thus replicated the pattern of accelerating deforestation occurring across the global south, as development aspirations and debt crises increased pressure on natural resources to generate revenue.

Ministers of government also considered tourism as a strategy to further diversify and expand the national economy. Prior to this time, the prime minister had accorded low priority to tourism, wary of its neocolonial potential; he sought to prevent Belize from becoming a "nation of waiters and busboys" (Wilk 2006:177). Despite this official stance, an American entrepreneur had opened a "jungle camp" in central Belize during the 1950s, attracting sport fishermen and trophy hunters interested in bagging exotic species such as jaguars and crocodiles (BTB n.d.; Johnson 1998:77–79). During the 1960s, a small marine tourism enclave had emerged on Ambergris Caye, the largest caye, capitalizing on its location just a half-mile from the Mesoamerican Barrier Reef. This spectacular reef system, the second longest in the world, runs the entire length of Belize. In 1971, an episode of the U.S. television series *The Undersea World of Jacques Cousteau* featured the "Blue Hole," a collapsed volcano on a Belizean atoll, which Cousteau pronounced one of the top ten dive destinations in the world. The TV episode and the endorsement generated increasing international interest in Belize as a dive destination (BTB n.d.).

As cabinet ministers embraced tourism more enthusiastically, they established the Belize Tourism Board (BTB). They charged the BTB with expanding the tourism industry geographically beyond the largest caye to provide development opportunities to other regions of the country and developing a Belizean "brand" to market the country as a destination (GIS 1982).[1]

## The Biodiversity Crisis

At the same time, accelerating extinctions catalyzed efforts by Northern conservation NGOs to counter species loss by creating protected areas across the world. The decade between 1985 and 1995 saw unprecedented growth in protected areas, which came to occupy nearly 12 percent of the world's land surface (Brockington et al. 2008:1, 38). Tropical forests became objects of special concern, perceived as extremely important—but extremely endangered—global resources: important as counters to global warming and reservoirs of biological diversity; endangered because of their rapid destruction (Slater 2003; Takacs 1996). As a result of heightened concern for biodiversity, Belizean forests attracted increasing international attention.

Despite the acceleration of forest-to-agriculture conversion in response to the debt crisis, the Forestry Department estimated that 70 percent of Belizean lands remained forested. These lands formed part of the largest contiguous area of tropical forest north of the Amazon, extending across the borders of Belize, Mexico, and Guatemala (Jacobs and Castañeda 1998:v).[2] Significant for their biodiversity, Belizean forests also served as watersheds that protected the Mesoamerican Barrier Reef.

As northern conservation NGOs sought out critical conservation opportunities across the world, Dr. Archie Carr III, assistant director at the Wildlife Conservation Society (WCS) in New York, perused hunting magazines for insights into the status of threatened species in specific locales.[3] An account of jaguar hunting in Belize caught his eye. Jaguars had become endangered or extinct across much of their traditional range because of habitat loss and human predation. Were they more abundant in Belize? Carr contacted the Belize Audubon Society (BAS), the oldest and largest conservation organization in Belize, to offer a study of Belizean jaguars.

The president of the BAS consulted with staff in the Ministry of Natural Resources, who expressed interest. Thus, in 1983, the WCS hired wildlife ecologist Alan Rabinowitz to assess the relative density of jaguars throughout the country and identify areas with high potential for protecting jaguars (Rabinowitz 2000:6–7). Rabinowitz found evidence that jaguars were abundant in the large expanses of "unspoiled wilderness" in Belize and identified a promising area for jaguar protection: the Cockscomb Basin of southern Belize. "The potential for conservation was tremendous," Rabinowitz asserted, "and the time to act was now" (Rabinowitz 2000:13). Wealthy investors were razing forest to establish citrus plantations or cattle ranches near the Cockscomb, while Maya *milperos* cleared small parcels to cultivate subsistence and cash crops. Tourism entrepreneurs were also promoting trophy-hunting expeditions.

## The Belize Audubon Society

In this instance, Belize Audubon Society leaders played a role that would become familiar, as brokers between Northern conservation NGOs and Belizean government officials. The Belize Audubon Society was founded in 1969, and its members represented the social elite of Belize City. They were connected to one another through kinship, professional relationships, and the joy they derived from monthly bird-watching field trips.[4] BAS members included both Belizeans and foreigners, primarily from the United Kingdom or the United States. Regardless of their countries of origin, half of its founding members were current or former high-ranking civil servants, whose networks included civil servants and elected leaders (Waight and Lumb 1999:3–6). For example, James Waight, who served as president of the Belize Audubon Society for its first seventeen years, spent his working life in the Ministry of Natural Resources, rising to the position of surveyor general of Belize. Other BAS members had similar career trajectories. Their number included officers from government departments including Forestry, Archaeology, Tourism, Planning, Fisheries, and Lands and Surveys (Waight and Lumb 1999:5–7). Two founding BAS members were sisters of Peoples United Party (PUP) leader George Price, who served five terms as prime minister of Belize, and the long-serving first president of the BAS was the Prime Minister's brother-in-law.

BAS efforts to direct the conduct of government officials predate by decades the devolution of state responsibilities associated with neoliberal policies. The society's leaders sent frequent letters to the Minister of Natural Resources and his staff, requesting protection for threatened species such as jaguars, manatees, and jabiru storks. BAS also advocated for protection of critical wildlife habitat, resulting in the declaration in 1977 of seven small Crown Reserves on mangrove cayes to protect rookeries (Hartshorn et al. 1984:98). These Crown Reserves joined Half Moon Caye, which had been declared a Crown Reserve in 1928 to protect the nesting grounds of the red-footed booby. However, these Crown Reserves were protected on paper only; there was no management.

Both reserves and rare species could serve as tourist attractions, BAS leaders asserted, citing frequent bird-watching tours to Belize organized by conservation NGOs from the United States. BAS leaders sometimes invited state officials to join these excursions to observe for themselves the interest foreigners took in Belizean wildlife. On one occasion, three BAS leaders, joined by the research director of the U.S. National Audubon Society, hosted the Chief Forest Officer, Forestry's Conservation Officer, the Secretary of the Tourism Bureau, and the Chief Information Officer on a trip to Crooked Tree Lagoon. The lagoon was an important wetlands habitat for local and migratory birds, for which the BAS had requested protection. The Chief Information Officer subsequently wrote in glowing terms in the government's monthly news magazine about the birdlife experienced on the excursion and the confidence of the U.S. Audubon Research Director that protecting the lagoon could offer "a sure financial return," as "growing numbers of tourists" seek opportunities to explore the "fascinating natural world" (GIS 1973). Through these engagements, BAS members began to constitute a market for protected Belizean nature in the imaginations of state officials.

Just as Belizean BAS members warmly welcomed U.S. Audubon associates into their social circles, their Audubon contacts integrated BAS leaders into their networks of conservation NGOs, including other Audubon chapters, the World Wildlife Foundation-US (WWF-US), and the Wildlife Conservation Society (WCS). BAS leaders sought information and advice from their North American partners on issues ranging from pesticide use to petroleum refining to traffic in animal pelts. BAS leaders shared this information with staff in the Ministry of Natural Resources, as they pushed for and shaped Belizean regulatory policies (Waight and Lumb 1999:62–64). BAS officers were also involved in drafting the Wildlife Protection Act and the National Parks System Act, both of which were passed into law within two months of Belizean independence. Sometimes, BAS leaders assembled funding for Belizean conservation efforts. In one case, the BAS secured funds to enable the Belizean government to purchase privately held lands to establish a natural monument, winning contributions from the World Wildlife Fund–US, the Nature Conservancy, the National Audubon Society–US, and multiple smaller conservation organizations (Waight and Lumb 1999:126).

## Governing Nature: Conservation NGOs and the State

Encouraged by Rabinowitz's evidence of a significant jaguar population in Belize, the WCS funded a longer study in 1983–1984 in the Cockscomb Basin. In the first large study of jaguars carried out in a tropical forest habitat, Rabinowitz trapped and sedated jaguars to collect data on their sex, life stage, size, and weight, before placing radio collars around their necks to track their movements. He collected scat and recorded paw prints to learn more about their food sources and habits. The Cockscomb appeared to offer a promising site for jaguar protection: a rugged, heavily forested area adjacent to the Maya Mountains that run the length of southern Belize. The Cockscomb was designated as state land.

Rabinowitz wrote letters to government officials to request protection for the Cockscomb's jaguar population and made periodic trips to Belmopan, the capital, to meet with them in person. However, he lamented, his letters were rarely acknowledged, and when he visited government offices, his "pleas for Cockscomb were greeted with compassion and concern, but nothing was done" (Rabinowitz 2000:316).

Meanwhile, BAS leaders strategically used their personal and professional relationships with ministers, permanent secretaries, and department heads to make the case for jaguar protection, sometimes accompanied by Rabinowitz or Dr. Carr from the WCS. BAS leaders did not focus their efforts on a generic entity—"the state." Rather, they targeted officials with whom they had relationships, those responsible for natural resources or tourism, and those recognized as especially powerful. The latter included cabinet ministers, because the cabinet wields most of the power to set policies in the Belizean political system.[5] BAS leaders also lobbied public officers in the Ministry of Natural Resources, the administrative unit most involved in shaping and implementing environmental policy. Overseeing the departments of agriculture, forestry, and lands, the Ministry of Natural Resources pursued a contradictory set of charges: its staff was simultaneously responsible for catalyzing agricultural development, maximizing timber revenues, preventing "haphazard" clearing of forests, protecting watersheds and wildlife, and managing national parks (Hartshorn et al. 1984:122). BAS leaders worked to educate the Minister of Natural Resources, the Permanent Secretary, and department heads within the Ministry of Natural Resources about the global significance of Belize's jaguar population and the conditions required to protect it. Collaboration between the WCS and the BAS combined the data, expertise, and prestige of the WCS with Audubon leaders' personal and professional relationships and reputations.

However, as conservationists advocated for jaguar protection in the Cockscomb Basin, other actors were pursuing logging interests in the Cockscomb. The basin had been logged by a local family from 1937 to 1962. After a direct hit by a hurricane in 1961 leveled its forests, logging ceased in the Cockscomb for a decade. Timber extraction recommenced between 1970 and 1976, and another concession was let to two Americans through 1984 (Emmons et al. 1996:14–15). A 1984 study designated the Cockscomb among the "principal forest lands" of Belize, citing a Forestry Department timber survey conducted in the late 1970s that revealed dense concentrations of hardwoods (Hartshorn et al. 1984:94–95). Logging licenses were granted, and U.S. investors were negotiating with representatives from the Ministry of Natural Resources and the Forestry Department to launch a plywood manufacturing operation in the basin.

Further, wealthy agricultural entrepreneurs were bulldozing forests around the eastern perimeter of the Cockscomb to plant citrus orchards and expand cattle operations, and some were eying lands within the Cockscomb for future expansion. A land use survey carried out in the 1980s identified some lands in the Cockscomb Basin with "considerable agricultural potential" (King et al. 1989:29). Residents of several predominantly Mopan Maya villages situated on or near the eastern rim of the basin already cultivated crops, hunted, fished, and harvested forest materials for housing, food, and medicinal purposes within the Cockscomb. Although the Cockscomb was designated as state property, state officials had made no effort to exclude residents of these Maya communities from the basin. One community, Quam Bank, located on the basin's eastern rim, had requested from the Lands Department 2,000 acres of land within the Cockscomb for small-scale swidden agricultural production.

BAS leaders arranged for George Schaller, Wildlife Conservation Society director, and Archie Carr III, the assistant director, to meet with officials in the Ministry of Natural Resources. Pressing for protection of the Cockscomb, they won a promise from the Minister that the Belizean government would consider designating the Cockscomb Basin a Forest Reserve. In the meantime, the ministry imposed a moratorium on the distribution of lands within the Cockscomb Basin until the jaguar study was completed, instructing the Lands Commissioner to turn away requests for land in the basin (Rabinowitz 2000:232).

As Rabinowitz's research drew to a close, BAS president James Waight arranged an opportunity for Rabinowitz and Carr to present the research results to the entire cabinet and make a pitch for protection of the Cockscomb. In a two-hour lecture over lunch in October 1984, Rabinowitz explained his research methods and presented his findings on jaguar numbers, ranges, behaviors, and diet. The relatively healthy jaguar population in Belize was critical at a global scale, he asserted, because the jaguar had virtually disappeared from most of its traditional range (Rabinowitz 2000:321–322).

Rabinowitz asserted that rainforest was an economic asset to a country only when left intact, emphasizing the Cockscomb's critical roles as a watershed. He warned that rain forest soils are highly erodible; thus, forest clearance would result in erosion, with silt ultimately being deposited on the barrier reef. The silt would kill corals, damaging the marine ecosystem and the fishing industry that depended on it. Logging, "slash-and-burn" agriculture, and large-scale clear-cutting of forest for citrus and cattle production were driving "massive deforestation," he continued. "A few may benefit in the short term, but the populace will suffer in the years to come" (Rabinowitz 2000:320).

Rabinowitz framed these predicted ecological disasters in economic terms: "Yes, I wanted Cockscomb preserved for jaguars, I told them bluntly, but forgetting about the jaguars, if it was not protected, the consequences would be economically disastrous" (Rabinowitz 2000:320). Because the Cockscomb's forests slow and regulate the release of rainwater into three major rivers, he warned, their destruction would lead to flash flooding that would wipe out bridges along the Southern Highway (Rabinowitz 2000:321).

Advocacy for the creation of a protected area for jaguars in the Cockscomb Basin coincided in time with the debt crisis and IMF structural adjustment programs in Belize, which had intensified pressure on natural resources to generate revenues. For two decades, the Belizean government had promoted a development strategy based on the conversion of forested lands to export agriculture, and the Lands Department had distributed state lands to farmers who would clear their forest cover to cultivate export crops, including large parcels near the Cockscomb Basin. Now, conservation advocates were asking cabinet ministers to weigh the importance of the Cockscomb for protecting jaguars against its potential for timber production or conversion to agriculture.

As the prime minister polled the assembled cabinet members, the ministers inquired whether they might combine jaguar protection and watershed protection with "high-grade" logging, seeking to optimize the economic value of Belizean forests. Yes, the WCS representatives replied, as long as no hunting or settlement were allowed within the basin (Rabinowitz 2000:321). The prime minister turned to the Minister of Natural Resources and instructed him to move ahead with protection for the Cockscomb (Rabinowitz 2000:322).

However, the presence of the Mopan Maya community of Quam Bank within the Cockscomb complicated implementation of this decision. Because settlement was prohibited in protected areas, designation of the Cockscomb as a protected area would require the community's expulsion. Neither the residents of Quam Bank nor any of the other Maya communities near the Cockscomb had been incorporated into discussions concerning the possible creation of a protected area in the Cockscomb. In a meeting with Lands Department staff in the capital in pursuit of their request for 2,000 acres in the Cockscomb, Quam Bank leaders were informed of the moratorium on land distribution in the Cockscomb and advised that no one else could move into the basin. On a later trip to the capital, they were told they would not be granted land within the basin, because of efforts to create a protected area. However, neither elected officials nor Ministry of Natural Resources staff wanted to evict them. "The Indian problem," as Rabinowitz framed it, stood in the way of conservationists' objectives: "The government would not physically move the Indians from Cockscomb, nor could they allow legal designation of the area as a forest reserve while there were still residents there" (Rabinowitz 2000:332–333).

By late 1984, conservationists found themselves racing against time: Prime Minister Price had called elections for December of that year, and the odds were against another PUP electoral victory. The permanent secretary in the Ministry of Natural Resources, a senior civil servant trained by BAS president Waight, ensured inclusion of "the Cockscomb issue" on the agenda for the final sitting of the legislature. "Though the Forestry Department was hesitant to act without the Indian question resolved," Rabinowitz explained, the Minister of Natural Resources had "decided to proceed, regardless" (Rabinowitz 2000:322–323).

"Strangely enough," Rabinowitz recounted, "the Indian problem resolved itself" (Rabinowitz 2000:333). While he was in the capital, Rabinowitz reported, he learned that the desire of Quam Bank's Mopan residents "to obtain schooling for their children and to have a church on land that they owned had overcome all else, and they had decided to all leave Cockscomb" (Rabinowitz 2000:333). Most of the families would return to Maya Centre, just outside the Cockscomb. "I immediately informed the government of their decision," Rabinowitz explained, "knowing it would speed matters up" (Rabinowitz 2000:333).

On December 2, 1984, the government declared the Cockscomb Basin a Forest Reserve and imposed a hunting ban within the reserve to protect jaguars. With this step, Belize became the first country in the world to establish a protected area for jaguar conservation.

Former Quam Bank residents narrate a very different sequence of events that culminated in what they describe as an eviction, which will be explored in the next chapter.

Although conservationists succeeded in getting the Cockscomb declared a Forest Reserve, they would have preferred a stricter form of protection. Forest Reserve lands can easily be "de-reserved" for agriculture. However, extant logging concessions for the basin prevented a higher level of protection. In reality, the Forestry Department was unable to uphold even the hunting ban it had declared for the Cockscomb Forest Reserve. Enforcement of wildlife protection laws was "virtually non-existent," due to the department's lack of personnel, vehicles, equipment, and training in wildlife management (Hartshorn et al. 1984:104). Further, in the same month that the Minister of Natural Resources established the Forest Reserve in the Cockscomb, he had also created the Crooked Tree Wildlife Sanctuary in north-central Belize, for which the BAS had also lobbied (Johnson 1998, 2015, 2019). However, in the midst of a debt crisis, reduced state budgets prevented the Ministry of Natural Resources from hiring, training, and equipping personnel to administer protected areas. Conservation activities fell under the jurisdiction of the Forestry Department, but that department was "understaffed, underfinanced, undertrained" and "in no position to take on this added responsibility" (Hartshorn et al. 1984:104).

Faced with the challenge of managing two large terrestrial protected areas, the Ministry of Natural Resources delegated management responsibilities for both to Audubon. A 1984 letter from the permanent secretary in the Ministry of Natural Resources authorized the Belize Audubon Society "to work along with the Forestry Department of the Government of Belize in the protection and management of areas designated under the Forestry Act and the National Parks and Refuges Acts" (Waight and Lumb 1999:33). The agreement granted permission to BAS to draft management plans for the government's approval and to implement such plans, "including the building of structures and other works on [the] land" and the appointment of wardens (Waight and Lumb 1999:33). However, the agreement allocated no funds to the BAS for managing the protected areas, and it expressly prohibited the BAS from collecting fees. Government officials were concerned that charging entrance fees for protected areas might deter tourists from visiting Belize.

Assuming these new responsibilities marked a major transition for the BAS. Up to this time, it had functioned as a membership organization with no paid staff. It had few expenses and a tiny budget derived from membership dues. Now, small grants from the Massachusetts Audubon Society enabled the BAS to open an office, hire its first part-time executive director, and provide him clerical support, as the society initiated efforts to manage the new protected areas in the Cockscomb Basin and at Crooked Tree Lagoon. The WWF-US provided funds to manage the Cockscomb, including hiring a warden, whose job was to stop traffic on the access road to prevent people from entering the reserve to hunt.

At the same time, the BAS also confronted another transition: just after the PUP government had designated the Cockscomb a forest reserve, national elections on December 14, 1984, brought the United Democratic Party (UDP) to power for the first time, ending twenty years of PUP rule. BAS members were concerned that the organization's strong ties to PUP leaders might work against the society under the new administration. However, the new UDP administration prioritized tourism development, announcing plans to transform the tourism sector into "a major contributor to the national economy" and a remedy to the country's balance-of-payments deficit (GIS 1985:6). This commitment to tourism made the BAS a valuable partner to the UDP administration.[6]

## Imagining New Commodities and New Markets

As the government embraced tourism, state officials commissioned a flurry of studies to guide development of the sector (Alexander 1985; Berl-Cawtran Consortium 1984; CTRDC 1985a, 1985b). These studies identified the enormous "deficits" Belize confronted compared with established tourism destinations. One deficit was infrastructural: only two of the country's "highways" were paved; the others were gravel roads. Only one hotel met international standards, and the country lacked water and sewage systems. Belize also had a marketing deficit: it had never launched a serious effort to "brand" itself for foreign tourists. Further, Belize had an information deficit: the government lacked data on the characteristics of tourists who visited Belize.

To address the information deficit, teams of consultants surveyed visitors to Belize to identify the kind of tourists drawn to Belize, their motivations for choosing Belize, and their expenditures while in-country (Morgan 1990). Based on their findings, consultants recommended that Belize develop a marketing strategy to target "jungle" or "adventure tourists." They pinpointed a potential market for Belizean adventure tourism among individuals from "middle to upper income levels" in thirteen states in the western United States, whose high-income, highly mobile, and adventurous populations offered "a sound market in which to launch an assault" (Alexander 1985:27). "Adventure" tourism would capitalize on growing interest in "tropical rainforests" in the global North and complement the reputation Belize was already developing for marine tourism (CTRDC 1985a:7).

As Anna Tsing has noted, the production of a commodity, the "object of consumers' desire," requires huge leaps of imagination (Tsing 2005:51). It is the work of the translator or "the power-crazed magician" to "conjure" consumer desires and imagine the possibility of profit (Tsing 2005:52, 57). Belize Audubon leaders had worked for two decades to enable government leaders to envision Belizean flora and fauna as a potential tourism commodity, as they invited government officials to join them on birdwatching expeditions with conservationists from the United States. U.S. conservationists themselves had reinforced the possibility of "selling" Belizean nature, as they asserted the existence of growing numbers of nature lovers like themselves, eager to experience Belizean wildlife. Because most Belizean elected officials were not themselves birders or nature enthusiasts, initially the idea that people from the global North would travel to Belize to experience forests—denigrated as "bush" by many Belizeans—seemed ludicrous. Cabinet ministers were already market-rational subjects, but they had to be convinced that standing forests could generate revenues, that a market for standing tropical forests existed. U.S. conservationists' repeated performances of consumer desire to view Belizean wildlife, supported by the research of "experts" on tourist desires and demand, finally succeeded in "conjuring" a market for protected tropical nature in the imaginations of Belizean government officials.

The Belize Tourism Board responded with a campaign to promote Belize as "the Adventure Coast," "famous for its picturesque cayes and spectacular diving," but offering "equally exciting" activities in its "undiscovered and unspoiled" interior: "jungle walks to Mayan archaeological sites, canoe rides on exotic rivers, riding trails through rainforests, birdwatching and photography" (*Belize and the Barrier Reef Cayes: Profile*, n.d.). In a bid to position Belize as a "paradise for the environmentalist," the new Minister of Tourism announced a shift away from trophy hunting: "official policy will discourage game hunting to protect endangered species" (GIS 1985).

Coordinated marketing efforts by the BTB and the private-sector Belize Tourism Industry Association produced the desired results: tourist arrivals more than doubled between 1985 and 1990. During the 1960s, tourist arrivals had averaged around 11,000 annually. They rose to an annual average of 30,000 during the 1970s and reached 64,000 by 1980 (Barry 1992:50). However, tourist arrivals climbed sharply once the BTB launched its first marketing campaign, exceeding 207,000 by 1990 (King et al. 1993:87–88).

### From Forest Reserve to Wildlife Sanctuary

In 1985, BAS leaders learned from the Permanent Secretary in the Ministry of Natural Resources that a 3,640-acre parcel of land in the Cockscomb was no longer included in logging concessions and was thus eligible for a more secure category of protection. Because this parcel included the only access road into the Cockscomb, it provided a strategic opportunity to control vehicular traffic into the basin. It also included the site of the former logging camp, which offered an already-cleared space for tourism infrastructure, along with several deteriorating buildings. The BAS immediately requested its designation as a wildlife sanctuary.

Audubon leaders also mobilized allies from WCS and WWF-US to press cabinet ministers to designate the Cockscomb a wildlife sanctuary. Addressing the government's desire to increase tourism revenues, WCS representatives emphasized the tourism potential of a wildlife sanctuary in the Cockscomb. Rabinowitz returned to Belize to argue that Belizean tropical forests could generate more revenue standing through tourism than through logging or conversion to agriculture. The creation of a wildlife sanctuary in the Cockscomb "could bring in tourist dollars" (Rabinowitz 2000:354). BAS and WCS leaders sought to enable cabinet ministers to reimagine the Cockscomb as a tourist attraction rather than a source of timber or fertile land for agriculture.

As they promoted the creation of protected areas in countries across the global South confronting debt crises, conservationists had developed market-based mechanisms to fund conservation without drawing on public coffers. Structural adjustment packages that accompanied IMF loans to indebted countries required states to slash state budgets and spending, limiting the resources that could be allocated for protected areas management. The priority accorded to debt repayment applied pressure on political leaders to utilize natural resources to generate revenues, especially foreign exchange, that could be used to pay debts (Hartwick and Peet 2003; Igoe and Brockington 2007). Thus, conservationists promoted tourism to protected areas as a market-based mechanism to fund protected areas in endangered ecosystems through the expenditures of Northern nature tourists, rather than with state funding.

Ecotourism emerged as a concept and a buzzword in this context, underwritten by twin assumptions: that the market would set a price that reflects the true value of protecting endangered ecosystems and that economic-rational actors will only conserve natural resources that have monetary value (Brockington et al. 2008:111; Liverman and Vilas 2006:332; West 2005). Beyond generating revenues to fund management of protected areas, proponents of ecotourism emphasized that tourism would generate the foreign exchange indebted countries needed to repay their creditors. Ecotourism thus endowed protected areas with cash value, offering to nature "the opportunity to earn its own right to survive in an increasingly marketized world economy" (McAfee 1999:3, italics deleted).

As the UDP administration worked to expand tourism to Belize, WWF-US officers linked jaguar conservation to this goal. They offered to fund tourism infrastructure in the Cockscomb: an improved access road, hiking trails, accommodations, a visitors' center. However, such a commitment would require stronger legal protection for the reserve. WWF-US would not commit more funds "while there was a possibility that the government would grant a new timber concession cutting right through the jaguar's habitat" (Rabinowitz 2000:354). While seeking designation of the Cockscomb as a forest reserve, WCS staff had agreed that logging and jaguar protection could be compatible. Now, the WWF-US offered funds for tourism infrastructure only if logging were prohibited.

Conservation NGOs thus sought to direct the conduct of government officials by offering resources that would help to produce the Cockscomb as a tourism commodity, if the Belizean government strengthened its protection for the basin. The NGO offer represented an option whose only expense for the Belizean state was the opportunity cost of forgoing timber extraction or conversion to agriculture. Political leaders accepted the deal. In February 1986, the Minister of Agriculture, Forestry and Fisheries signed a statutory instrument designating this 3,640-acre parcel as the Cockscomb Basin Wildlife Sanctuary (CBWS).

Hailed as the world's first "jaguar reserve," the creation of the CBWS won great acclaim for the Minister of Natural Resources and his cabinet colleagues. The WWF-US offered congratulations, accompanied by grants to the BAS to fund the promised tourism infrastructure in the Cockscomb, including signage, gates, and trails (Waight and Lumb 1999:159). The Jaguar car company donated $100,000 to support the conservation of its namesake; their funds were used to purchase the buildings that had housed logging operations in the Cockscomb and refurbish them for use as tourism facilities (Watt 1989). Prince Philip, then president of WWF-International, celebrated the creation of the sanctuary by visiting the Cockscomb, where he planted a mahogany tree and enjoyed a birding tour, before dining with the prime minister (Watt 1989). The International Union for the Conservation of Nature declared the designation of the CBWS "the major achievement in cat conservation for the triennium" (Emmons et al. 1996:20). The UDP newspaper publicized these accolades, reporting, "Belize has earned the thanks and respect of the entire world for its jaguar reserve and enlightened conservation policies."[7]

The WWF-US also funded development of the first management plan for the Cockscomb Basin Wildlife Sanctuary. In March 1987, Forestry Department officials, the BAS Executive Director, international conservation NGO donors, and researchers active in the Cockscomb participated in a workshop to prepare a three-year plan to guide sanctuary management. The plan prioritized the development of tourism infrastructure for the Cockscomb, including upgrading the access road;

constructing a visitor center, lodging, and a potable water system; and developing the first brochure to promote the CBWS. BAS used this plan as the basis for a subsequent proposal to WWF-US that resulted in an additional grant of $25,000 to implement the plan. Part of this funding would also support an education program targeting Maya communities surrounding the reserve (Emmons et al. 1996: 22; Waight and Lumb 1999:158–159).[8]

WWF-US officers made multiple visits to Belize each year to track progress in implementing the CBWS management plan. They also engaged state agencies on these visits, offering training and salary support for conservation hires in the Forestry Department. At the time, the Forestry Department had about fifty-four permanent staff members, two of whom were designated as conservation officers. WWF staff encouraged Forestry Department leaders to submit a proposal for "institutional strengthening," and, on a 1990 visit, the president of WWF-US delivered a grant of US$120,000 to the Forestry Department's Conservation Division to build capacity for protected areas and wildlife management.[9] Northern conservation NGO funding thus subsidized and defined priorities for the Forestry Department as well as the BAS.

Amazingly, despite the international acclaim surrounding the creation of the world's first "jaguar sanctuary," the sanctuary was large enough to accommodate only a single jaguar (Emmons et al. 1996:20). Hence, the praise heaped upon Belizean ministers of government at the sanctuary's creation might best be understood as a strategy by conservation NGOs to encourage further, more meaningful, steps. Visiting WWF-US and WCS officers urged government officials to expand the CBWS, and Prince Philip advocated for the sanctuary's expansion during his visit to the CBWS.[10] However, although the UDP administration embraced the international accolades for its "enlightened conservation policies," conservation NGO officers made little headway in their campaign to expand the CBWS. In fact, at the same time, agricultural entrepreneurs and a cabinet minister were pushing to "dereserve" land within the Cockscomb Basin for agriculture.

After 1989 elections returned the PUP to power, international conservation donors renewed their efforts to convince the new administration to expand the sanctuary. In 1990, the Minister of Natural Resources signed a statutory instrument enlarging the sanctuary to encompass the entire Cockscomb Basin, 102,000 acres. Although this action responded to NGO advocacy, it also reflected the growing importance of tourism to the Belizean economy. The PUP newspaper dedicated an entire page to the expansion of the CBWS, reproducing in full the speech delivered by the Minister, which positioned the PUP administration as stewards of ecosystems of global importance. Expansion of the CBWS was, the Minister declared, "another act on the part of my government to fulfill our commitment to protect, enhance and preserve our natural resources and environment," for "our national development and for the future of the earth."[11]

The president of the WWF-US attended the ceremony marking the sanctuary's expansion. Lauding the minister for "setting an example for the entire world to emulate," she declared, "It is not often that a country takes a step as important for

Photo 1. The Cockscomb Basin; formation for which basin is named is at left.
Credit: Tony Rath, Naturalight Productions.

conservation as Belize takes today under your leadership" (Waight and Lumb 1999:162). She pledged additional funds to support BAS management of the expanded sanctuary.

By expanding the sanctuary, cabinet ministers appeared to abandon the possibility of timber extraction in the Cockscomb or the basin's possible conversion to agriculture, deciding in favor of conservation and ecotourism. Though some cabinet ministers have subsequently sought to have lands excised from the sanctuary for conversion to agriculture, conservation NGOs have rallied other ministers, especially ministers of tourism, to oppose these efforts. In fact, in 1997, the subsequent UDP administration expanded the CBWS to 120,000 acres, adding a parcel to connect the CBWS to a nature reserve to its south to create a continuous corridor of 250,000 acres under strict protection (Waight and Lumb 1999:163), (see photo 1).

## NGO Government Targets "The State"

As Northern conservation organizations became increasingly engaged in conservation efforts in Belize, the Belize Audubon Society served as a critical partner. The BAS brokered relationships between ministers and administrative staff in the Belizean government and an expanding network of transnational NGOs, intergovernmental organizations, and development donors through which resources and expertise for conservation circulated. As the BAS and its transnational allies

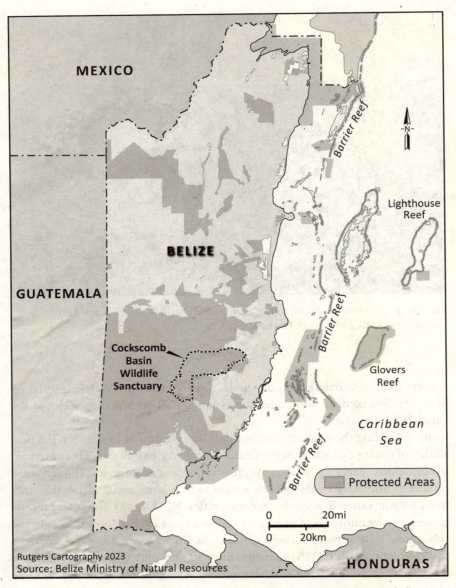

Map 3. Expanse of protected areas in Belize (all categories of protection included). Credit: Michael Siegel, Rutgers Cartography 2023.

succeeded in convincing the Belizean government to establish the CBWS and other protected areas, large swaths of Belizean territory and Belizean nature came to be governed by this alliance of conservation NGOs (see map 3). The BAS received additional grants from international donors to support and expand its conservation work. These grants funded the development of tourism infrastructure in protected areas, training for growing numbers of protected areas staff, and environmental education for the Belizean public, especially communities near protected areas (Emmons et al. 1996:22; Waight and Lumb 1999:189–191).

Scholarship on the "neoliberalization of nature" has noted a trend toward the devolution of responsibility for environmental management from state to nonstate actors. Studies of the expanding role of NGOs in managing natural resources have typically cast resource-dependent rural communities as the target of environmental government; in the next chapter, I explore this dynamic in Belize. In contrast, this chapter has explored how environmental government in Belize, carried out by a transnational network of conservation NGOs, targets the conduct of state officials, reversing the usual expectations about whose conduct is to be conducted. Further, although analysis of government-by-NGO has typically focused on the nation-state as the "spatial container" for operations of government (Ferguson and Gupta 2002:994), in this case, the devolution of environmental management from state to nonstate actors involved transnational networks that extended beyond the boundaries of the Belizean nation-state.

The transnational alliance of conservation NGOs involved in managing the Belizean environment deployed ecotourism, a market-based mechanism for protecting endangered ecosystems, to persuade government officials to create protected areas. Conservation leaders helped cabinet ministers and civil servants recognize the potential for intact forests to be fashioned into a new commodity—endangered, but protected, tropical biodiversity—that could generate new revenue streams by attracting a kind of tourist said to represent a particularly high-value market: the ecotourist. NGOs cast protected areas as the necessary foundation for a Belizean ecotourism product that could successfully compete for international consumers against other destinations. Further, they offered, the creation of protected areas and their transformation into consumable commodities would not require government investment; conservation NGOs would fund construction of the infrastructure required to facilitate tourism.

In response, government officials established protected areas in Belizean forests, wetlands, and reefs. Elected officials from both Belizean political parties embraced protected areas conservation as a means to produce a competitive Belizean ecotourism product capable of attracting high-value tourists. The glowing rhetoric of a 1991 policy document departed dramatically from the earlier designation of forests as "idle lands" that contributed nothing to national development. Forests were now recognized as "remarkable assets," "extraordinary natural wonders" that could "significantly contribute to the welfare" of all Belizeans through ecotourism (Ministry of Tourism and the Environment 1991:2).

However, the Ministry of Tourism and the Environment was explicit about the market-based rationale of the government's actions in favor of conservation. A 1992 report explained, "The importance of the tourist sub-sector, which is currently the second leading foreign exchange earner, provides the direct monetary rationale for enacting environmentally sensitive policies. Belize is a tourist destination growing in popularity as the global demand for eco-tourism increases. Environmental degradation in Belize will result in the country becoming less attractive as a destination, thus depriving it of needed foreign exchange" (DOE 1992:3).

## "Branding" Belize: Producing a Commodity, Conjuring a Market
### Ecotourism

The success of an ecotourism strategy to fund conservation and generate development required the production of both ecotourism commodities and ecotourists, who would constitute "the market." Although responsibility for managing protected areas had been devolved to NGOs, cabinet ministers decided that the government would take responsibility for branding and marketing Belize as a tourism destination, assigning this work to the Belize Tourism Board (BTB).

Early efforts by the Belize Tourism Board to commodify Belizean nature, especially its forests, had cast the experiences Belize offered as "adventure," "jungle," or "nature" tourism. However, by the 1990s, the term "ecotourism" had emerged as a buzzword that both reflected and shaped a trend in tourism production and demand. Seeking to increase the sustainability of both conservation and tourism, advocates for ecotourism initially defined the concept as travel to "natural areas" that contributed to conservation outcomes (Boo 1990; Ceballos-Lascurain 1987). Ecotourism definitions became more rigorous and more oriented toward environmental and social justice principles as the decade progressed (Medina 2012). In 1990, scholars and advocates for ecotourism founded The Ecotourism Society (later The International Ecotourism Society, TIES) to shape the definition of ecotourism and to promote, facilitate, and monitor its implementation. In 1993, TIES leader David Western defined ecotourism as "responsible travel to natural areas that conserves the environment and sustains the well-being of the local people" (Western 1993:8).

Belizean political leaders and private-sector entrepreneurs quickly embraced the term "ecotourism" to characterize the Belizean tourism product. Tourism entrepreneurs set about producing accommodations and activities that would be recognizable as ecotourism. The prime minister rearranged cabinet portfolios to create a Ministry of Tourism and the Environment, signaling the link between tourism development and conservation. The Ministry of Tourism and the Environment hosted a global conference on ecotourism, hoping to attract attention to Belize as an ecotourism destination and learn from the ecotourism experts who attended.

Staff in the Ministry of Tourism and the BTB sought guidance from The Ecotourism Society on how to implement and market ecotourism, and TIES director Megan Epler-Woods visited Belize multiple times to identify opportunities and assess Belizean efforts. Airport surveys conducted by ecotourism advocates indicated that 51 percent of travelers to Belize "considered natural history an important factor in their decision to visit, and 63 percent actually toured a protected area during their stay" (Boo 1990:xvi). Experts identified "ecotourists" as highly educated urban professionals, who were relatively more affluent than "mass tourists." According to tourism experts, ecotourists were "high-value" but "discerning" consumers (Wight 2001), willing to stay longer in a destination and pay more than mass tourists for high-quality experiences. Ecotourists or nature tourists were also described as "more accepting of conditions different from home" than other types of tourists, a potential plus for Belize, which lacked tourism infrastructure (Boo 1990:13). A study completed on Belizean tourism development in 1989 asserted, "Belize cannot and should not compete with mass tourism destinations such as Mexico and the Bahamas because of its lack of an elaborate tourism infrastructure and the uniqueness of its product.... Belize tends to appeal to a much more limited tourist market, the constituents of which are sophisticated, educated, and in middle- to high-income brackets. Indeed, Belize should concentrate on cultivating low-impact, high-spending tourism and seek to develop into an up-market adventure destination" (BTB 1993:2–3).

To attract "high-value," "up-market" tourists, conservationists asserted, the creation of protected areas was critical. Formal protection would index both the quality of Belizean nature and the country's commitment to sustaining that quality (Medina 2012). The government extended protected status to nearly one third of the country's total land territory and declared several marine reserves. The state also sought and won recognition for the Belizean portion of the Mesoamerican barrier reef as a UNESCO World Heritage Site.

In addition to signaling the pristine quality of Belizean nature, terrestrial protected areas in forests and wetlands would differentiate the Belizean ecotourism product from the offerings of more established tourism destinations in the Caribbean. Rather than competing directly with more developed Caribbean destinations, Belize could package beach and reef tourism assets with inland rain forests and wetlands to set Belize apart as a uniquely rich and biodiverse destination (GIS 1973).

Accordingly, a marketing campaign launched by the BTB and the new private-sector Belize Tourism Industry Association cast Belize as "Mother Nature's Best-Kept Secret" (Stinson 2017). Highlighting the significant proportion of Belizean lands and waters under protection and casting Belizean flora and fauna as "secret" emphasized the pristine quality of Belize's barrier reef and tropical forests. The BTB represented the country as an ecotourism destination that was "green" in every sense of the word, from its spectacular natural endowments to the state's commitment to biodiversity conservation, to the country's "rustic and simple" tourism infrastructure, "perhaps lacking in sophistication but certainly not in charm" (BTB 1993:46). Pitching Belize's rudimentary tourism infrastructure as proof of its commitment to sustainable, low-impact tourism transformed what had been a deficit into an asset.

Marketing materials capitalized on the status of the CBWS as the world's only "jaguar sanctuary," promoting the CBWS as the country's flagship terrestrial park. Images of jaguars began to appear on nearly every brochure, print advertisement, and video promoting Belize. An explosion of upscale hotel and ecolodge construction along the southern coast of Belize led to the emergence of two tourism enclaves offering "reef and rainforest" experiences. In fact, research on tourists to Belize revealed that although 70 percent were motivated by Belizean nature, the largest segment wanted to experience tropical nature during the day but relax in comfort in the evening (Palacio and McKool 1997); the new coastal enclaves matched these desires.

BTB marketing specialists targeted the few tourism wholesalers who had begun to specialize in promoting Belize. More broadly, they also targeted newspapers in metropolitan areas deemed by tourism experts to have high numbers of potential ecotourists and magazines likely to be read by tourists who could be attracted to one of Belize's "product lines": *Skin Diver, Sierra, Outside, Audubon, Sport Fishing, Islands,* and *Condé Nast Traveler* (BTB 1993).

### The "Mundo Maya"

In the early 1990s, Belize also joined a regional initiative to market a third "product line" in addition to reef and rainforest: Maya culture. The regional tourism promotion project began in 1988 and culminated with the 1992 signing of an incorporation agreement for the "Mundo Maya" (Maya World). Based on the extent of ancient Maya occupation of Mesoamerica, the Mundo Maya encompassed Belize, El Salvador, Guatemala, Honduras, and several Mexican states. All five countries contributed funds to collectively market the region, capitalizing on popular narratives and images associated with the advanced civilization that flourished in Mesoamerica during the first millennium.

The initiative highlighted Maya culture, past and present, as Mesoamerica's comparative advantage relative to all other tourism destinations. Mundo Maya promotions linked the ancient and contemporary Maya and situated the Maya in relation to the region's natural assets:

> Once the domain of one of the most intriguing ancient civilizations ever to develop in the Americas, the Maya World awaits discovery.
>
> More than 2,000 years ago ... the Maya built magnificent cities of pyramids, temples and observatories where sages scanned the heavens and predicted solar eclipses. They invented a calendar more precise than the one we use today, utilized hieroglyphics, and were the first culture in the Americas to employ the zero in their calculations. They were also artists, their skill evident in a legacy of exquisite carvings, pottery, and murals.
>
> Temples now lie silent, but their ancient architects are not forgotten. Their descendants still inhabit the area, speaking the old languages and respecting the customs of their ancestors.... Today, visitors can meet the living Maya in their villages and markets; watch them work timeless symbols into their textiles and even share a colorful saint's day celebration that brings an entire community to life.
>
> Like their forefathers, the Maya hold their land sacred; they are at one with nature, and it's easy to see why. Breathtaking landscapes crowd the 500,000-square-kilometer Maya World. Mountains, jungles, mighty rivers,

caves, palm-lined beaches, islands, and an immense coral reef, make the Maya World one of the most geographically varied areas on the planet. Such richness is rivaled only by the diversity of the region's flora and fauna.

The Maya possess a magnificent cultural and natural heritage and they welcome visitors to their world—a world waiting to be discovered.[12] (MMO n.d.)

In the wake of marketing campaigns that featured protected Belizean nature and vibrant Maya culture, tourism grew to become the largest contributor to Belizean gross domestic product (GDP). Tourism accounted for nearly 16 percent of GDP by 2005, with overnight tourist arrivals consistently surpassing 230,000 between 2006 and 2008 (BTB 2008; Richardson 2007:27). A decade later, overnight tourist arrivals had risen to nearly 490,000, while cruise tourists accounted for a million additional visits. Ecotourism thus achieved the goals set by government ministers and the promises offered by consultants: it diversified and expanded the national economy beyond agricultural exports, generated foreign exchange required to service debts and purchase imports, and incorporated new regions of the country into the development opportunities offered by tourism.

### BAS Fiscal Crisis and Its Resolution: Deepening Market Rationalities

Despite the success of ecotourism, the BAS confronted a financial crisis in the early 1990s. As it assumed responsibility for managing seven protected areas, BAS staffing had multiplied; including wardens for these protected areas, BAS staff had grown to more than thirty. Transnational conservation NGOs had been eager to fund initial management for Belizean protected areas and the construction of tourism infrastructure, but they were not willing to pay for management of protected areas in perpetuity. Ecotourism was premised on the use of revenues generated through tourist entrance fees and concessions to fund long-term park management, without tapping public coffers. However, the comanagement agreement between the government and the BAS did not permit the BAS to charge entrance fees for the parks it managed, because government officials were concerned that entrance fees would deter tourists from visiting Belize. After grants to fund tourism infrastructure had been expended, BAS was unable to cover the costs of managing the protected areas for which it was responsible.

Transnational conservation NGOs responded by partnering with development donors in a pair of studies to investigate the cause of Audubon's fiscal crisis. The studies diagnosed the financial base for protected areas as "wholly inadequate." "Tourism is the most buoyant component of the national economy at the current time and is based on the health and quality of the natural environment," one study noted. However, the "user pays" principle had not been applied to protected areas in Belize. Because entry to protected areas was free, "protected areas have been subsidizing the tourism industry, while their management has been left critically short of funds" (Programme for Belize and InterAmerican Development Bank

1995:96). This was represented as a failure to sufficiently extend market rationalities to nature: protected areas had not been fully commodified; rather, tours of protected areas functioned as commodities, while protected areas merely subsidized those tours without garnering any monetary return. State prohibitions on charging entrance fees were preventing protected areas from operating in an economically rational manner.

Both reports recommended deepening the application of market rationality to protected areas to enable tourism revenues to pay for management of protected areas. They prescribed the institution of entrance fees and the creation of the Protected Areas Conservation Trust, financed by a conservation fee levied on air travelers to Belize (Aukerman and Haas 1992; Programme for Belize and Inter-American Development Bank 1995). An additional study sponsored by the WWF-US addressed ministers' concerns that such fees would deter tourists from visiting Belize. Surveys of tourists to Belize revealed that they were willing to pay entrance or conservation fees if the resulting revenues were applied directly to conservation efforts (Lindberg and Enriquez 1994). This provides a clear example of reliance on the market as a site of veridiction regarding policy decisions: tourists' willingness to pay additional fees to support conservation indicated the correctness of a policy to impose entrance fees.

However, despite these studies, cabinet ministers held to their no-fee policy. Thus, BAS president Therese Rath and BAS board member Jean Shaw, both ecotourism entrepreneurs, ratcheted up the pressure. The two of them traveled to the capital to meet with the Minister of Natural Resources and the Minister of Tourism, bearing signs that read, "This Park Closed Due to Lack of Funds." If the BAS were not allowed to charge entrance fees for the protected areas it managed, they warned, they would post these signs at park entrances and return responsibility for managing the protected areas to the Forestry Department.

This threat finally catalyzed government approval for the collection of entrance fees. In May 1995 the government signed a statutory instrument to permit the BAS to charge entrance fees at the protected areas it managed (Waight and Lumb 1999:35). In September, the government established the Protected Areas Conservation Trust to support conservation work, funded by a conservation fee imposed on international air travelers to Belize.[13] In November 1995, representatives of the Ministry of Natural Resources, the Forestry Department, and the Belize Audubon Society signed a five-year comanagement agreement that authorized the BAS to collect entrance fees to fund its management activities (Waight and Lumb 1999:34).

Subsequently, a new round of international grants supported the implementation of a funding model for protected areas fully based on market-generated revenue streams. A European Union grant funded the implementation of entrance fees in BAS-managed protected areas, and a USAID grant channeled through the WWF-US funded construction of a new dormitory, composting toilets, and solar-powered electrical water systems in the Cockscomb to accommodate paying tourists (Waight and Lumb 1999:166, 193).

## Analysis

Although cabinet ministers performed an act of sovereignty in designating the Cockscomb a protected area, they quickly devolved management of the Cockscomb to BAS, whose conservation NGO allies funded preparation of the park for tourism. Although the devolution of governmental responsibilities to NGOs is often cited as a key dimension of neoliberal reforms, I argue that subjection to market rationalities is the real centerpiece of neoliberal environmental government in Belize. Political leaders' embrace of ecotourism as an integrated conservation and development strategy rendered their policy decisions subject to the leisure expenditures of international ecotourists, counted upon to fund conservation and generate economic development. Predictions and research data regarding the preferences and priorities of Northern nature tourists, which revealed that "undisturbed nature" is their top motivation for travel to Belize (Kwan et al. 2010:12), directed the conduct of state officials and their production of a Belizean "brand."[14]

Belize Audubon Society leaders and staff began as "environmental subjects" committed to biodiversity conservation (Agrawal 2005). However, reliance on ecotourism to sustain protected areas conservation also subjected them to the market for tropical rainforest experiences. Conservationists have thus had to operate as market-rational subjects, responding to the desires and consumption choices of Northern nature tourists, to pursue conservation goals within the opportunities and constraints posed by ecotourism as a technology of neoliberal environmental government.

CHAPTER 4

# Governing through the Market

## MANAGING TROPICAL NATURE AND MAYA COMMUNITIES

As the Belize Audubon Society (BAS) assumed responsibility for managing the Cockscomb Basin Wildlife Sanctuary (CBWS), it also became responsible for managing the communities on its perimeter. This chapter explores Audubon's entanglements with the nearby community of Maya Centre, whose members had lost access to subsistence resources upon which their livelihoods had depended, when the sanctuary was established. Losing access to subsistence resources, their livelihoods became increasingly subject to market exchange. Audubon pursued two strategies to win villagers' support for the protected area, offering an education campaign grounded in the western scientific concept of "ecosystem" and leveraging their increasing reliance on markets by incorporating them into ecotourism.

### Mopan Migration to the Stann Creek District

The communities most affected by the state's designation of the Cockscomb as a wildlife sanctuary were Mopan Maya villages, established by migrants to the Stann Creek District from the Toledo District. State efforts to privatize reservation lands in Toledo had disrupted customary systems of land management in Maya villages, prompting some Maya to migrate northward along the newly constructed Southern Highway, a gravel road that provided the first land link between the Toledo District and the rest of Belize. During the 1970s, Mopan migrants established several new villages in the Stann Creek District. These communities settled on uncultivated land and then requested state recognition and lands. Because the state prioritized the expansion of agricultural production, Lands Department officials often granted recognition to these communities and provided agricultural lands to them.

In 1976, several extended families established the settlement of Maya Centre on uncultivated lands at the junction of the Southern Highway and a logging road into the Cockscomb Basin. The community was situated on and surrounded by privately held lands, some under large-scale citrus or rice production, others still forested. The former offered opportunities for wage labor, the latter for subsistence agriculture. The

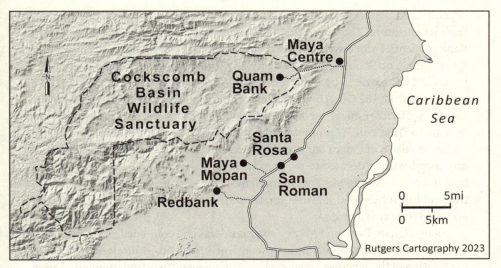

Map 4. Cockscomb Basin Wildlife Sanctuary and surrounding Maya communities. Credit: Michael Siegel, Rutgers Cartography 2023.

nearest lands claimed by the state were several miles to the west, in the Cockscomb. After clearing small plots of land and planting corn in the forested hills between the village and the eastern rim of the Cockscomb, community leaders traveled to the capital to petition Lands Department personnel for these lands (see map 4).

In 1978, several families left Maya Centre to establish a new settlement, Quam Bank, five miles upland on the eastern rim of the Cockscomb. Here the land resembled the well-drained hills they had farmed in Toledo, and small-scale logging operations in the Cockscomb provided sporadic opportunities for wage labor. Quam Bank leaders also traveled to the capital to request 2,000 acres of land from the Lands Department for their community.

After pursuing these requests for land across repeated trips to the Lands Department and several years, Maya Centre was finally allocated a large parcel of lands in the coastal plain to the east of the village, rather than the hilly lands they had requested. These lands were too waterlogged to support subsistence crops like corn and beans; they had been earmarked for banana or citrus production, whose expansion the government was actively promoting. Quam Bank found its land request blocked by the efforts of the BAS and the Wildlife Conservation Society (WCS) to protect the basin.

### Eviction

Creation of the Cockscomb Basin Wildlife Sanctuary restricted access to resources on which the Mopan Maya villages on its eastern perimeter had depended. While most communities had acquired land outside the basin of sufficient quality to enable cultivation of subsistence staples, Quam Bank and Maya Centre were more dependent on the Cockscomb's resources and thus experienced the greatest impact from its enclosure. The imposition of the sanctuary led to the eviction of Quam Bank residents. Families who were living at Quam Bank when the government designated the Cockscomb a forest reserve recall a vastly different chain of events from the ones narrated by Rabinowitz, the WCS jaguar researcher. "One day we get a paper from the Government saying we have to leave at a certain time," a former Quam Bank resident explained. "They don't even give help to move. We just have to go. That's all" (Emmons et al. 1996:27). This account is consistent across former residents of Quam Bank, challenging Rabinowitz's assertion that community members had decided to move of their own accord to access schooling and land to build a church. Most of Quam Bank's 112 residents returned to Maya Centre, doubling its population. However, the state did not expand the amount of land allocated to Maya Centre.

Though Quam Bank and Maya Centre residents had combined subsistence production with cash crop cultivation or wage work, their descriptions of life prior to the creation of the sanctuary refer explicitly to independence from markets. A man who had lived most of his childhood in the Cockscomb explained, "It was self-sustaining. We planted sugar cane; we processed sugar. We made our cooking oil from the cohune nut. We raised chickens. We grew vegetables, corn, beans, rice. Anything that you can think about, we grew it on our own. We hunted for game meat; we did a lot of fishing. We didn't depend on stores. We produced our own." A man whose family had stayed in Maya Centre echoed this sentiment: "[We] used to live along with the forest," he recalled. "We, our parents, our grandparents, we grow things to eat, almost anything that we use. We don't know about supermarkets. We never go to the supermarket."

Indeed, James Gregory's research in the Toledo community from which Maya Centre and Quam Bank residents had migrated documented their ability to produce livelihoods with little recourse to markets. Each farmer cleared and burned a plot of well-drained land to plant wet-season corn, which would then be fallowed for a period of years before reuse to regenerate soil fertility and kill weeds and grasses. Each household also planted a dry-season corn crop on low-lying lands. Households relied on forested lands for hunting, harvesting wild plant foods, and cutting materials to build and maintain houses (Gregory 1984:16–18). As colonial and later national administrators promoted the production of cash crops, Maya farmers seized the opportunity to earn income, producing rice, corn, beans, and pigs for urban consumers. They also participated in labor markets when work became available. However, since markets for labor or crops in southern Belize were sporadic, usually seasonal, and often fickle, most Maya farmers took advantage of opportunities to earn cash incomes without sacrificing the security provided by the production of subsistence staples (Gregory 1984:190; Osborn 1982:26; Zarger 2009). Although the Maya of southern Belize were market subjects to a degree, subsistence cultivation and access to forest resources made them less subject to markets than most Belizeans.

However, the state's enclosure of the Cockscomb Basin terminated access to lands that both Maya Centre and Quam Bank residents had used for agriculture, hunting, fishing, and collecting housing materials. Since subsistence crops would not thrive on the waterlogged lands allocated to Maya Centre, the state's enclosure of the Cockscomb forced Maya Centre and Quam Bank residents to purchase staple foods with cash, rendering them increasingly dependent upon market exchange to meet their basic needs.

## The Production of Environmental Subjects

Both the protection of the Cockscomb and its commodification as a tourism product required the collaboration of the communities on its perimeter. Ecotourism experiences are particularly vulnerable commodities, because consumers must travel to consume ecotourism experiences in the places where they are produced. With continual access to both the product and its consumers, residents of communities near protected areas can damage the "pristine nature" on offer or disrupt tourists' experiences. Thus, the cooperation of people who live near a protected area is necessary to produce an ecotourism commodity sufficiently attractive to compete effectively on international markets.

As a result, in addition to governing the CBWS, the BAS would have to govern the communities on its perimeter. Residents of these communities, who had not been consulted in creating the reserve, complained that the government had accorded greater significance to the needs of jaguars than to the needs of its Maya citizens. Either patrols would have to keep them out of the park, or the BAS would need to win their consent.

Though some have cast the devolution of responsibility for managing protected areas from states to nonstate organizations as the "privatization of sovereignty" (Igoe et al. 2010), BAS staff did not see their organization as a stand-in "sovereign," a legitimate enforcer of law; neither, they were certain, would rural Belizeans. As one BAS president put it, "the person conducting illegal activities does not recognize an NGO [nongovernmental organization] as a law enforcement agency, and that's a fact. Nothing can change that."

Rather than attempting to coerce villagers into compliance with the restrictions imposed by the protected area, the BAS thus sought to recruit them as "environmental subjects," who "care for, act, and think of their actions in relation to" the environment (Agrawal 2005:164–165). My analysis extends Arun Agrawal's application of the analytic of governmentality to decentralized forms of environmental governance (Agrawal 2005). Agrawal identified participation in decentralized regulatory practices as a mechanism that transformed rural people into environmental subjects disposed to regulate their own behavior and the behavior of others vis-à-vis the environment: as villagers patrolled forests or served on forest councils, they came to perceive forests as vulnerable and in need of human protection. I expand this approach in several ways. I situate NGO efforts to shape the environmental subjectivities of Mopan villagers in relation to the culturally and historically specific forms of knowledge and subjectivity that villagers already held. Further, although Agrawal's environmental subjects emerged as an unintended outcome of decentralized regulatory practices, I examine efforts to produce environmental subjects as an explicit policy aim. This is important, because conservation donors increasingly prioritize environmental subject production as an integral dimension of projects they fund, in the guise of "capacity-building" or the provision of a "stake" in conservation (Goldman 2005). In addition, I attend to the *content* of environmental subjectivities.

As I examine the production of environmental subjects, I am also concerned with how the resulting subjectivities oriented the *agency* of villagers who were their targets. Although Foucault focused little on agency, offering only cryptic assertions about "resistance," his double formulation of "the subject" provides an entry point for theorizing the mutual constitution of agency and subjection. The subject is "subject to someone else by control or dependence, and tied to [their] own identity by a conscience or self-knowledge" (Foucault 1982:212). The second part of this definition points to subjection as the starting point for the capacity to exercise agency: the subject/agent can pursue interests or projects only once they "recognize" them as "their own." This recognition involves the "paradox of subjectivation": "the very processes and conditions that secure a subject's subordination are also the means by which [they become] a self-conscious identity and agent" (Butler 1990, 1997; Mahmood 2005:17). Because the production of subjects involves the ascription of interests and commitments, subjection both opens and imposes possibilities for the exercise of agency. Thus, agents are subjects, formed and enabled through the exercise of power. Purposeful actions can only be understood as an outcome of prior processes of subject-making, through which interests and commitments have been ascribed to an individual as their own; this constitutes the "self-knowledge" to which Foucault refers (Medina 2004:13).

Further, the first part of Foucault's formulation, "subject to someone else by control or dependence," points to the agency of the "someone else" who seeks to direct the commitments and conduct of others. Within the domination/resistance binary in which agency is equated with resistance, efforts to subject others have not been counted as agency. In contrast, I explore both the agency involved in efforts to produce subjects and the agency exercised by the resulting subjects themselves.

The Audubon Society's earliest engagements with communities involved visits by the Executive Director to each village to explain the laws that regulated the new wildlife sanctuary: no cultivation, no hunting, no fishing, and no harvesting of forest materials. However, knowledge of the law did not lead to compliance: villagers continued to hunt and fish in the Cockscomb.

In 1986, the BAS hired the first warden, a former Quam Bank resident now living in Maya Centre, to control the gate they had installed on the access road into the basin. His job was to stop hunters from entering the Cockscomb. In 1987, Audubon hired a park director from Maya Centre, who oversaw the growth of a warden staff, also drawn primarily from Maya Centre. Highlighting the priority accorded to ecotourism, during the sanctuary's early years its growing warden staff *did not patrol*. Instead, they transformed the CBWS into an ecotourism commodity. Wardens wielding machetes slashed trails through the forest and then labored to keep them clear. They posted informational signs, dug latrines, refurbished buildings from the Cockscomb's logging era to make an office and a bunkhouse, and built a water supply system.

When wardens did begin to patrol, the BAS trained them to deploy persuasion rather than prosecution to stop their co-villagers from hunting or fishing in the sanctuary. "The Audubon doesn't take immediate action for people who do illegal things," explained one warden. "They always have patience to explain." Later, the BAS launched a concerted education campaign that presented the ecological rationales for protected areas conservation, grounded in Western science and aesthetics.

Maya residents of villages near the reserve already possessed extensive ecological knowledge of the plants and animals native to this area; they had relied on forest resources for their livelihoods. They had cultivated, encouraged, or collected a wide range of plants for food, medicine, and fiber; trapped game animals and fished using plant-based poisons; and built and furnished houses using posts, poles, and rough boards cut from the forest, lashed together with vines and covered with cohune palm thatch (Gregory 1984). In addition to their wide-ranging ecological knowledge of forest plants and animals, Mopan understood themselves to be enmeshed in social relationships with powerful beings known collectively as *Witz-hok*. The Mopan terms *witz* and *hok* refer to hills/mountains and valleys, respectively, but the Witz-hok are not simply geological features. Rather, they are nonhuman beings considered the "owners" or "keepers" of lands, plants, animals, and rain. Mopan individuals, families, or communities engaged the Witz-hok by giving respect, *tzik*: burning copal incense, making offerings of food, and reciting prayers to ask permission to use the resources they required (Gregory 1984:23). They also sought the goodwill of the Christian god, who might exert power over the Witz-hok (Gregory 1984:25–26). Based on research in Toledo in the early 1980s, Anne Osborn noted the importance that Mopan accorded to their relationships with these nonhuman forces: "The Maya see themselves as having an important part in the scheme of the universe," she concluded (Osborn 1982:96).

However, conservationists were unaware of the integral relationships that bound Mopan communities to the forested landscapes in which they lived. Instead, the BAS environmental education campaign began from the assumption that Mopan villagers needed to be taught about the complex webs of interconnection among humans, flora, and fauna that characterized tropical forests.

### *The Education Campaign*

*Ecological Value of Protected Areas Conservation.* A Peace Corps volunteer assigned to the CBWS initiated the formal education program. Trained as a wildlife biologist, he collaborated with scientists conducting research in the Cockscomb to develop slideshows that justified protection for the Cockscomb using concepts from Western science. When the Park Director was hired, he inherited the task of educating communities surrounding the reserve, adapting these slideshows.

The presentations introduced the ecosystem concept from Western science to portray tropical forests as vibrant, yet vulnerable, assemblages of plant and animal species, in which the vitality of all parts is integral to the survival of the entire system.[1] Highlighting images and data collected by foreign scientists who conducted research in the Cockscomb, the slideshows demonstrated the methods by which foreign scientists had collected and analyzed data in the Cockscomb to explain how scientists had identified the constituent parts of the Cockscomb's ecosystem and the complex interconnections among them. This explained the priority conservationists had placed on jaguars: as "apex animals" sitting atop the rain forest ecosystem, their survival depended on—and served as an indicator of—the overall health of Belizean rainforests and their fauna. The ecosystems concept offers a culturally specific way of apprehending nature and producing knowledge about it; although ecosystems resemble Mopan worlds in their complex integration of species, the integrants of the networks, the nature of the relationships among them, and the roles accorded to humans differ.

Additionally, the education campaign highlighted the ecological value of the Cockscomb's forests as watersheds for major river systems through a slideshow developed for adults and, later, a skit performed by wardens for schoolchildren. Forested watersheds protected villagers' own source of water for drinking, bathing, and washing. At a larger scale, these watersheds also protected the health of the Belizean marine ecosystem, including the barrier reef, which sustained the nation's fishing and marine tourism industries. Describing the relationship between forests and reef as "part of a big process," the Park Director warned his co-villagers, "When we came here, all this area was in high forest, and now it is not like that. The forest is being cut down all around us. This area is a watershed, and if the trees are all cut, once you start the process of erosion you can't stop it. It will have effects all the way out to the reef."

Casting villagers' prior agricultural activities in the Cockscomb as threats to ecosystems of national importance, these arguments exhorted the Mopan to embrace restrictions on their use of forest resources from the Cockscomb, abandon practices that Western conservationists deemed environmentally destructive, and become stewards of forest and marine ecosystems by abstaining from use of forest resources. However, Mopan villagers rejected the subject position of "environmental threat." The Park Director recalled, "The people said, 'Yes, the forest is being cut down, but we are not responsible for that. Rich people are!'" While BAS undertook its education campaign, tangled heaps of bulldozed trees burned for days just north of the village, on hundreds of acres of land that elites were converting from forest to cattle production. Village residents found ludicrous the charge that their small plots of corn posed serious threats to Belize's marine ecosystem or that responsibility for protecting Belize's marine resources rested with them.

Although Raymond Bryant suggests that concepts from Western science are often deployed as means of inducing rural people "to appreciate the scientific—and hence 'incontestable'—basis of protected area designation" (Bryant 2002:283), BAS efforts to teach villagers about interconnections among species using the ecosystem concept were not compelling to Maya Centre residents. Most community members rejected the very assumptions that oriented the education campaign: that they lacked knowledge about the complex webs of relationships that sustain forests and that their traditional agricultural practices rendered them environmental threats.

*Aesthetic Value of Protected Areas Conservation.* Beyond the value of the environmental services provided by the Cockscomb's forests, the education campaign attributed intrinsic value to the Cockscomb's flora and fauna, a value largely aestheticized through emphasis on "seeing" as the privileged means for experiencing jaguars or rain forests and appreciating their worth (see Neumann 1998:19–24; Vivanco 2006). This form of vision is situated, of course; it represents the gaze of Northern nature tourists, who consume forests aesthetically, rather than through crop production or hunting (Urry 1990). While BAS members shared the gaze of Northern nature tourists, most Belizeans did not.

The Park Director screened a Belizean television program about the CBWS in the communities around the sanctuary (Great Belize Productions 1988). Originally broadcast on a Belize City television station, the program introduced the CBWS to a Belizean public unfamiliar with and unappreciative of Belizean forests. The program opens with a striking image of the sun setting over the Cockscomb's forests, as the narrator asserts that the Cockscomb is "one of the last places on Earth where jaguars still thrive in large numbers," positioning the Cockscomb in a global context and scale. Images of the equipment used in the WCS jaguar study followed, accompanied by assertions that scientific data supported the sanctuary's creation.

Then, the program cuts to footage of tourists—White people without Belizean accents—in the forest, gesturing animatedly upward, binoculars in hand, as one tries to help the others locate a bird he has sighted. These foreigners perform an unfamiliar, culturally specific way of interacting with the forest: "seeing" (West et al. 2006:252). Asserting the intrinsic value of jaguars and other facets of tropical nature, the program introduced the significance of "seeing" as a means of apprehending that value, providing a vehicle for villagers to begin to understand—and perhaps exercise—the gaze of Northern ecotourists.

The Belizean narrator performs this desired transition herself, as she hikes a trail in the sanctuary with a park warden. She marvels at ceiba trees towering overhead and leaf-cutter ant trails underfoot, worn bare of vegetation by the passing of tiny ant feet. Although she does not encounter a jaguar, the warden points to paw prints left in the mud by one of the Cockscomb's smaller cat species, a jaguarundi, which she inspects excitedly. The narrator's expanding capacity to "see" ant trails and paw prints marks her growing recognition of the forest's intrinsic worth. By the end of the program, she recognizes the "natural riches" of the Cockscomb as national "treasures." As the program concludes, the narrator warns, "In the past, we've been lucky. Low population has meant that these treasures were never destroyed. But with economic development happening all around us, there is no guarantee that these natural riches will be so untouched in the future." Fortunately, she adds, the Cockscomb and other protected areas have been created to "enable our grandchildren to experience our heritage firsthand." Thus, while the narrator situates Belizean rain forests as global "treasures," she positions herself and her viewers as national subjects, protecting Belizean natural heritage for the good of "our grandchildren."

After viewing the slideshows and television program, members of each target community were transported to the sanctuary to "see" the Cockscomb's flora and fauna for themselves, perhaps in new ways. However, while Mopan villagers recognized the subsistence value of forests, the commercial value of their hardwoods, and the configuration of tree species that indicated soils with high agricultural potential, most Maya Centre residents did not embrace the tourist gaze. The assertion that forests had cash value as "scenery" was as novel to them as it had initially been to government officials.

### *Leveraging Market Subjectivities*

The Audubon Society also sought to leverage Maya Centre residents' expanding market subjectivities to win their support for the CBWS, asserting that ecotourism to the sanctuary could generate incomes for villagers, whose livelihoods now depended on access to cash. Audubon's hiring of five or six men from Maya Centre as wardens was a first step to make this true. Audubon also organized training to enable another half dozen young men to work as tour guides in the sanctuary. For these positions, the BAS targeted former Quam Bank residents and the few villagers with high school degrees and the associated English-language facility. Women were not hired to work in these capacities, in part because gendered Mopan cultural expectations circumscribe women's movements to domestic and village spaces and discourage interactions with unrelated men (see McClusky 2001). However, Audubon's Executive Director had been inspired by the market for native weavings and jewelry in the U.S. Southwest, which he had observed while participating in a training seminar. He encouraged women from Maya Centre to sell their own handicrafts to generate income from tourism to the reserve. Some village women began to sell the embroidered blouses that Mopan women traditionally wore or jewelry fashioned from locally made clay beads; later, they expanded their repertoire to include slate carvings, baskets, and other types of artisanry.

Because all visitors to the CBWS had to pass through Maya Centre, where a warden manned the gate that controlled entry to the sanctuary, village women sent their children to the gate to sell their handiwork to tourists. These sales channeled cash into the homes of villagers who were increasingly dependent on cash income to purchase food and other necessities. However, conflicts ensued as neighbors competed to display their wares, and craft sales conflicted with children's attendance at school. In response to criticism from co-villagers for taking a job in the sanctuary, the Park Director sought to organize the community to take greater

Photo 2. Members of Maya Centre Women's Group. Credit: Dirk Francisco/BAS, published in *Producciones de la Hamaca* by Judy Lumb.

advantage of the economic potential of tourism to the CBWS. "It became an issue, why am I in Cockscomb, when we know it is not in our favor?" he explained. "I told them, 'That's the point I want to make! It's not in our favor, but maybe we can make it work.'"

Though village men were unwilling to cooperate with him, he worked with a group of women to organize a craft cooperative in 1988. The women cajoled their reluctant husbands to provide labor to build a gift shop at the entrance of the CBWS access road. Each group member was assigned a shelf to display her work, and members took turns running the shop. The Park Director pressed the BAS to relocate the sanctuary's entrance gate and guest register to the women's gift shop. Though initially reluctant to cede responsibility for monitoring traffic into the sanctuary to the women's group, the BAS ultimately agreed. With all tourists now required to stop at the shop to register, the women's sales increased markedly (see photos 2 and 3).

Initially, only a few women joined the group and shared responsibility for the gift shop. The time they spent minding the shop was a source of conflicts with husbands, who were unhappy that their wives were absent from home or concerned about their wives' interactions with other men. The women themselves perceived the time spent managing the gift shop as somewhat onerous. However, over time, more women joined the group and began to produce crafts, a task they could combine with other household work in their homes. They preferred this option to

Photo 3. Maya Centre Women's Group Gift Shop. Credit: Laurie Kroshus Medina.

working for wages outside the community or not having access to cash at all. As membership in the group expanded, the burden of managing the gift shop decreased for each member, with each woman taking responsibility for only a couple of days each month. Husbands also became more accustomed to their wives taking a turn in the gift shop over time, and marital conflicts over women's participation decreased. Women assert that the income their families derived from craft sales contributed to their husbands' decreasing complaints. One woman described how she had answered her husband's grumblings by threatening to withdraw from the women's group: "When these problems arise, I tell him if it is so much of a problem I can stop going in there." She told him she would love to just sit and wait for him to give her money, "if you are tired of my help." This suggestion ended the discussion, because he did not want the family to lose her income.

As the number of tourists visiting the sanctuary grew, most households in Maya Centre began to earn income from tourism to the reserve. Concerted marketing by the BTB and the BTIA increased tourist arrivals in Belize, and the Cockscomb became a day trip from new upscale coastal resorts in southern Belize. Visits to the Cockscomb increased to more than 4,000 annually (BTB 2006). Over time, every household in Maya Centre became integrated into tourism to the reserve in one form or another. Eight to ten men, some with limited English proficiency, worked sporadically as porters on multiday expeditions far into the sanctuary offered by a North American tour operator. A number of young men found jobs on the grounds crews at resorts in the nearby coastal tourism enclaves. Steady work as a warden or at a coastal resort enabled a few men to accumulate sufficient cash to launch their own businesses by building a thatch-roofed cottage or two, selling meals, or purchasing a used vehicle to transport tourists to the reserve. However, since most tourists who visited the CBWS originated in the upscale coastal enclaves, the requirement that all visitors stop at the women's group gift shop to register was critical to villagers' ability to transact exchanges with them. By 1993, members of the women's craft cooperative averaged US$1,168 in annual income. Considering that women's wages are, on average, lower than men's, this figure compared favorably with the nation's per capita GDP of US$1,562 (Lindberg and Enriquez 1994:63).

## Neoliberal Environmental Government

The state's assignment of management responsibilities for the sanctuary to the BAS may resemble what scholars have called "the privatization of sovereignty" (Igoe et al. 2010). However, a closer look reveals that no single "sovereign" controls the fate of the CBWS or the communities on its perimeter. Rather, after the state's creation of the park, the exercise of sovereignty was eclipsed by the practice of "government," efforts to shape conduct indirectly by "arranging conditions" to bring protected nature and rural communities into market exchange.

As Foucault asserts, governmental power—rule through the market—"gets a hold on" the individual "to the extent, *and only to the extent*, that he is a *homo economicus*" (Foucault 2008:253, emphasis added). The state's sovereign act of enclosing the Cockscomb, drastically limiting Mopan villagers' access to subsistence resources, was a critical step in expanding the extent to which homo economicus could "get a hold on" Quam Bank and Maya Centre residents. The displacement of Maya Centre residents from resources in the Cockscomb deprived them of opportunities to produce their own subsistence and created the conditions in which market forces and market rationalities could be brought fully to bear on villagers' decisions and actions. Subsequently, the BAS played on villagers' market subjectivities to recruit them into conservation commitments. This strategy worked. Villagers had made frequent incursions into the CBWS during its early years. However, as tourist consumption of tropical nature became important to their livelihoods, Maya Centre residents became increasingly committed to protecting the flora and fauna of the Cockscomb. They recognized that they could comply with the restrictions imposed by the protected area to produce an ecotourism commodity capable of attracting Northern tourists, or they could disregard these restrictions and bear the economic consequences if tourists judged the CBWS undesirable.

Although the BAS education campaign sought to elicit appreciation for the aesthetic and ecological value of the protected area and engender nonmarket commitments to conservation, these efforts were much less effective than markets at shaping villagers' environmental subjectivities. Concepts and methods from Western science are often deployed as means of inducing rural people "to appreciate the scientific—and hence 'incontestable'—basis of protected area designation" (Bryant 2002:283). However, the campaign's assertions of ecological value, conveyed through the concepts and practices of Western science, did not resonate with Mopan villagers. Instead, most Maya Centre residents rejected the very assumptions that oriented the education campaign: that they lacked knowledge of the forests in which they lived and that their traditional agricultural practices rendered them environmental threats. Although Maya Centre residents came to recognize the economic opportunities afforded by the tourist gaze, based on "seeing" as a means of engaging the natural world, few adopted this gaze as their own. The former Park Director recalled with frustration villagers' assertion, "We don't understand the conservation part of the Cockscomb, but we understand the economics of the park!"

While only 58 percent of Maya Centre residents reported having been in favor of the CBWS when it was established, 92 percent of Maya Centre residents expressed support for the reserve by 1993; 75 percent cited tourism benefits as the reason for their support (Lindberg and Enriquez 1994:84). Growing community support for the sanctuary manifested itself in respect for the ban on hunting. "People stopped hunting back there, because they were making a little money," a long-serving warden asserted. "Now they are making plenty." Other wardens and BAS staff concurred with this assessment.

Other village residents echoed this analysis. A teacher explained, "People have understood that the only reason these tourists are coming is that they want to see what is back there. And if they can keep it intact, then they will be able to still sell their crafts." A former Quam Bank resident, who had become a tour guide, agreed: "At the beginning I was disappointed." We didn't know what conservation meant or "what it can bring us." Later, he continued, when tourists began to travel to the Cockscomb, "from that point up to now, we found out that it's a good thing that we moved. Otherwise, government could have just sold the land to a foreigner or to a big agriculture company, and then they would be destroying our area there. But now it's a reserve, and that is good. The environment is in a safe position: we are saving the lives of many wildlife species, plants. And at the same time that we are preserving them, we are making money. It's good for the economy as well. All the villagers are benefiting from it." Thus, I argue, villagers' application of "the rationality of the market, the schemas of analysis it offers and the decision-making criteria it suggests" (Foucault 2008:323) to govern their own conduct more effectively regulated their actions regarding resources in the Cockscomb than did patrolling wardens or threats of punishment.

Some may argue that this market-rational valuation of protected nature does not warrant the label "environmental subjectivity." However, taking seriously Agrawal's definition of an environmental subject as someone whose "self-interest is cognized and realized in terms of the environment" (Agrawal 2005:164–165), the calculating, market-rational subject described above is revealed as a very particular kind of environmental subject: an appropriately neoliberal one.

It is important to state explicitly that the imposition or embrace of market subjectivities did not simply displace or erase other forms of subjectivity. Subjects are located in multiple, intersecting social positions, and the subjectivities they take on and perform are thus complex and multifaceted. Recent impositions layer over more deeply rooted positionings. Maya Centre residents' emerging environmental subjectivities thus reflected their prior positionings. As parents weighed past subsistence security against the cash incomes they now earned from tourism to the reserve, they lamented having to purchase their food. However, they expressed satisfaction at being able to invest in high school education for their children. Few adults in the village had had an opportunity to complete high school. Now that their ability to self-provision through subsistence production had been curtailed, Maya Centre residents valued education as an increasingly important asset for their children, and tourism revenues enabled more Maya Centre families to send their children to high school. As non-elites, villagers also shared a belief that the most likely alternative to the Cockscomb's enclosure would not have been Mopan ownership of these lands but rather their allocation to agricultural elites. Thus, protecting the Cockscomb enabled villagers to earn income as self-employed tourism entrepreneurs, which they preferred to working for wages on elite-owned plantations (Medina 2005). Women, in particular, valued the increased voice and autonomy their income from craft sales accorded them within their households.

### Governing *for* the Market, Governing *through* the Market

This book began with the story of a group of ecotourists unable to reach the Cockscomb because a fallen tree blocked the access road. "Park closed until further notice," a sign posted on a nearby tree announced. Women from Maya Centre had felled the tree, and market rationalities had oriented their agency in doing so. The women recognized that obstructing the operation of "the market"—preventing the CBWS from functioning as a commodity—would be an effective means to compel Audubon to dialog with them. However, a deepening sense of themselves as the bearers of Indigenous rights also shaped their actions. At the time, conflicts over land use and land tenure in southern Belize had escalated, and Maya organizations had filed a legal petition claiming Indigenous rights to the lands Maya communities traditionally used, mapping those lands in support of their claim. The territories mapped as areas of traditional use by Maya Centre and other communities around the Cockscomb included portions of the CBWS, despite government officials' designation of these lands as state property (TMCC and TAA 1997). Belizean political leaders had refused to address the Maya claim.

Amid heightened tensions concerning rights to land, the BAS had taken several actions that threatened villagers' tourism-based livelihoods. In 1995, when the Audubon Society had won permission to charge entrance fees at parks it comanaged, tensions emerged over who would collect these fees. The Maya Centre Women's Group wanted to collect the entrance fees at their gift shop, elite tourism entrepreneurs wanted to be able to sell tickets at their hotels, and Audubon staff wanted to collect the fees at park headquarters. To generate additional revenue through overnight stays, Audubon built a new dormitory inside the reserve in 1996, which lodge owners in Maya Centre perceived as competition. The Park

Director had also left his position, and BAS had hired a new director from another village bordering the reserve. Maya Centre women worried that the new director might allow women from his village to sell crafts inside the reserve, in competition with the Maya Centre Women's Group gift shop. The last straw came in 1997, when a BAS Executive Director moved the sanctuary's entrance gate and guest register up into the reserve. Many women believed the requirement for all tourists to stop at their gift shop to register was critical to their economic success, which also underwrote their increased voice in household decisions.

In response, a group of women "came together, got their axe, and went up the road," explained one villager. "They cut a big tree and crossed it flat on the road." The tour operator whose group was stopped by the fallen tree notified the BAS, and Audubon staff immediately contacted Maya Centre seeking explanation. Villagers demanded that BAS meet with the whole community to discuss their concerns. Although BAS leaders prioritized wildlife and habitat protection, the NGO's ability to achieve its conservation goals in the sanctuary depended on the generation of tourism revenues to finance park management, sustain state support for protected areas conservation, and win the consent of nearby communities. Recognizing the market-oriented imperatives that BAS leaders confronted, villagers forced Audubon to negotiate by impeding the operation of the market, rather than by threatening the sanctuary's flora and fauna.

Although the state had been unwilling to manage the protected area for the past decade, at this point the head of the Forestry Department suddenly expressed willingness to exercise force to keep the sanctuary open. "We will send in troops, take over, patrol!" he asserted. Given the critical role accorded to protected areas in the Belizean ecotourism "brand" and the flagship status of the CBWS itself, Forestry's willingness to ensure the continued production and sale of the CBWS as a tourism commodity reflected a commitment to govern *for* the market.

Three Audubon representatives and the Chief Forest Officer traveled to Maya Centre. At Forestry's request, a police officer accompanied them. Villagers expressed surprise at the involvement of the police: they had underestimated the state's commitment to the operation of the market for protected nature in southern Belize. However, a new Audubon Executive Director, who had participated throughout the 1990s in international conferences on best practices concerning relationships between "peoples and parks," won permission from the Chief Forest Officer to negotiate with villagers.

BAS and state delegations met in the village school with some fifty Maya Centre residents. Many villagers complained that they were not benefiting sufficiently from the sanctuary; they advocated for reclaiming lands in the Cockscomb to farm. A young woman who had lived in the Cockscomb as a child and now had children of her own recalled, "The people in Maya Centre wanted to close the reserve, because some people benefit from it, but some people do not benefit. So, most of the people say that it's better if we close it and then we start to farm those lands again. But when the Belize Audubon came, he told us that it was not better for us, because if the people from Maya Centre close the reserve, then we won't have money. Yes, we will have farming, but where will our children be in the future?" Thus, BAS representatives countered by contrasting subsistence security, based on the production of corn in the Cockscomb, with cash income derived from participation in global markets for nature. They asserted that participation in the market for ecotourism provided opportunities for villagers' children that subsistence security could not, including high school educations, which required cash for tuition, uniforms, and books.

Although some community members wanted to close the sanctuary permanently, villagers who had invested in tourism opposed efforts to dismantle the reserve. Instead, they sought to increase the economic benefits villagers derived from tourism to the CBWS. A man who had acquired a vehicle to ferry tourists to the sanctuary restated his grievances in a later interview:

> Audubon wanted to start a restaurant up there. They wanted to start a craft shop up there. They wanted to do almost everything up there. They wanted to start charging Maya Centre people for going up there. And all these things I protest[ed] against.... I can remember what they said at the time [the sanctuary was created], that if we were to leave, to come and live here, they would turn that place into tourism someday, which is true; that is good. And they said that when the tourists come, we will guide them, we would feed them, we would bike them, we would horse ride them, we would canoe them, we would put them up, we would do almost everything. They would bring the tourists, leave them here, and we would take care of them. But that is not true. Because when people come now, they already have a package tour. They have their own air-conditioned bus. They have their own tour guide. They have their food. They don't want anything from the people here.... How else can we benefit from the tourism?

This complaint underlined the degree to which Maya Centre relied on the requirement that those air-conditioned vans full of box-lunch-toting tourists from the coastal tourism enclaves stop at the women's group gift shop to register. This provided villagers' only point for market exchange with many tourists to the reserve.

Members of the women's group proposed a series of actions to ensure that Maya Centre, and especially its women, benefited from tourism to the sanctuary. They began with vehement demands that Audubon return the gate and guest register to their gift shop. The women also called for their group to be given sole responsibility for collecting park entrance fees by selling tickets to the reserve in their gift shop. Both actions would channel tourists into their gift shop and facilitate craft sales. Further, to prevent competition, the women insisted that no craft sales be allowed inside the CBWS. The women also sought a voice for villagers in hiring decisions for the CBWS and priority for Maya Centre residents, who, they argued, had lost more than other villages at the reserve's creation.

In response, the Audubon Executive Director proposed that they create an Advisory Committee, comprising representatives from Audubon, Forestry, and the community, to resolve the issues raised by the community. After lengthy debate among themselves in Mopan, villagers who sought to increase Maya Centre's income from the sanctuary prevailed over those who wanted to close the reserve. The community agreed to participate in the advisory committee, and six villagers were appointed to serve, representing the women's group, tour guides from the community, the school, and both churches in the community.

Over the months that followed, the advisory committee negotiated the return of the reserve's entrance gate and guest register to the women's group gift shop. The committee also agreed to locate ticket sales for the sanctuary at the gift shop, with the women's group retaining 10 percent of ticket revenues. This concession ensured additional income for the women's group. BAS representatives opposed Maya Centre's demand for preference in hiring at the reserve, arguing that other communities around the CBWS should also derive economic benefits from the sanctuary. The committee reached a compromise: Maya Centre representatives would propose qualified candidates from their community for *some* positions, and the BAS would select from among them. The integration of village representatives into an advisory committee and the concessions made by the BAS reflected emerging norms in global conservation circles that favored community participation in comanaging parks and the extension of economic benefits to communities near protected areas to secure their support for conservation (Tsing et al. 2005).

Notably, the focus of the advisory committee's efforts at comanagement of the sanctuary was not wildlife or resource management but rather the distribution of tourism revenues. Villagers demanded to be included in comanaging the reserve neither to regulate themselves, as the literature on decentralized environmental management might lead us to expect (Agrawal 2005; Li 2005; Neumann 2001; Schroeder 2005), nor to regulate resource use, but rather to regulate access to the economic opportunities created by the reserve.

By 2002, the number of visitors to the Cockscomb had reached 5,000 to 6,000 annually, and all households in Maya Centre were earning income from tourism. That income was not evenly distributed within the community; however, the broad range of activities carried out in the sanctuary by diverse entrepreneurs provided an equally broad range of employment and entrepreneurial opportunities to village residents with varied sets of resources and skills. Some men worked as wardens or assistants to wildlife researchers. Three households had been able to mobilize sufficient economic resources to build two- to three-room lodges, and three had purchased used vehicles to ferry tourists to the reserve. Male members of households with fewer monetary resources and less English-language facility worked as porters on occasional multiday expeditions far into the sanctuary; a few women worked occasionally as cooks for groups of tourists or researchers staying in the reserve. Several men worked as tour guides in the sanctuary. A number of young men had also found employment at resorts in nearby coastal tourism enclaves. Since most tourists who visited the CBWS originated in these enclaves, rather than staying in Maya Centre, the requirement that all visitors stop at the women's group gift shop to register was critical to villagers' ability to extract economic benefit from them through craft sales. The women's group claimed a membership of over 90 percent of the village's women in 2002, and its members reported earning as much as US$200–300 per month, at a time when mean income in Belize was US$417 per month (CSO 2001:23). Further, the women's group collectively earned US$4,500–US$5,000 per year from ticket sales, with which it helped to fund the village primary school.

## Analysis

In the conflict over entrance fees and villagers' closure of the sanctuary, state officials, NGO staff, and Mopan villagers each governed their own conduct and sought to govern one another's conduct by applying market rationality to orient their own actions and predict and shape the actions of others. Maya Centre residents' exclusion from subsistence resources had intensified their market subjectivities, which in turn oriented their exercise of agency, shaping the form of their protest and their demands. State officials threatened to exercise sovereignty to govern *for* the market, but Audubon's response was "governmental" in nature, seeking to resolve the conflict through the application of market rationality rather than force. By making concessions, "arranging conditions" so as to protect and increase villagers' market access, the BAS ensured the continued integration of sanctuary and community into market exchange and their continued subjection to market rationalities, governing *through* the market.

Maya Centre residents' challenge to the BAS cannot be categorized as resistance in any straightforward way, because villagers' agency was oriented by the intertwined market and environmental subjectivities imposed and/or cultivated through the combined actions of the state and the BAS. The complaints and demands that villagers voiced in the 1997 conflict demonstrated that Maya Centre residents understood the principles Audubon had applied to conduct their conduct: their subjection to markets for nature was expected to generate environmental subjectivities. Deploying the very logic articulated by proponents of neoliberal conservation, villagers asserted that the BAS must increase the economic benefits they received from conservation, to win or sustain their support for the reserve.

Thus, although the state devolved responsibility for managing protected nature in the Cockscomb to a conservation NGO, management of both the sanctuary and the residents of nearby villages devolved in more significant ways to "the market" through the implementation of ecotourism. After the act of state sovereignty that evicted the Mopan Maya residents of Quam Bank from the Cockscomb, environmental government came to consist in "arranging conditions" so as to incorporate the sanctuary and Maya Centre residents into market exchange and bring market rationalities to bear on villagers' actions. As villagers became incorporated into the global market for ecotourism—through the sale of crafts or services or through wage labor at coastal resorts—their conduct came to be governed through the market. More precisely, villagers came to apply "the rationality of the market, the schemas of analysis it offers and the decision-making criteria it suggests" to govern their own conduct in relation to the sanctuary. This resulted in villagers abandoning hunting to support and sustain the successful production and sale of protected-nature-as-commodity.

As Audubon became dependent on ecotourism to fund its conservation agenda, its personnel also became increasingly subject to market exchange, as participants in the production and sale of protected-nature-as-commodity. Consequently, BAS staff increasingly governed their own behavior through the application of market rationalities.[2] The analytic of governmentality reveals how the deployment of the "truth of the market" rearranged material constraints and incentives in ways that subjected both those who sought to govern and the people they targeted to the consumption choices of Northern ecotourists.

CHAPTER 5

# Contested Histories and Histories of Contestation in Southern Belize

This chapter examines the origins of struggles over land tenure in southern Belize, which escalated in the last decades of the twentieth century. The government sought to exercise sovereignty over the south by implementing development projects that would transform lands collectively managed by Maya communities into private property. State actors also granted concessions to transnational companies for timber extraction and oil exploration and established protected areas on lands used by Maya communities but designated by the government as state property. In response, Q'eqchi' and Mopan Maya mobilized to secure the lands they traditionally used. In alliance with North American Indigenous rights advocates, Mopan and Q'eqchi' leaders launched a mapping project to demonstrate the extent of their land use as a basis for their claim. They also petitioned the Belize Supreme Court for recognition of their land rights as Indigenous people.

## British Efforts to Exercise Sovereignty in Southern Belize: Mapping, Counting, and Indirect Rule

As chapter 2 demonstrated, southern Belize was largely outside of European control for most of the colonial period. Spanish forces captured and forcibly relocated some native people westward to territories under Spanish control, but they never established a permanent presence in these lands.

Britain claimed this territory in the early 1800s and won recognition for its claim in the 1859 treaty with Guatemala. However, British colonial administrators knew virtually nothing of this region beyond the coast. In 1859, the colony's superintendent reported, "The southern portions of our territory have never been explored, and according to the Crown Surveyor they contain inhabitants who . . . have never yet been seen by European or creole" (Wainwright 2015:126). Maps drawn prior to 1900 substantiate this assertion, misplacing major topographical features of Toledo's interior (Wainwright 2015:126). Despite the near complete absence of the state from Toledo, most of the district's land was designated as state property. During the late 1800s and early 1900s, several large agricultural estates began operations in Toledo, but most failed for lack of labor (Wilk 1997:56). Officials welcomed Mopan and Q'eqchi' migrants from Guatemala in the late 1800s, viewing them as potential labor for agricultural or logging enterprises.

The 1872 Crown Lands Ordinance had authorized the designation of "Indian reservations," but the colonial government created only one reservation in Toledo prior to 1900, at San Antonio. After establishing a Forestry Department in 1923, colonial officials acted to "stop the destruction of valuable mahogany forests" by restricting Maya fire-based agriculture to reservations (Van Ausdal 2000:17). The Forestry Department launched an effort to map the trails and "areas of Indian occupation" in Toledo, enlarging the San Antonio reservation and establishing additional reserves for each Mopan or Q'eqchi' settlement discovered and mapped (ICMW 1941). During a logging boom in Toledo during the 1930s, the Forestry Department conducted an agricultural census in 1931 and used its data to redraw and expand the reservations to reflect actual Maya land usage, which had shifted since the mid-1920s. The Forestry Department repeated the recalibration of land to people in 1936 and 1939 to keep up with changes in the extent and location of Maya land use (ICMW 1941; Wilk 1997:68).

As these recalibration exercises suggest, colonial administrators were unable to regulate Maya land use, despite assertions of state ownership over most lands in Toledo. Reservation boundaries were never clearly demarcated, and Q'eqchi' and Mopan farmers extended their land use far beyond the reserves, with the state redrawing the reservations to reflect Maya land use. Further, in the absence of a colonial bureaucracy in the south, colonial officials replicated in Belize the strategy of indirect rule practiced elsewhere across the British Empire: they relied on leaders of Maya communities' own system of self-governance to collect the annual rents levied on parcels within the reservations (Bolland 1987). The British used the Spanish term *alcalde* to refer to these community leaders; Q'eqchi' and Mopan communities have their own terms for these leaders and the institutions through which they govern themselves.

Even though colonial heads of departments lacked knowledge of the inhabitants of Toledo's interior, they recommended sweeping interventions to "improve" their lives and livelihoods. Before addressing these recommendations, it is worth taking account of the institutions through which Mopan and Q'eqchi communities managed their lands and relationships to set the context for the struggles that emerged around state development policies.

### Mopan and Q'eqchi' Worlds: Relations and Practices of Respect

In the Mopan socionatural world, the hills and valleys are—or are inhabited by—living forces, Witz-hok, whom humans must engage in relationships of respect, *tzik*. "Tzik"—respect—is a transitive verb that is innately relational: one acquires the tzik relations necessary to live well by giving tzik to those beings to whom one owes it. Tzik is "an attitude of religious deference ... given in the form of human action" (Danziger 2001:96). A key organizing principle for Mopan is that everyone owes tzik to beings upon whom their survival and well-being depend. For any individual, this category includes parents, aunts and uncles, godparents, and substantially older siblings. This category also includes the "owners" or "keepers" of the hills and valleys (Witz-hok), sun and rain, animals, and plants, along with the Christian god and Catholic saints, who have been brought into the circle of tzik relationships through human practice (Danziger 2001; Saqui 2012).

A Q'eqchi' cosmovision resonates with this Mopan worldview, revolving around relationships between humans and *Tzuultaq'a*—hills and valleys—described by James Stinson as "other-than-human persons" (Stinson 2017:212).[1] Both Mopan and Q'eqchi' hold to a relational ontology in which proper human personhood is achieved through the performance of respect for the beings—both human and nonhuman—upon whom one depends for well-being. As Hillary Kahn describes, for Q'eqchi', "respect is a relationship and an action" (Kahn 2006:63). The term *naleb'*, which Stinson associates with respect, "is not simply knowledge or a set of moral values, but is above all else, a way of living and being," specifically a way of being *in relation to* other selves (Stinson 2017:205–206). In this sense, personhood "is an attribute of being cultivated and recognized ... through the establishment of social relations" (Stinson 2017:207; Wilson 1995).

Showing respect to both human and other-than-human persons involves using appropriate terms of address and an appropriate language of supplication, humbly requesting permission, and asserting one's need to use resources under the control of the Witz-hok or Tzuultaq'a. Carefully husbanding those resources and using only what one needs are also ways of giving respect. Requests for permission to use lands or hunt animals involve offerings or acts of sacrifice, including burning copal incense, providing food, and practicing sexual abstinence (Stinson 2017; Wilk 1997). These performances of respect are most elaborated around milpa production of corn, the most significant crop (Baines 2016; Saqui 2012).

Through performances of respect, an individual knits together a social network upon which he or she can depend, integrating kin, community members, and Witz-hok or Tzuultaq'a. These social relationships are integral to milpa production of corn. For example, the relationships a young Mopan man establishes by offering respect to elders and Witz-hok ensures that elders with whom he has a tzik relationship will provide the knowledge and guidance he requires in the moment in which he needs it (Danziger 2001; Saqui 2012). Further, the networks Mopan and Q'eqchi' create by giving respect allow households to mobilize collective work groups for the most labor-intensive phases of milpa corn production, clearing land and planting (Downey 2010).

Maya communities in Toledo manage collective decisions and tasks that extend beyond the boundaries of individual households or reciprocal labor exchanges through the Alcalde System. Through the Alcalde System, villages regulate access to land to ensure that all households in the community have access to the resources they need to sustain themselves: a well-drained plot of land for the main rainy-season corn crop, a low-lying plot for a dry-season corn crop, and access to fresh water and forest resources. Although the specific rules for allocating lands may vary across villages, the processes, principles, and institutions upon which the Alcalde System is based are shared across communities. Nor do practices vary by language affiliation, as many villages have both Mopan and Q'eqchi' residents.

Annually, each farmer marks, clears, and plants a rainy-season cornfield; after this crop, the plot will be fallowed for five to seven years before reuse. A farmer who clears high bush from a parcel of land and cultivates it has the right to reuse that parcel, a right that may be passed to heirs. Likewise, farmers who plant permanent tree crops on a parcel may be recognized as having rights to that parcel and the trees in perpetuity. Because community members know who has rights to which parcels of land, conflicts over land are rare; however, the alcalde is responsible for resolving disputes that arise, in consultation with community members through the institution of the Village Meeting. Communities also manage common spaces within the community through the Alcalde System (Wilk 1986).

In addition, Maya communities regulate village membership through the Alcalde System. People seeking to join a community and work lands held by that community must request permission from the alcalde, who consults with community members through the Village Meeting. If members of the community know the individual or family seeking to join the village and can vouch for their character, they are usually permitted to move into the community and cultivate village lands. If disputes arise between communities over shared lands and resources or the boundaries between villages, the alcaldes of the communities involved are responsible for negotiating a satisfactory compromise, in consultation with their communities. Because it is the alcalde who has the authority to convene the Village Meeting, overtures from outside the community would also engage the community through the alcalde (see photo 4).

Photo 4. San Jose Village, Toledo District. Credit: Laurie Kroshus Medina.

## Anti-Milpa Discourses and Development Projects

None of these relationships, principles, or logics have been legible to state policymakers. Colonial assessments of Maya agriculture generated during the first half of the nineteenth century defined milpa production as primitive, inefficient, and destructive (Van Ausdal 2000:54–56). Of course, the anti-milpa perspective that shaped colonial policies for Toledo was not exclusive to British Honduras; discourses that denigrated swidden agriculture circulated throughout the British Empire at this time (Bhandar 2018; Van Ausdal 2001:593).

As the logging boom in Toledo ended in the late 1930s, colonial authorities shifted their priorities for Toledo. Personnel from the newly established Agriculture Department targeted Toledo for cash crop production to feed the colony's urban population (Van Ausdal 2000:53–54). Forestry officials remained concerned about Maya farmers' use of fire to prepare milpas, which they saw as destructive. Failing to recognize the rotational nature of Maya agriculture, with farmers fallowing lands after use before clearing the parcel anew, they cast the Maya milpa system as a form of "predatory nomadism," in which each Maya farmer cleared a new parcel of "virgin" forest each year, voraciously destroying the forest (Wainwright 2007). Officials in the Agriculture Department deemed milpa production inefficient; they sought to instill more intensive forms of cultivation in Toledo and to shift the priority from subsistence to cash crops. Both agriculture and forestry experts blamed the reservations for perpetuating the practices they deemed destructive and inefficient. Proposing permanent cultivation as a remedy, they determined that permanent cultivation would require the conversion of reservations into private landholdings (Wainwright 2007:83–87).

Efforts to transform production in Toledo to meet the colony's food needs occurred in phases. In 1949, the colonial state established a Marketing Board to spur production of urban staples by purchasing, processing, and distributing crops such as corn, rice, and beans (Wilk 2006:139). In the 1960s, the colonial administration built the Southern Highway, a gravel road that provided the first land link between Toledo and the rest of the colony, to facilitate the transport of staple crops to urban markets. Though colonial administrators deemed it an "all-weather road," heavy rains regularly submerged its low bridges for hours or days at a time. Nonetheless, the road drew Maya out of more remote areas of the district to establish new villages along the highway with easier access to markets (Wilk 1997:70), (see map 5).

After British Honduras became self-governing, Peoples United Party (PUP) elected officials adopted the discourse and policies of colonial administrators, denigrating milpa agriculture and blaming the reservations for its continuation (Van Ausdal 2000:55). During the first decade of Belizean self-government, a period when 86 percent of the lands in Toledo District were designated as state lands by the government, political leaders took steps to abolish the reservations and privatize land in southern Belize, seeking to replace milpa agriculture with permanent cropping on individually owned parcels (Hoffman 2021:68; Van Ausdal 2001).

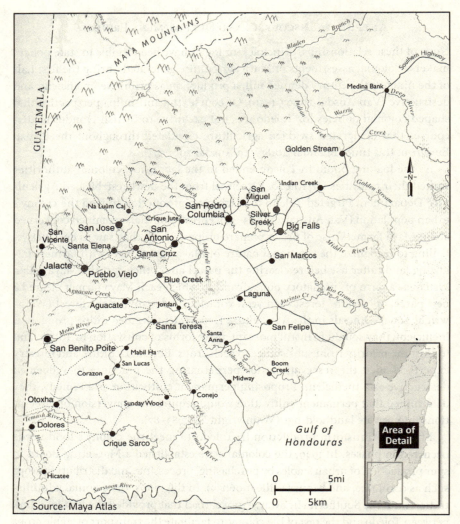

Map 5. Maya communities in the Toledo District, adapted from *Maya Atlas*, North Atlantic Books. Credit: Michael Siegel, Rutgers Cartography 2023.

Confronted by Maya resistance, in 1974 the government retreated from its plans to simply abolish the reservations (Gregory 1984). However, legislators and Lands Department officials continued to offer leasehold parcels to individual Maya farmers, both within and outside the reservations (Van Ausdal 2000:59). This strategy was possible, because the Lands Department designated both reservation lands and most nonreservation lands in Toledo as state property. State officials reportedly pressured Maya farmers to apply for leases by warning that their control of land was tenuous without an official government lease. An additional incentive offered was the suggestion that farmers could use individual lease lands as collateral for loans to purchase agricultural inputs to intensify production.

State-issued leases for lands to individuals generated tensions within Maya communities: leases decreased the amount of land a community managed collectively, increasing pressure on the remaining lands held by the community (Gregory 1976, 1984; Howard 1977; Van Ausdal 2001:594). The tensions were exacerbated by the fact that Maya farmers who received leases for individual parcels of land rarely relied on those parcels alone for their livelihoods. They typically continued to access other community lands—a wetter parcel, for example, for dry-season corn production—to sustain their families throughout the annual cycle of planting and harvesting.

The self-governing state also pursued its agenda of land privatization through a series of development projects that prioritized the production of cash crops using more intensive cultivation techniques on individual holdings (Van Ausdal 2000, 2001). These projects aimed to integrate both Maya farmers and lands into markets, establishing a market for land in Toledo. These development projects provide another example of state actors governing *for* the market, creating markets where they had not previously existed. Beyond remaking Maya agriculture and transforming land tenure in Toledo, PUP leaders envisioned these projects as vehicles for the governing party to signal its commitment to developing the rural south.

Leases for private parcels of land also served as key resources in an expanding patronage system, through which the governing party sought to expand its support (Vernon 2022; Wainwright 2007:206). Political party clientelism, launched with the advent of self-government after 1964, expanded postindependence, as the United Democratic Party (UDP) emerged as a viable political alternative to the PUP. Once Belize had become independent, substantive policy or ideological differences between the parties diminished, and the parties increasingly competed to win votes through the provision of patronage to supporters (Vernon 2022).

At the same time, the PUP government strongly promoted the implementation of a Village Council System in rural villages across Belize. PUP leaders envisioned the Village Council System as a mechanism through which the government could provide resources such as roads, schools, or potable water systems to communities to win their support. Village council members—and possibly whole communities—might thus be integrated into party patronage relations.

However, Toledo residents expressed dissatisfaction with the self-governing Belizean state by consistently electing representatives from opposition political parties. The PUP carried national elections for twenty years after the beginning of self-government in 1964, but Toledo elected representatives from opposition parties in 1964, 1969, 1974, and 1979. PUP efforts to privatize the reservations and sideline the Alcalde System in favor of village councils provoked contestation and mobilization by Mopan and Q'eqchi'. Maya communities viewed the Alcalde System as the means by which they governed themselves and their lands and resources; in contrast, they recognized village councils as instruments of political parties and their expanding patronage networks.

## Belizean Indigenous Mobilization in Global Context

Maya activists date Maya political mobilization in Toledo to 1978, when the Toledo Indian Movement emerged to oppose state efforts to privatize reservation lands and undermine the Alcalde System. Maya leaders accused the Belizean state of the "systematic destruction of Maya culture" and sought to develop new opportunities to generate income for Maya communities that built on—rather than seeking to alter—Maya agricultural practices (TMCC and TAA 1997:3). Belizean political leaders tried to suppress and discredit the organization, fearful of its "radical" potential (Van Ausdal 2000:72). To counter this portrayal, the organization changed its name to the Toledo Indian Cultural Movement in 1984 and then became the Toledo Maya Cultural Council (TMCC) in 1985.

Maya mobilization in Belize occurred in the context of an emerging global Indigenous movement. During the 1960s and 1970s, American Indian and First Nation activists in the United States and Canada mobilized to demand self-determination, in response to government projects that aimed to terminate tribal governments and assimilate native peoples to dominant national norms (Engle 2010:52). By the mid-1970s, North American Indigenous groups were expanding and formalizing alliances, establishing the International Indian Treaty Council in 1974 and the World Council of Indigenous Peoples (WCIP) in 1975 (Brysk 2000:100; Engle 2010:52). In 1978, the Indian Law Resource Center emerged from a legal aid organization that had served American Indian groups, with a mission of extending legal and technical assistance to Indigenous groups in Latin America (Brysk 2000:88).

In Latin America, programs to assimilate Indigenous peoples to Eurocentric norms, as well as serious human rights violations against Indigenous peoples, prompted European scholars to organize the International Work Group for Indigenous Affairs (IWGIA) in 1968. In 1971, a group of Latin American anthropologists critiqued Latin American countries' policies of assimilation in the Barbados Declaration, demanding that Latin American states guarantee Indigenous peoples' right to lands, their right to govern themselves "in accordance with their own traditions," and their right "to be and to remain themselves, living according to their own customs and moral order free to develop their own culture" (Bartolome et al. 1973:268). Indigenous activists from Latin America began to speak on their own behalf in international forums, rejecting the assimilationist goals of indigenist policies in the region. Calling on Latin American states to recognize the "plurinational, multicultural, and multilinguistic" nature of their societies, they mobilized to reassert, reclaim, and revitalize Indigenous cultures and identities (de la Peña 2005; Engle 2010:92). During the 1980s, Indigenous groups from across South America also organized broad alliances (Engle 2010:92).

The United Nations became an important venue for Indigenous organizations to present their grievances. In response to Indigenous mobilization, in 1969 the UN Sub-Commission on the Prevention of Discrimination and Protection of Minorities commissioned a study of discrimination against Indigenous populations. Its report was damning (Daes 2011:11–12). From 1973 to 1982, the UN Decade for Action to Combat Racism and Racial Discrimination prompted a series of international conferences on racism, including a 1977 conference on discrimination against Indigenous populations in the Americas. Representatives of sixty Indigenous peoples from fifteen countries attended the conference, focusing global attention on the conditions they confronted as Indigenous peoples. A second international conference on Indigenous peoples in 1981 focused specifically on land issues (Niezen 2003:44–45). Indigenous organizations expanded their access to UN forums, with the International Indigenous Treaty Council securing consultative status at the United Nations in 1977, followed by the World Council of Indigenous Peoples, the Indian Law Resource Center, and the Indian Council of South America (Brysk 2000:99; Engle 2010:75).

In response to growing Indigenous advocacy, the UN Economic and Social Council authorized the creation of a Working Group on Indigenous Populations (WGIP) in 1982, comprising five human rights experts who represented the major world regions (Daes 2011:12). The WGIP convened annual two-week meetings that attracted representatives of Indigenous groups from around the world, who sought to make their struggles known. Across time, similarities among the threats that representatives of Indigenous groups denounced before the WGIP contributed to a growing awareness among Indigenous peoples that they shared the experience of being culturally distinct from the dominant populations in their societies as well as the experience of being oppressed because of that cultural distinctiveness (Niezen 2003:47).

Belizean Maya leaders traveled to international forums convened by the IWGIA and the WGIP to denounce the Belizean government's actions to abolish the reservations, privatize reservation lands, and withdraw recognition for Maya traditional forms of governance (IWGIA 1984; Van Ausdal 2000:73). In 1984, the Toledo Maya Cultural Movement joined the World Council of Indigenous Peoples, and in 1985, Primitivo Coc, an officer in the renamed Toledo Maya Cultural Council, was elected to lead the Coordinadora Regional de Pueblos Indigenas (Regional Coordinator of Indigenous Peoples, CORPI). CORPI and the WCIP both called on the Belizean government to recognize the authority of the Maya Alcalde System and to acknowledge that reservation lands were the property of the Maya people (Mesh 2017:171).

At this time, the Belizean government had resumed the distribution of leases for lands to individual Maya, as well as alienating lands used by Maya communities to non-Maya investors. For example, in 1986, the government granted one hundred acres of land to a foreign company to develop citrus orchards on lands claimed by the village of San Felipe. Shortly thereafter, the government announced the launch of the Toledo Small Farmer Development Project, which aimed to privatize Maya reservation lands to enable leaseholders to access credit (Van Ausdal 2001:594–596). Criticizing these actions for launching "a serious erosion of Maya land holdings," the Toledo Maya Cultural Council proposed creation of a Maya homeland to defend Maya collectively held lands. In 1988, the TMCC petitioned the government for a half million acres of land in Toledo District to create that homeland, which would replace the reserves and accord collective ownership rights to Mopan and Q'eqchi' Maya (Van Ausdal 2000:81; Wilk 1991:235).

The government rejected this petition, and government leaders invoked dominant narratives of Belizean history to deny Q'eqchi' and Mopan claims to indigeneity. Insisting that the Q'eqchi' and Mopan were immigrants from Guatemala, government officials maintained that Q'eqchi' and Mopan should be treated like all other Belizeans: they should apply as individuals for parcels of state-owned land on lease.

## The 1990s: State Attacks on Maya Lands and the Alcalde System

In 1992, the Belizean legislature passed the National Lands Act, reasserting the state's right to eminent domain in the reservations. The government also took further steps to impose village councils on all rural communities in Belize, facilitating the intrusion of partisan competition and clientelism into all villages (Vernon 2022:101). Maya communities were concerned that the Village Council System, which is highly partisan in nature, would provide an avenue for political parties and their competing patronage systems to win adherents and divide community members. They worried this would undermine the power Maya communities wielded in governing themselves through the Alcalde System, shifting power to the state or to political parties.

In 1992, the alcaldes of some of the larger villages began to organize across their communities; then, they reached out to incorporate all Maya communities across the district. After several months of planning, they formally established the Toledo Alcaldes Association (TAA), whose membership includes the first and second alcaldes from all Maya villages in Toledo. These officials are selected—and can be removed at will—by their communities. One of the TAA's objectives was to advocate for the continued operation of the Alcalde System in the face of state efforts to shift power to village councils. The TAA enabled alcaldes and the communities they represent to act in concert to respond to issues that affect all communities. The alcaldes are responsible for representing the views of their respective communities in deliberations at TAA assemblies; they are also responsible for representing discussions at TAA assemblies back to their villages, so that deliberations at TAA General Assemblies and deliberations in Village Meetings can inform one another.

Meanwhile, TMCC leaders participated in international Indigenous rights forums, where they expanded and deepened their networks of allies. They forged a significant relationship with the Indian Law Resource Center (ILRC), a U.S.-based nonprofit organization founded and staffed by Indigenous legal experts, who mobilized the law to secure Indigenous rights. The ILRC was committed to extending its legal and technical assistance to Indigenous groups in Latin America. With their ILRC partners, TMCC leaders explored the idea of establishing a Maya homeland.

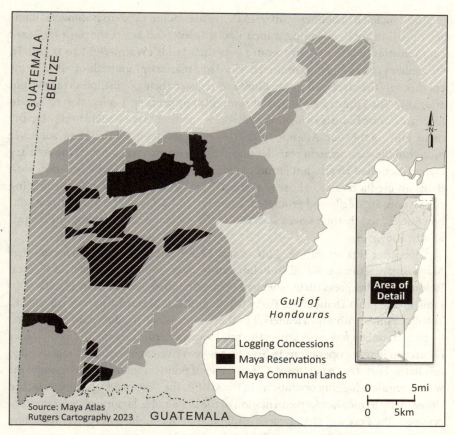

Map 6. Extent and overlap of reservations, logging concessions, and lands used and claimed by Maya communities in Toledo District, adapted from *Maya Atlas*, North Atlantic Books. Credit: Michael Siegel, Rutgers Cartography 2023.

Then, in 1993, the Belizean state issued logging concessions for over a half million acres of land in Toledo (TMCC and TAA 1997:122). The concessions included lands designated as reservations as well as other lands used by Maya communities that would be part of the proposed Maya homeland. Commencement of logging by one foreign concessionaire, Atlantic Industries, in the Columbia River Forest Reserve in 1995 galvanized Maya opposition. The logging represented a dual affront to Maya communities: the concessions ignored Maya claims to these territories, and the logging activities degraded the forest and contaminated water supplies for downstream villages (see map 6). The Toledo Alcaldes Association created a Reservation Lands Committee to study the legal status of the Indian reservations, selecting a charismatic young schoolteacher, Julian Cho, to chair the committee (Wainwright 2007:178). Members of the Reservation Lands Committee traveled to all Maya villages in the Toledo District to mobilize Maya to pursue collective Indigenous land rights (Wainwright 2007:246).

Cho contacted major newspapers in Belize to denounce the environmental damage caused by foreign logging companies in Toledo and assert the need for Maya communities to attain secure tenure over their lands (Wainwright 2007:177). In December 1995, as logging continued, Cho led a march by hundreds of Maya farmers through the streets of Punta Gorda to register their opposition (Wainwright 2007:179). The Forestry Department responded by sending a delegation to Toledo to tour Atlantic Industry's logging operations, inviting Maya leaders to accompany them. During the tour, Atlantic Industries managers revealed that they had never even read the management plan developed for their concession, which the Forestry Department had clearly not enforced. Maya leaders shared this admission with Belizean media houses, whose reporting drew national attention to the logging concessions in Toledo and prompted conservation NGOs such as the Belize Audubon Society to ally themselves with the TMCC to oppose the concessions (Wainwright 2007:179).

Soon after this revelation, TMCC and TAA officers and the leaders of other Maya organizations traveled to Belmopan to meet with the Minister of Natural Resources and express their vehement opposition to logging on Maya lands. Subsequently, United Democratic Party prime minister Manuel Esquivel traveled to Toledo to meet with Maya leaders, but these discussions produced no resolution.

In fact, only a few weeks after the revelations of enforcement and compliance failures in logging operations in Toledo, the government announced massive layoffs in the Forestry Department. Clearly, even if political leaders had possessed the will to regulate logging operations in the CRFR, the Forestry Department lacked the capacity to monitor implementation of the sustainable logging plan for the concession.[2] The Forestry Department responded to the public outcry over its failure to enforce sustainability protocols in Toledo by closing Atlantic Industries' sawmill. However, the department allowed the company to continue logging, and the company opened a new sawmill at another location (Wainwright 2007:179).

In addition to the logging concessions, Prime Minister Esquivel and his cabinet had initiated plans for a $100 million project to pave the Southern Highway, upgrading the gravel road that connected the two southern districts to the rest of the country. Mopan and Q'eqchi' anticipated that the value of land in the south would rise as the region became more accessible, and they feared that a land grab would ensue, with the government leasing or selling lands on which Maya livelihoods depended (TMCC and TAA 1997:175). In 1996, the TMCC pressed the Inter-American Development Bank, a principal funder of the road project, to halt funding until the Belizean government addressed Mopan and Q'eqchi' land claims. The bank responded by delaying the loan until the prime minister committed to resolving Indigenous land tenure and environmental concerns. Then, it approved funding for the Southern Highway project, and construction commenced, without waiting for those concerns to be resolved.

In late 1997, the TMCC learned that the Ministry of Energy had also granted concessions for oil exploration on reservation lands and other lands used by Mopan and Q'eqchi' in Toledo. This represented another attack on Maya control over the lands they traditionally used: under Belizean law, oil extraction rights are guaranteed to the concession holder if commercially viable oil deposits are found.[3]

## Maya Responses: Mapping the Land Claim via the *Maya Atlas*

In December 1995, the Reservation Lands Committee reported its findings to the TMCC membership and announced plans to map Maya lands (Wainwright 2007:246). At that meeting, TMCC members elected Julian Cho and other members of the Reservation Lands Committee to leadership positions in the TMCC. Cho, who became chair of the TMCC, was charismatic, capable of engaging villagers, state officials, and international interlocutors alike. Under his leadership, the TMCC became increasingly visible and active across national and international scales. He forged a close relationship with the chairperson of the Toledo Alcaldes Association, Santiago Coh, and the two leaders traveled together internationally to draw attention to land issues in southern Belize and lobby organizations to support the Maya cause and apply pressure on the Belizean state (Wainwright 2007:247). Participating in international conferences and meetings of the UN Working Group on Indigenous Populations, they engaged Indigenous allies in North, Central, and South America. Collaborations with more experienced Indigenous organizations helped them to get meetings with officials at the Inter-American Development Bank, the World Bank, the U.S. State Department, the Inter-American Commission on Human Rights, the Inter-American Foundation, the National Congress of American Indians, and environmentalist organizations (Wainwright 2007:197). With assistance from the North American Indian Law Resource Center, the TMCC and the TAA launched a dual strategy to secure legal recognition for a Maya homeland: a mapping project and a petition to the Supreme Court of Belize.

Participants in the Maya movement in Toledo had considered mapping Maya lands since the mid-1980s, but the events of the 1990s made the project increasingly urgent. The Toledo Maya Cultural Council and the Toledo Alcaldes Association collaborated to produce an atlas that would make Maya land use visible to support their land claim. Working with the Indian Law Resource Center, the TMCC won funding from the MacArthur Foundation and the Inter-American Foundation to undertake a community mapping project that would delineate the extent of the lands used by Maya communities to produce livelihoods. On the advice of ILRC staff, they contracted with geographers at the University of California, Berkeley, for cartographic training and mapmaking support (TMCC and TAA 1997:138).

Each Maya community in southern Belize designated its own mapmaker. The mappers and their village alcaldes attended cartographic training workshops with geographers from the University of California, Berkeley, in June and July 1996. They decided on the features they would include on their maps and the symbols they would use to represent them, and Maya mappers learned to use GPS units to align their maps with government maps. Then, each community mapper prepared a map

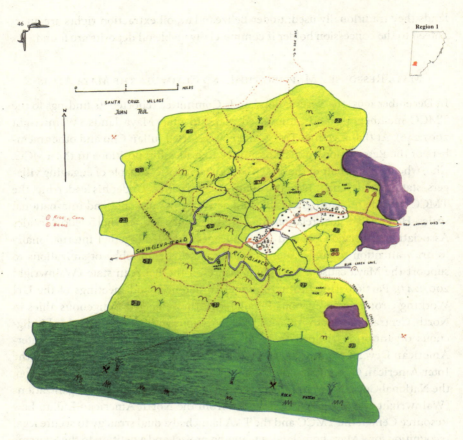

Photo 5. Map of Santa Cruz Village from *Maya Atlas*, North Atlantic Books. White area represents the village, light green indicates areas of milpa cultivation, purple shows low areas where dry-season corn is cultivated, and dark green represents forests where villagers hunt and collect forest products.

of his communities' land use, both inside and beyond the reservations.[4] The maps showed the lands used by each village for swidden agriculture and demonstrated the extent of the lands they used for hunting, fishing, and collecting forest resources. The community maps were aggregated to demonstrate the expanse of Maya lands in southern Belize, as defined by Maya land use. The TMCC and TAA submitted two of the maps, one showing the aggregate extent of Maya customary land use in Toledo and the other showing the extent of the logging concessions, with the Supreme Court petition (see photos 5 and 6). They submitted the entire *Maya Atlas*, published in 1997, in subsequent cases.

In addition to the maps, the *Maya Atlas* included narratives that articulated Maya claims to the lands they used. Countering the government's rejection of Mopan and Q'eqchi' indigeneity, the atlas emphasized continuity and connections between ancient and contemporary Maya. "The Toledo District has been Mayan

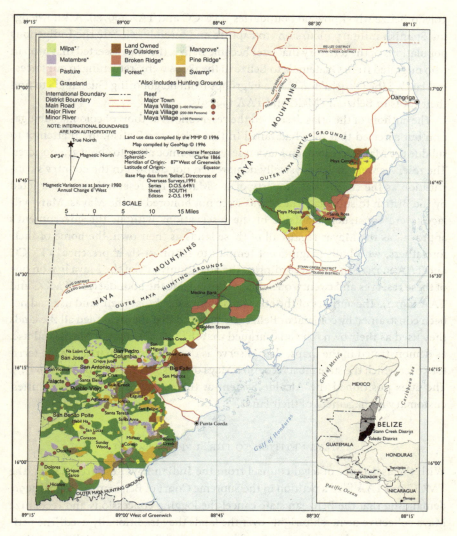

Photo 6. Aggregate Maya land use/land claim from *Maya Atlas*, North Atlantic Books.

territory for many centuries," the atlas asserted. "Mayan people were the first to occupy and use the land for subsistence agriculture. Four thousand years ago, the Maya were occupying the land that is now known as Belize" (TMCC and TAA 1997:14). Defining the contemporary Maya of Toledo as "the direct descendants of the ancient Mayas," the atlas cited their continuous use of Maya temples for religious purposes as "testimony to their connection with the past" (TMCC and TAA 1997:3).

Addressing dominant narratives of Belizean history, which cast all contemporary Belizean ethnic groups as immigrants, the atlas's authors asked, "How can we, Mayas, be considered immigrants? We are the original inhabitants of

Toledo Belize who know no boundaries" (TMCC and TAA 1997:2). Acknowledging Spanish military incursions to capture and forcibly relocate the Indigenous populations of the territory that later became Belize, the atlas asserted that Mopan who migrated from Guatemala to Belize in the 1800s were "returning to our ancestral lands"; the Q'eqchi' too "came in groups from neighboring Guatemala to find their roots in Belize" (TMCC and TAA 1997:9).

The authors of the atlas described the reservations as tools of colonial subjugation but asserted that they had failed in this role: "The British, in an attempt to subdue the Mayas, created ten Maya reservations amounting to about 77,000 acres. The reserves were never physically demarcated nor defined in the country's constitution as the communal property of the Mayas. The reservations constructed by the British to subjugate the Mayas were not honored by the Mayas. Many villages were constructed outside of the reservations without the government's approval, as the Mayas regard all of these lands as their own, the home of their forefathers, who built magnificent temples to manifest their presence" (TMCC and TAA 1997:7). In fact, according to the atlas, "only 51% of the Maya live on one of these reserves and twenty-one villages are outside the boundaries" (TMCC and TAA 1997:1). The authors of the atlas thus emphasized that their land use had not been constrained by colonial or Belizean states and that they regarded all the lands they used as their own. The atlas argued that the actual extent of Maya land use, as demonstrated in the maps, should serve as the basis for demarcating the territory over which the state must recognize Maya ownership (TMCC and TAA 1997:7). The atlas positioned the Alcalde System at the center of Maya communities' customary management of their lands.

## Maya Petition to the Supreme Court

With the assistance of legal counsel from the Indian Law Resource Center, the TMCC and TAA filed a petition in the Supreme Court of Belize in December 1996, demanding that the Belizean state cancel the logging concessions and recognize Maya collective ownership rights over the lands they traditionally used. The petition drew on developing international law regarding Indigenous rights to articulate a novel legal theory that Indigenous land rights "arise from and are commensurate with the customary land tenure patterns of the Toledo Maya" (Anaya 1998:19). This legal argument, developed by S. James Anaya, a professor of law and affiliate of the Indian Law Resource Center, had the immediate aim of halting logging on lands used by Mopan and Q'eqchi.' However, it had the larger goal of achieving secure collective title to the lands used by Mopan and Q'eqchi' communities in southern Belize.

On January 13, 1997, the Supreme Court's Judge George Meerabux announced that he would try the case via written submissions and ordered the two sides to submit their arguments and evidence. The Maya legal team submitted their documents, but the government did not.

During this time, logging continued in Toledo District. Thus, on April 17, 1998, the TMCC and the TAA petitioned the Supreme Court for an injunction to suspend all logging concessions within lands claimed by the Maya. The petition was scheduled for a hearing on May 19, 1998, but the hearing was adjourned indefinitely in response to a request from the attorney general's office. It was never rescheduled.[5]

With litigation in Belize blocked, on August 7, 1998, the TMCC and the TAA filed a complaint against the Government of Belize with the Inter-American Commission on Human Rights (IACHR). A body of the Organization of American States (OAS), the IACHR is empowered to investigate allegations of human rights abuses by OAS member states and issue advisory decisions. This case is the focus of chapter 6.

During that same month, general elections ousted the UDP and returned the PUP to power. The new PUP prime minister, Said Musa, opened talks with Maya leaders concerning land issues. However, in November 1998, in a shocking turn of events, TMCC chairperson Julian Cho was found dead (Wainwright 2007:275). An investigation by the police medical examiner into the cause of his death determined that he had died of a blow to the head. The investigation concluded that Cho had sustained that blow to the head in an accidental fall down a cement staircase while he was alone. This explanation was widely rejected by Maya, who believed that Cho had been murdered by someone acting at the direction of powerful figures whose interests he had challenged. Negotiations between the government and Maya organizations came to a halt.

## Analysis

Efforts to exercise sovereignty and territorialize the British Honduran colonial state included the creation of property in lands, both state property and private parcels. Colonial officials wielded claims of state ownership of lands in Toledo to establish reservations and forest reserves, authorize resource extraction, and sell or lease lands as private property. Later, the colonial state and then the self-governing Belizean state both sought to exercise sovereignty by "developing" southern Belize, focusing on the transformation of reservation lands into individual private properties for intensified agricultural production. Although these actions by state officials involved the performance of sovereignty to extend the state property system to Toledo, once again, the state exercised sovereignty to govern *for* the market: the aim of this strategy was to incorporate both land and Maya farmers more fully into markets for land, labor, and agricultural commodities.

State development and land privatization efforts—transforming lands collectively managed by Maya communities into private property, granting concessions for logging and oil exploration, and enclosing lands in protected areas—were accompanied by attacks on the Alcalde System through which Maya communities had long governed themselves, as the government sought to impose the

Village Council System on Maya communities. These actions provoked mobilization by Maya communities to contest control—and ownership—of the lands and resources on which they depended. Blocked from pursuing justice within the Belizean legal system, the Maya and their North American allies turned to the judicial bodies of the Organization of American States. The next chapter follows the Maya claim through the Inter-American Commission on Human Rights, situating the claim within the context of international struggles to produce Indigenous rights to lands.

CHAPTER 6

# The Production of Indigenous Rights

## INDIGENOUS ADVOCACY IN THE UNITED NATIONS AND THE INTER-AMERICAN HUMAN RIGHTS SYSTEM

This chapter explores Indigenous activism to define and codify Indigenous rights in international law, beginning with crafting written standards in the United Nations (UN), the Organization of American States (OAS), and the International Labor Organization (ILO). When state opposition weakened or delayed approval for these standards, Indigenous advocates turned to existing human rights instruments and "strategic litigation" to produce Indigenous rights. Within the UN system, Indigenous advocates relied on the right to cultural integrity guaranteed by human rights covenants; strategic litigation in the Inter-American Human Rights System was forced to rely on the right to property, protected by inter-American treaties and the constitutions of American states. The Maya land claim played a significant role in the strategic litigation that produced an inter-American jurisprudence on Indigenous rights to lands and territories.

Most anthropological analysis of the production of international human rights laws has focused on the conflicts, negotiations, and alliances involved in drafting and implementing rights instruments within the UN context (Merry 2006b; Muehlebach 2001, 2003; Niezen 2003; Riles 2000). This chapter broadens anthropological inquiry into the production of rights by engaging strategic litigation and judicial decisions as a site for the production of Indigenous rights. This reflects a significant trend: "Litigation has been increasingly important in securing Indigenous rights in the last few decades. In both domestic courts and international jurisdictions, Indigenous peoples have persuaded courts to recognize certain of their key rights, setting precedents that have been used by other Indigenous groups around the world" (Baldwin and Morel 2011:121; Medina 2016). Litigation resembles a contentious conversation, with claims, counterclaims, and judgments that weigh the merits of the competing arguments. Such judgments, as a former president of the Inter-American Court of Human Rights asserted, do not only settle disputes; they also state "what the law is" (Tanner 2009:988).

101

## Indigenous Mobilization:
### Seeking Self-Determination as "Peoples"

The struggle for Indigenous rights must be understood in relation to movements for decolonization that surged across the world in the mid-twentieth century. As demands for self-determination by colonized peoples gained increasing support, the UN General Assembly passed a Declaration on the Granting of Independence to Colonial Countries and Peoples in 1960. This declaration affirmed, "All peoples have the right to self-determination; by virtue of that right they freely determine their political status and freely pursue their economic, social and cultural development."[1] This right and this wording were subsequently incorporated into the two 1966 human rights conventions that provide the legal framework for implementing the 1948 Universal Declaration of Human Rights: the International Convention on Civil and Political Rights (ICCPR) and the International Convention on Economic, Social, and Cultural Rights (ICESCR). In each of these conventions, the right of peoples to self-determination is the lone collective right.

During the 1960s and 1970s, when Native American and First Nation activists in the United States and Canada mobilized in opposition to assimilationist policies, they did so as "peoples" demanding the right to self-determination enshrined in the 1960 UN Declaration and the 1966 human rights conventions (Engle 2010:52). During the 1970s and 1980s, Indigenous activists in Latin America also rejected the region's assimilationist policies, calling on Latin American states to recognize the "plurinational, multicultural, and multilinguistic" nature of their societies (de la Peña 2005; Engle 2010:92).

In 1982 the UN Economic and Social Council responded to growing Indigenous advocacy by establishing a Working Group on Indigenous Populations (WGIP), comprising five human rights experts representing the major world areas (Daes 2011:12). The Working Group heard complaints of human rights violations against Indigenous peoples at annual sessions that attracted representatives from Indigenous groups across the world. In 1985, the WGIP also began drafting a UN Declaration on the Rights of Indigenous Peoples to establish an international standard concerning the rights of Indigenous peoples. Seeking redress for dispossession and forced assimilation, Indigenous peoples demanded standards to protect their rights to their lands and territories and their distinctive languages and cultures (Burger 2011:43). Indigenous organizations prepared two statements of principles that offered a foundation for the declaration, one adopted at a 1984 meeting of the World Council of Indigenous Peoples attended by hundreds of representatives of Indigenous groups, the other submitted in 1985 by North American Indigenous organizations (Daes 2011:13–16).

The WGIP chair drew upon these statements of principles to prepare the first draft of a UN Declaration on the Rights of Indigenous Peoples (UNDRIP). Debate in the WGIP over the language and content of the declaration extended from 1987 to 1993. The process of drafting UN rights declarations or conventions involves representatives of states from across the world who negotiate every word of their content. While representatives pursue their own state's agendas, they also aim to produce a document that enjoys broad support from most states (Merry 2006b; Riles 2000). The legitimacy of the norms spelled out in the resulting documents is grounded in this very process of negotiation and compromise and the international consensus that slowly emerges (Merry 2006a:102). Achieving consensus is the overwhelming objective, because international law has no centralized authority to enforce its content. Legal positivism, the dominant perspective in international legal theory, casts every state as a sovereign power constrained only by rules to which it consents. Thus, international laws derive their force from the international consensus they express, which the process of their drafting helps to create.

Representatives of Indigenous peoples were involved to an unprecedented degree in drafting the UNDRIP. They insisted on recognition as colonized peoples, who shared the same right to self-determination as all other peoples under international law (Muehlebach 2003:252). Indigenous activists accorded a range of meanings to the term "self-determination," focusing on the ability of Indigenous peoples to shape the institutions through which they are governed and to work through those institutions to effect meaningful policy decisions on an ongoing basis (Anaya 2004:97–184; Corntassel and Primeau 1995; Daes 2000, 2001; Engle 2010:67–99; Thornberry 1993). Few sought to exercise self-determination by forming independent Indigenous states, although some sought to retain independent statehood as an option (Engle 2010:67–99). The WGIP acceded to Indigenous peoples' insistence on the right to self-determination, appropriating the wording of common Article 1 from the ICCPR and the ICESCR as Article 3 of the draft UNDRIP (Daes 2011:33): "Indigenous peoples have the right of self-determination. By virtue of that right they freely determine their political status and freely pursue their economic, social and cultural development."[2]

The draft UN declaration explicitly linked Indigenous cultures and territories. Asserting Indigenous peoples' "collective right to exist" in both physical and cultural senses, the draft declaration articulated Indigenous peoples' right "not to be subjected to forced assimilation or destruction of their culture," their right to "maintain and strengthen their distinct political, legal, economic, social and cultural institutions," and their right to "manifest, practice, develop and teach their spiritual and religious traditions, customs, and ceremonies." Indigenous representatives defined control over their ancestral lands as the foundation for the exercise of all other rights, an essential basis of Indigenous peoples' survival and way of life (Daes 2011:17, 20, 26). Thus, Articles 25 through 30 of the declaration affirmed Indigenous peoples' right to the lands, territories, and resources they have traditionally owned, occupied, or used and linked that right to "the right to maintain and strengthen their distinctive spiritual relationship" with those lands and territories.[3]

A small number of state observers expressed opposition to Indigenous use of the term "self-determination," casting it as a threat to the sovereignty and territorial integrity of their states. The strongest opposition came from former British colonies with a history of treaties that recognized Indigenous peoples as sovereign: Canada, the United States, New Zealand, and Australia insisted on language to limit the right to self-determination (Engle 2010:5, 48).[4] However, Indigenous representatives considered the right to self-determination nonnegotiable; thus, the draft declaration became "mired for years" in debates over inclusion of this right (Engle 2010:4).

In 1993, the WGIP finally approved a Draft UN Declaration on the Rights of Indigenous Peoples at a session attended by nine Indigenous NGOs and 500 individuals representing another 121 Indigenous organizations (Brysk 2000:129). In 1994, the UN Sub-Commission on the Prevention of Discrimination and Protection of Minorities approved the draft and forwarded it to the UN Commission on Human Rights. The commission established a working group to consider the draft, and the declaration languished for more than a decade while its content, especially the language on self-determination, was debated.[5]

A parallel process unfolded in the Organization of American States (OAS). In the late 1980s, the Inter-American Commission on Human Rights (IACHR) determined that inter-American human rights instruments did not protect rights specific to Indigenous peoples, and in 1989, the OAS General Assembly authorized the IACHR to draft a regional declaration on the rights of Indigenous peoples (IACHR 2000). The commission solicited comments from both governments and representatives of Indigenous groups about the rights that should be included, and, again, Indigenous peoples insisted on the right to self-determination. The draft American Declaration on the Rights of Indigenous Peoples (ADRIP) affirmed Indigenous peoples' right to cultural integrity and respect for "all their ways of life, cosmovisions, spirituality, uses, customs, norms, traditions, forms of social, economic and political organization" (ADRIP, Article 13). The draft declaration also affirmed Indigenous peoples' right to legal recognition of their own "modalities and forms of property, possession, and ownership of their lands, territories, and resources" (ADRIP, Article 25) and the right to "maintain and strengthen their distinctive spiritual, cultural, and material relationship with their lands, territories, and resources" (ADRIP, Article 25). In 1997, the commission submitted the draft declaration to the OAS General Assembly, which established a working group of member states to study it. However, U.S. and Canadian opposition prevented the proposed declaration from being brought to the General Assembly for a vote for nearly two decades (Rodriguez-Piñero 2011).

As the draft UN and OAS declarations were being debated, similar initiatives began in the International Labor Organization (ILO), the only international body with an existing convention on Indigenous people. The convention had been adopted in 1957 to protect Indigenous peoples in the process of their assimilation into dominant national cultures and systems (de la Peña 2005; Tennant 1994), and its assimilationist language elicited strong objections from Indigenous organizations. In 1986, the ILO began work on a convention to replace it. Indigenous peoples demanded that the new ILO convention recognize them as "peoples" rather than "populations." States objected to use of the term "peoples," because of the right to self-determination associated with that term. State representatives again raised objections that guarantees for Indigenous self-determination could lead to the formation and secession of independent Indigenous states, threatening the territorial integrity of existing states (Niezen 2003:70). After three years of debate, a compromise finally permitted the convention to recognize Indigenous peoples as "peoples," followed by the caveat that this appellation "shall not be construed as having any implications as regards the rights which may attach to the term under international law" (ILO 169). This compromise enabled the convention to advance to adoption in 1989.

ILO Convention No. 169 of 1989 Concerning Indigenous and Tribal Peoples in Independent Countries affirmed Indigenous peoples' right to cultural integrity and grounded Indigenous cultures in Indigenous territories. The convention required state parties to protect Indigenous peoples' customs and traditions, their institutions, and their "social, cultural, religious and spiritual values and practices" (ILO 169, Articles 2, 5). Article 4 called for states to adopt "special measures" that might be required to enact and ensure these protections. Regarding lands, the convention stipulated, "governments shall respect the special importance for the cultures and spiritual values of the peoples concerned of their relationship with the lands or territories . . . which they occupy or otherwise use, and in particular the collective aspects of this relationship." It directed governments "to identify the lands which the peoples concerned traditionally occupy, and to guarantee effective protection of their rights of ownership and possession" (ILO 169, Article 14). Thus, in addition to affirming Indigenous peoples' right to cultural difference, the convention grounded Indigenous cultures in Indigenous territories and articulated the collective nature of Indigenous peoples' rights.

The direct impact of ILO 169 was limited by the ILO's structure, with representation from states, employers' associations, and labor unions: complaints to the ILO must be brought by one of these constituent categories. However, the ILO convention played a significant indirect role through the Indigenous movement's "turn to human rights" (Engle 2010).[6]

Through their involvement in drafting the declarations and the ILO convention, Indigenous advocates produced international Indigenous rights and defined their content. Their efforts simultaneously constituted a particular conceptualization of Indigenous cultures. Indigenous activists appropriated the concept of "culture" and defined it in a manner intended to capture, in a generic way, the "difference" that distinguished Indigenous lifeways from the lifeways of the larger societies that marginalized them. The conceptualization of culture they advanced was "territorializing," defining Indigenous cultures as integrated systems of practices, relationships, meanings, and beliefs grounded in Indigenous lands and territories (Muehlebach 2003). This understanding of culture was incorporated into the draft UN and OAS declarations and elaborated more fully in ILO 169.

## The Turn to Human Rights and the Right to Culture

With the draft UN and OAS declarations stalled and the ILO convention of limited direct utility, some Indigenous leaders began to deploy existing human rights instruments to secure Indigenous rights (Anaya 1991). Human rights instruments had inserted individual rights-bearers into international law, previously the exclusive province of states. Now, Indigenous rights advocates sought to advance the collective rights of Indigenous peoples by mobilizing protections for culture contained in the ICCPR and the International Convention on the Elimination of Racial Discrimination (ICERD) (Anaya 1991). These were the first conventions to recognize the right of minorities to their distinct cultures, a right rejected by states in the drafting of earlier rights standards (Stamatopoulou 2011). Both covenants also had treaty bodies, comprising independent rights experts, to monitor states' compliance (Muehlebach 2003:256). Further, both covenants enjoyed broad support: the ICCPR has 172 state parties; the ICERD has 179.

Indigenous advocates began to submit complaints to the UN Human Rights Committee, which reviews states' progress in implementing the ICCPR. The complaints alleged state violations of Article 27 of the ICCPR, which stipulates, "In those States in which ethnic, religious or linguistic minorities exist, persons belonging to such minorities shall not be denied the right, in community with the other members of their group, to enjoy their own culture, to profess and practice their own religion, or to use their own language" (ICCPR 1966).[7] Although Indigenous rights advocates sought recognition as "peoples" rather than as "minorities," their deployment of Article 27 to make claims led to some successes, and success encouraged continued use of this strategy (Engle 2010:114).

The Human Rights Committee initially responded to Indigenous complaints on a case-by-case basis, but in 1994 the committee issued a General Comment to clarify how ICCPR Article 27 applies to Indigenous peoples. Noting the protection provided by Article 27 for the rights of individuals to enjoy their own culture, the General Comment asserted that culture "may consist in a way of life which is closely associated with territory and use of its resources," noting, "This may particularly be true of members of Indigenous communities" (UN HRC 1994). Acknowledging that "the rights protected under article 27 are individual rights," the Human Rights Committee nonetheless noted that some rights depend on "the ability of the minority group to maintain its culture, language or religion." This may require "positive measures by States . . . to protect the identity of a minority and the rights of its members to enjoy and develop their culture and language and to practise their religion, *in community with the other members of the group*" (UN HRC 1994, emphasis added).[8]

Indigenous legal activists also brought claims to the Committee on the Elimination of Racial Discrimination (CERD), the treaty body for the 1965 International Convention on the Elimination of Racial Discrimination. Because they sought the rights of "peoples" rather than only the rights of minority citizens, Indigenous advocates focused on the ICERD's broad assertions regarding equality and nondiscrimination (Engle 2010:119). In 1997, the CERD issued a General Recommendation to clarify how the convention applies to Indigenous peoples specifically. The General Recommendation called on state parties to respect the distinct culture and way of life of Indigenous peoples and to enable Indigenous communities to "practice and revitalize their cultural traditions and customs." Directly addressing Indigenous rights to lands and territories, the General Recommendation also called on state parties "to recognize and protect the rights of Indigenous peoples to own, develop, control and use their communal lands, territories and resources" and to ensure that "no decisions directly relating to their rights and interests are taken without their informed consent" (UN CERD 1997).

Thus, the human rights experts who authored the HRC General Comment and the CERD Recommendation embraced the characterization of Indigenous cultures elaborated by Indigenous advocates themselves during the drafting of the UN, OAS, and ILO standards, advancing this territorializing vision of Indigenous cultures. As a result, the ICCPR and the ICERD became critical tools for making Indigenous claims to lands. Further, because human rights are almost universally accepted as "settled norms" by states, the use of existing human rights instruments generated less controversy than efforts to draft new Indigenous rights instruments (Donnelly 2003:1, 38). The mobilization of human rights standards to protect culture thus became the dominant legal strategy for making Indigenous claims (Engle 2010:102).

The subject of Indigenous rights that emerged over the 1980s and 1990s is thus a collective, culture-bearing subject, whose right to cultural integrity requires collective control over traditional lands with which Indigenous peoples sustain relationships that are not only economic but also spiritual (Stavenhagen 2008:35). If the practice of culture requires an ongoing relationship with particular lands or territories, then severing this relationship violates a group's capacity and right to exist (Muehlebach 2003:256). The draft UN Declaration on the Rights of Indigenous Peoples articulated cultural rights in at least seventeen of its forty-six articles (Stamatopoulou 2011:389).

## Strategic Litigation and the Right to Property

Recourse to the review processes of UN human rights treaty bodies represents one dimension of the human rights strategy deployed by Indigenous rights advocates to produce international Indigenous rights. Strategic litigation emerged as a complementary tactic focused on the development of a jurisprudence on Indigenous rights through petitions to international judicial bodies (Baldwin and Morel 2011:121). Indigenous rights advocates from the U.S.-based Indian Law Resource Center allied with Indigenous communities to file legal claims in domestic courts and the judicial bodies of the Inter-American Human Rights System. These claims elicited judicial decisions that developed into the most extensive jurisprudence on Indigenous rights globally.

The Organization of American States (OAS) and its judicial bodies are the primary vehicles for constituting human rights and state obligations in the American hemisphere. The OAS Charter obligates all member states to uphold the provisions of the 1948 American Declaration on the Rights and Duties of Man, and the Inter-American Commission on Human Rights (IACHR) investigates complaints alleging violations of the American Declaration. However, IACHR decisions are not legally binding; they are "advisory." The IACHR can refer cases to the Inter-American Court of Human Rights (IACtHR), a judicial body with a narrower scope but greater authority. The court adjudicates complaints alleging violations of the 1969 American Convention on Human Rights, and its decisions are legally binding for the twenty state parties that have acceded to the court's jurisdiction.[9] Belize is not among them. Although the commission and the court thus have distinct jurisdictions, they collaborate to ensure coherence and consistency in the jurisprudence of the Inter-American System.

While the proposed American Declaration on the Rights of Indigenous Peoples languished due to U.S. and Canadian objections to Indigenous demands for self-determination, inter-American judicial bodies forged a path around this impasse by generating a body of jurisprudence on Indigenous rights in the hemisphere. They did so in response to petitions crafted by Indigenous legal advocates who sought to secure the rights of Indigenous groups they represented and to elaborate a regional jurisprudence on Indigenous rights in the process. A 1995 complaint against Nicaragua initiated this strategy, and the petition from the Maya of Belize followed soon after.

In UN treaty bodies, Indigenous advocates had pursued a strategy grounded in the right to culture, protected by the ICCPR and the ICERD; however, inter-American human rights instruments did not include protections for culture (Shelton 2013:968). Both the American Declaration and the American Convention did guarantee property rights, however, as do the constitutions of OAS member states. Lawyers thus grounded Indigenous rights litigation in the Inter-American System in the right to property. This strategy was deeply ironic: the institution of private property had enabled the dispossession of Indigenous peoples' lands and territories from the beginning of colonization into the present. Indigenous advocates sought to invert this use of property rights.

Historically, efforts to include a right to property in human rights instruments had been controversial. Those who saw human rights as a means to protect the vulnerable opposed the designation of property as a human right, arguing that property rights protected the rich and powerful, that is, the propertied (van Banning 2002:8). Further, they asked, how can property be considered a human right, when so many people are unable to access property (van Banning 2002:6)? However, representatives of the United States had pushed to protect private property as "vital to a market economy," arguing that "property and contract jointly form the basis of exchange and trade, on which market economies are built" (van Banning 2002:2). At one point, representatives of the United States tried to insert property into an article protecting life and liberty, but representatives of other states objected to according equal weight to life and property, and the proposal was withdrawn (van Banning 2002:42). Such disagreements led to the exclusion of a right to property from the 1966 human rights covenants, but the American Declaration and the American Convention on Human Rights both included the right (van Banning 2002:43–45, 59–60).

## Awas Tingni v. Nicaragua

Development of an inter-American jurisprudence on Indigenous rights began with a petition by the Indigenous Mayagna community of Awas Tingni to the Nicaraguan courts in 1995 to halt a logging concession the Nicaraguan state planned to grant for lands claimed by the community. Nicaraguan law does not only guarantee rights to property; it also explicitly recognizes Indigenous communal land tenure. However, provisions for Indigenous communal tenure had not been implemented, and the lands claimed by Awas Tingni and other Indigenous communities had never been demarcated and titled. The petition was denied, and Awas Tingni appealed to the Nicaraguan Supreme Court.

When the Nicaraguan Supreme Court did not respond promptly, Awas Tingni petitioned the Inter-American Commission on Human Rights. S. James Anaya, a professor of law affiliated with the U.S.-based Indian Law Resource Center (ILRC), served as lead counsel for the community. The legal argument in the petition relied on the right to property guaranteed by Article 23 of the American Declaration on the Rights and Duties of Man, which states, "Every person has a right to own such private property as meets the essential needs of decent living and helps to maintain the dignity of the individual and of the home."[10] It also invoked the declaration's nondiscrimination guarantee, which declares "all persons" "equal before the law . . . without distinction as to race, sex, language, creed or any other factor."[11] The petition also cited the cultural integrity clauses of the ICCPR and the ICERD to support the right of Awas Tingni to have its collective property recognized and demarcated, and Anaya also drew upon language from ILO 169 and the draft American Declaration that identified Indigenous rights to lands and territories as foundational for Indigenous peoples' ability to sustain their cultures. Although Nicaragua was not a party to ILO 169, and the draft declaration had not yet received a vote, Anaya argued that these standards represented an emerging global consensus that was binding on all states.

In March 1998, the IACHR decided in favor of Awas Tingni, adopting much of the legal theory advanced by Anaya in the petition (Anaya and Grossman 2002). The commission ruled that the American Declaration's protections for property guarantee Indigenous peoples' right to property in land on the basis of their longstanding use, regardless of their lack of a state-issued legal title.[12] Following the jurisprudence of the European Court of Human Rights and the International Court of Justice, the IACHR applied an evolutionary method of interpretation, which treats human rights treaties as "live instruments," whose protections must be considered in relation to current human rights standards developing internationally.

This allowed the commission to invoke the ICCPR, the ICERD, ILO 169, and the OAS and UN draft declarations as indicators of emerging international norms, as it interpreted and applied the American Declaration's protections for property. Citing these standards' guarantees for Indigenous peoples' ownership rights in lands they have traditionally used and their recognition that Indigenous peoples' cultures involve special relationships with their collectively held lands and territories, the IACHR determined that Indigenous property rights "originate from traditional patterns of land tenure."[13] The commission directed the Nicaraguan government to cancel the logging concessions, demarcate the lands traditionally used by Awas Tingni, and issue a communal title for those lands to the community.

When the Nicaraguan state failed to fully implement these directives, the commission submitted the case to the Inter-American Court of Human Rights in June 1998, invoking the property guarantees of the American Convention. In its 2001 judgment, the Inter-American Court determined that Nicaragua had violated Awas Tingni's right to property under the American Convention. Also using an evolutionary method of interpretation, the court applied the American Convention's right to property in light of protections for cultural integrity guaranteed by the international covenants and the UN and OAS draft Indigenous rights declarations (Rodriguez-Piñero 2011:462).[14] The judges thus affirmed the commission's assertion of the cultural importance of collective property in land for Indigenous peoples, declaring, "Indigenous groups, by the fact of their very existence, have the right to live freely in their own territory; *the close ties of Indigenous people with the land must be recognized and understood as the fundamental basis of their cultures, their spiritual life, their integrity, and their economic survival. For Indigenous communities, relations to the land are not merely a matter of possession and production but a material and spiritual element which they must fully enjoy, even to preserve their cultural legacy and transmit it to future generations.*"[15] Casting Indigenous peoples' relations to their traditional lands and territories as simultaneously material and spiritual, fundamental to both their economic and cultural survival, the court thus linked Indigenous peoples' right to property to their right to cultural integrity.

On this basis, the court ordered Nicaragua to demarcate and title the lands of Awas Tingni and other Indigenous communities "in accordance with their customary laws, values, customs and mores."[16] The decision was hailed internationally as groundbreaking, "the first legally binding decision by an international tribunal to uphold the collective land and resource rights of Indigenous peoples in the face of a state's failure to do so" (Anaya and Grossman 2002:1). The Awas Tingni decision "paved the way for the elaboration of a specific, distinct body of jurisprudence regarding Indigenous peoples" (Rodriguez-Pinero 2011:463).

## Maya Indigenous Communities v. Belize

The strategy for constituting Indigenous rights via strategic litigation intersected with the conflicts that had pitted Mopan and Q'eqchi' Maya against the Belizean government. A team of attorneys affiliated with the Indian Law Resource Center had been working with the Toledo Maya Cultural Council (TMCC) and the Toledo Alcaldes Association (TAA) to support their land rights claim, and in December 1996, they filed a petition in the Supreme Court of Belize on behalf of the TMCC and the TAA. Accusing the Belizean government of violating Maya communities' rights to property, guaranteed by the Belize constitution, the petition sought to halt logging operations on lands traditionally used by the Maya. The Supreme Court did not act on this petition. Thus, on August 7, 1998, the Maya and their legal representatives petitioned the Inter-American Commission on Human Rights, alleging violations of the property guarantees in the American Declaration on the Rights and Duties of Man.

The Maya case was strikingly similar to the Nicaraguan case, with Indigenous communities seeking to halt state-sanctioned logging concessions on lands they claimed. However, there were also important differences between the cases. Nicaraguan law accorded communal land rights to Indigenous peoples, but Belizean law contained no provisions for Indigenous collective property. Additionally, as a former British colony, Belize participates in the common-law system, a body of law originally developed in England based on judicial decisions, custom, and precedent. During the colonial period, British officials applied the common law to Britain's colonies, and many former British colonies continue to use and develop this body of law as independent countries. Judges in any common-law country may refer to judicial decisions from other common-law jurisdictions across the world as precedents to guide their own judgments. Thus, the Belizean Maya case could expand the reach of emerging inter-American Indigenous rights jurisprudence across world regions, while the common law's recognition of native title on the basis of customary tenure could strengthen the language of inter-American jurisprudence.

On October 5, 2000, the IACHR declared the Maya petition admissible and called on the Belizean government to suspend all permits, licenses, and concessions for logging, oil exploration, and other natural resource development on lands used by Maya communities in Toledo, while the commission investigated the claims.[17]

Within a week, on October 12, 2000, Peoples United Party (PUP) prime minister Said Musa, on behalf of the Belizean state, signed an accord with Maya organizations in Toledo, the "Ten Points of Agreement." Point number six of this agreement recognized that "the Maya People have rights to lands and resources in southern Belize based on their long-standing use and occupancy" (Ten Points of Agreement 2000). The agreement set target dates for actions to address the urgent land needs of Maya communities and protect communal lands; however, state agencies did not meet these targets. Thus, in December 2001, the Maya asked the IACHR to rule in the case.

This request came just months after the Awas Tingni decision by the Inter-American Court. The Maya case, led by Anaya, the same attorney who had argued *Awas Tingni*, followed the legal logic of *Awas Tingni* but added common-law precedents concerning native title.

### The Maya Argument from International Law and the Common Law

Grounded in the American Declaration's right to property, the Maya petition asserted that the practice of Maya customary tenure gives rise to property, which the state is bound to recognize. Situating Belize as a common-law jurisdiction, where courts look to precedents from other common-law countries in the absence of relevant domestic jurisprudence, the petition invoked decisions from Australia and Canada to assert that the Maya have "aboriginal title" or "native title," a form of common-law ownership based on historical patterns of land use or occupancy.[18] The petition cited the landmark 1992 Australian case *Mabo v. Queensland*, which determined, "Native title has its origin in and is given its content by the traditional laws acknowledged by and the traditional customs observed by the Indigenous inhabitants of a territory."[19] Using the common-law doctrine of aboriginal title, attorneys for the Maya asserted that the lands used by the Maya were their property, based on their customary tenure practices; that is, Maya cultural practices *create* property. Failure to recognize Maya native title, the petition argued, would violate the American Declaration's guarantees for property as well as the fundamental legal principle of nondiscrimination.

Drawing on the ICCPR and the draft OAS declaration, the Maya petition identified an emergent cultural integrity norm in international rights law that obligated the Belizean state to recognize and protect Maya land rights, as "a function of its obligation to protect the integrity of the Maya culture, of which Maya land use patterns are an essential part."[20] The petition argued that the Belizean state's resource extraction in Toledo District imperiled "Maya land and resource uses, which are at the core of Maya culture," denying to Maya communities the right to "enjoy their culture and maintain its integrity."[21] Thus, attorneys for the Maya claimed, Maya control over their traditional lands is essential to protect the integrity of their culture.

Further, the petition asserted that ILO 169 and the draft UN and OAS declarations, all products of decades of discussion and debate, articulated an emerging international consensus regarding the existence and content of Indigenous rights, and that consensus now constituted customary international law and general principles concerning Indigenous land rights. This was a bold argument. Three sources of international law are generally recognized: international conventions, customary international law, and general principles of law. The content of conventions, written agreements binding upon the states that sign and ratify them, is relatively unambiguous; however, the content of custom and general principles is less clear cut. Customary law consists of *unwritten* rules that emerge through repeated practice, together with a belief that the practice is obligatory (Byers 1999); thus, the content of custom is often debated. Likewise, the content and basis of general principles is contentious: some jurists derive general principles from theories of natural law, while others apply positive law to define them as standards shared across national legal systems (Koskenniemi 2000). Though conventions bind only state signatories, and declarations—in themselves—are not binding at all, international customary law and general principles are binding on all states, despite their greater ambiguity (Medina 2016).

## *Evidence for Indigeneity and Customary Tenure*

The logic of their argument for Maya land rights required attorneys for the Maya to demonstrate that the Mopan and Q'eqchi' are Indigenous peoples who practice a form of customary tenure over their lands. To do so, they drew upon the *Maya Atlas* and affidavits from scholarly experts and four Maya leaders.

The *Maya Atlas* and the expert witness affidavits positioned the Mopan and Q'eqchi' as the descendants of the ancient Maya, who have, "for centuries, formed organized societies that have inhabited a vast territory—which includes the Toledo District of southern Belize—long before the arrival of the Europeans and the colonial institutions that gave way to the modern State of Belize."[22] The petition defined the contemporary Mopan- and Q'eqchi'-speaking people of the Toledo District as "the descendants or relatives of the Maya subgroups that inhabited the territory at least as far back as the time of European exploration and incursions into Toledo in the seventeenth and eighteenth centuries."[23]

The atlas presented evidence of the customary land use practices of the Mopan and Q'eqchi', graphically represented in maps that depicted the lands used by each village, including areas where milpas are planted, forested lands used for hunting, and sacred sites used for rituals.[24] The *Maya Atlas*, the petition asserted, demonstrates that Maya land use practices comprise "both subsistence and cultural elements that form a foundation for the life and continuity of the Maya communities."[25] The affidavits of Maya and expert witnesses corroborated this argument.

Taken together, the atlas and the affidavits affirmed the Mopan and Q'eqchi' of southern Belize as the collective culture-bearing subjects of Indigenous rights, tied to their traditional lands through both material and spiritual practices. Maya leaders' affidavits also attested to the damages caused by logging operations on lands traditionally used by the Maya, including disruptions to plant and animal life and damage to water sources that had negative effects on the livelihood practices fundamental to their cultural and physical survival.[26]

## *The Government's Response*

In response, legal counsel for the Belizean government sought to invalidate Mopan and Q'eqchi' claims to Indigenous rights by challenging their indigeneity. Drawing on common-law jurisprudence from Canada, counsel identified four criteria for indigeneity: the applicants for aboriginal title and their ancestors had to be (1) members of an organized society that (2) occupied the specific territory over which they assert aboriginal title, (3) to the exclusion of other organized societies, (4) at the time sovereignty was asserted by the colonizing power.[27] Government attorneys cited the dominant narrative of Belizean history to argue that the Mopan and Q'eqchi' did not meet these requirements: Spanish forces had emptied Belizean territory prior to British arrival, and Mopan and Q'eqchi' arrived as immigrants in the 1880s, after the establishment of British sovereignty over the territory.

Further, they argued, the presence of Garifuna communities on the coast of southern Belize from the early 1800s violated the criterion of exclusive occupation.

## The IACHR Decision

In October 2004, the IACHR ruled that the Mopan and Q'eqchi' are Indigenous peoples and that, as Indigenous peoples, they had rights to the lands they traditionally used. The commission determined that the evidence provided by expert affidavits and the *Maya Atlas* supported the petitioners' claim to Indigeneity. The commission noted that the government had presented no evidence to contradict the Mayas' ancestral connections to southern Belize.[28] Further, the commission invoked "information published by the State itself" that confirmed Mopan and Q'eqchi' claims to indigeneity, citing the official website of the Government of Belize. The website stated, "Numerous ruins indicate that for hundreds of years Belize was heavily populated by the Maya Indians, whose relatively advanced civilization reached its height between A.D. 250 and 900. Eventually the civilization declined leaving behind small groups whose offspring still exist in Belize contributing positively to the culturally diverse population."[29] These two sentences had been drafted for an audience of potential tourists, to whom the government sought to promote Belize as a tourism destination. Ancient Maya sites represented rarer commodities than either rainforests or reefs, and the touristic value of the contemporary Maya culture was enhanced by its direct connections to ancient Maya civilization. However, this portrayal of history directly contradicted the government's argument before the IACHR, and the commission interpreted it as state recognition of Mopan and Q'eqchi' indigeneity.

The commission also rejected the government's criteria for indigeneity. Instead, the judges applied the criteria articulated by ILO 169, which treats as Indigenous "peoples in independent countries who are regarded as Indigenous on account of their descent from the populations which inhabited the country, or a geographical region to which the country belongs, at the time of conquest or colonization or the establishment of present state boundaries and who, irrespective of their legal status, retain some or all of their own social, economic, cultural and political institutions."[30]

The commission did not engage Anaya's argument that ILO 169 and the draft UN and OAS declarations represented customary international law. Instead, it adopted the evolutionary method of interpretation used in *Awas Tingni* to apply the American Declaration's protection for property, drawing on the standards established by ILO 169 (which Belize had not signed) and the draft UN and OAS declarations (which had not yet been brought to votes in their respective General Assemblies).[31]

Citing *Awas Tingni*'s emphasis on the importance of land for the cultural survival of Indigenous communities, the commission declared that the property rights protected by the Inter-American Human Rights System are not limited to property already recognized by states or defined by domestic law: rather, "the right to property has an autonomous meaning in international human rights law." The jurisprudence of the Inter-American System, the commission continued, "has acknowledged that *the property rights of Indigenous peoples are not defined exclusively by entitlements within a state's formal legal regime, but also include the Indigenous communal property that arises from and is grounded in Indigenous custom and tradition.*"[32]

Based on the affidavits by Maya and scholarly experts, the commission recognized the existence of a system of customary land tenure in Maya communities, whose practices "are significant not only for the subsistence of the members of the Maya communities, but also provide a foundation for the cultural life and continuity of the Maya people."[33] By demonstrating their customary tenure practices, the commission determined, "the Mopan and Q'eqchi' Maya people have demonstrated a communal property right to the lands that they currently inhabit in the Toledo District."[34] The commission thus defined Maya cultural practices as the source of Maya property, and the lands and territories in which they practice Maya customary tenure as essential to Maya cultural survival.

The Belizean state had already conceded a similar point, the commission suggested, in the Ten Points of Agreement of 2000, which acknowledged Maya rights to lands and resources in southern Belize "based on their longstanding use and occupancy."[35] The commission deemed this acknowledgment by the state "formidable evidence of an enduring connection between the Maya people and lands in the Toledo District."[36]

The commission thus determined that Belize had violated Maya property rights, guaranteed by the American Declaration, by "failing to take effective measures to recognize their communal property right to the lands that they have traditionally occupied and used" and by granting logging and oil concessions for these lands "in the absence of effective consultations with and the informed consent of the Maya people."[37] The commission directed the government to demarcate and title "the territory in which the Maya people have a communal property right, in accordance with their customary land use practices" and to refrain from issuing concessions until these property issues were resolved.[38]

### International Significance of *Awas Tingni* and *Maya Indigenous Communities* Judgments

Via the *Awas Tingni* and *Maya Indigenous Communities* cases, Indigenous rights advocates judicialized their rights claims, using strategic litigation to establish an inter-American jurisprudence on Indigenous rights to lands and territories. This strategy circumvented the stalling tactics of states that had impeded the passage of UN and OAS declarations. Applying the evolutionary method of interpretation, the Inter-American Court and the IACHR interpreted the property guarantees of the American Declaration and the American Convention with reference to standards set by international conventions from outside the Inter-American System (ILO 169, the ICCPR, and ICERD) as well as the proposed UN and OAS declarations on Indigenous rights. The resulting judicial decisions advanced inter-American jurisprudence around the impasse created by state opposition to

Indigenous demands for self-determination. The judgments "clarified" the existence and content of Indigenous rights legal standards, beyond simply resolving land disputes, to explicitly articulate "what the law is" (Tanner 2009:988).

*Awas Tingni* was the first decision by an international judicial body to uphold Indigenous rights to collective lands; however, *Maya Indigenous Communities* was the first decision to uphold Indigenous land rights in a state with a legal framework that *does not recognize Indigenous communal land rights*. This heightened the judgment's significance: "the Commission reaffirmed that the international human right to property upholds Indigenous land rights such that, as a matter of international law, Indigenous land rights do not depend on prior recognition within the applicable domestic legal system" (Anaya 2004:172). Rather, the commission found Maya property rights to exist entirely on the basis of Maya customary patterns of land use and occupancy (Anaya 2009:285). This would have implications across American states and common-law countries that similarly lack legal recognitions for Indigenous communal land rights.

The *Awas Tingni* and *Maya Indigenous Communities* decisions circulated within the Inter-American System, shaping subsequent litigation within the hemisphere. In Indigenous rights cases from Paraguay, Ecuador, Honduras, and Panama, the commission cited the Maya lands decision as a precedent to affirm that Indigenous lands and territories are a form of collective property grounded in Indigenous customary tenure, and that the principle of nondiscrimination requires states to treat Indigenous modalities of property as legally equivalent to non-Indigenous forms of property (Medina 2016). Similarly, in its 2007 decision in *Saramaka People v. Surinam*, the Inter-American Court cited *Maya Indigenous Communities* as a precedent regarding the critical nature of Indigenous and tribal peoples' relationships to their lands and territories for their physical and cultural survival, affirming Indigenous peoples' right to prior consultation (IACHR 2010).

## Analysis

### Producing the Collective Culture-Bearing Subject of Indigenous Rights

Previous chapters explored how government, in the Foucauldian sense, produces "the market" and market-rational subjects of interest. This chapter examines the production of Indigenous rights and the collective, culture-bearing subjects of Indigenous rights.

In drafting UN and OAS declarations and ILO 169, Indigenous advocates demanded self-determination as peoples. They also deployed an explicitly territorializing conceptualization of culture to highlight a special relationship between Indigenous peoples and their lands and territories (Dannenmaier 2008). Although representatives from member states resisted the Indigenous demand for self-determination, they did not object to the conceptualization of Indigenous culture advanced by Indigenous activists.

While state actors stalled the progress of the draft UN and OAS declarations, Indigenous activists turned to existing human rights instruments, the ICCPR and the ICERD. Although these instruments had been drafted to protect the rights of *individuals*, Indigenous activists drew on their protections for cultural integrity to make them address Indigenous demands for *collective* rights. They again mobilized a definition of Indigenous cultures as territorialized practices that entail sacred and spiritual as well as economic-material relationships to lands and territories. UN treaty bodies adopted this view of Indigenous cultures in their oversight of ICCPR and ICERD implementation.

When Indigenous advocates turned to strategic litigation within the Inter-American Human Rights System, they were constrained to base their claims on the right to property guaranteed by inter-American human rights covenants. This reliance on protections for property forced the transformation of relatively expansive claims to "lands and territories" into narrower and more legalistic claims to "property." However, adopting an evolutionary method of interpretation, the IACHR and the Inter-American Court imported a right to culture from standards outside the Inter-American System. The significance of Indigenous customary tenure practices emerged at the intersection of the right to property with the right to culture, advancing the territorializing vision of culture Indigenous advocates had promoted in drafting the UNDRIP. Indigenous customary tenure practices articulated the material dimensions of Indigenous cultures with their cosmological aspects, establishing Indigenous peoples' distinctive relation to their lands. Inter-American judicial bodies identified the practice of Indigenous customary tenure, that is, the practice of Indigenous culture, as the *source* of Indigenous property in lands, rather than grounding Indigenous property in the property law of the state. Grounding Indigenous property in culture, which is inherently collective, also required the recognition of Indigenous property as *collective*, occupying an ambiguous middle ground between "property" and "lands and territories."

This vision of Indigenous cultures and the property interests created by the practice of Indigenous customary tenure were integrated into international law at the urging of Indigenous rights advocates themselves. The incorporation of this understanding of Indigenous cultures into law and jurisprudence, however, also relied on human rights experts on the HRC and CERD, state representatives who acquiesced, judges on inter-American judicial bodies, attorneys who crafted legal arguments, and Indigenous and expert witnesses.[39] Anthropologists were directly involved in defining culture only insofar as their expert testimony was embraced by attorneys and judges, though the conceptualization of Indigenous culture enshrined in law and jurisprudence was shaped in deep and diffuse ways by anthropological discourses on culture.

States' success in preventing full recognition of Indigenous peoples' right to self-determination protected the territories of existing states. Their acceptance of the territorializing definition of Indigenous cultures advanced by Indigenous advocates, however, altered the nature of the sovereignty states could exercise over those territories: inter-American jurisprudence and international law now required states to recognize and protect intertwined Indigenous cultures and lands as well as collective Indigenous legal subjects, who were present within state territory but not fully incorporated into state legal and property systems.

### Success and Danger: The Critical Conduct of Rights

Through these cases, Indigenous advocates successfully enshrined Indigenous rights to lands and territories in international law and jurisprudence; however, scholars warn, engagements with the law and rights present dangers (Sieder 2011b).[40] For example, pursuing litigation shifts the locus of struggles over Indigenous lands from Indigenous communities to the courts, sidelining the people with the most at stake while centering legal professionals and legal concepts and languages. The pursuit of rights through the law also reinforces the power of the state as the guarantor of rights (Speed 2008). As a result, even claimants whose rights are vindicated in the courts must contend with the power of the state to choose whether and when to enforce or ignore those rights. Rights strategies may also offer protections for Indigenous groups that have experienced marginalization without dismantling or transforming the structures that have marginalized them (Engle 2010; Wainwright and Bryan 2009). Worse, as Wendy Brown (2004) suggests, the pursuit of rights may limit people's ability to imagine alternative forms of struggle that might offer greater potential for dismantling the structures that have marginalized them.

Recognizing the complexity involved in the use of the law generally and rights specifically, I engage these cautions by applying a "both/and" rather than an "either/or" perspective. I also temper concerns that Indigenous engagements with rights and the law reinforce "state power" with recognition that "the state" is aspirational and performative, an achievement rather than a given, and "state power" is thus potentially more precarious than these critiques acknowledge. What is required, I suggest, is an analysis of the strategies and tactics deployed by differently positioned actors to make these dangers real or to avert them.

I approach Indigenous efforts to produce Indigenous rights via international law and jurisprudence as an example of what Ben Golder has called the "critical conduct of rights." Acknowledging the "both/and" nature of engaging rights and the law, the critical conduct of rights attempts "a contrary inhabiting" of rights discourse that works simultaneously "within and against it" (Golder 2015:21). The critic intervenes into existing formations of law, state, and power, seeking to use rights tactically to open space for alternatives, for "being otherwise" (Golder 2015:3, 22).

This approach recognizes that rights are unavoidably both emancipatory and regulatory (Sieder 2011b; Santos 2002). "Rights can enlarge, expand, or protect the sphere of action of subjects" and "bring new worlds and communities into being," but they also "constitute those very subjects and communities in particular ways and hence work to reinscribe them within existing forms of power" (Golder 2015:91).

Golder acknowledges, "The would-be rights claimant is not (and cannot ever be) in a simple position of mastery or instrumentalism vis-à-vis rights.... Rights produce subjects; they position, constrain, and conduct those who deploy them and subtly contour the subjectivity or self-understanding of the rights holder who is their supposed master" (Golder 2015:97). However, I would add, this predicament, the impossibility of occupying "a simple position of mastery" over rights, also applies to the actors who struggle to produce and perform "the state" and "state power." The outcome of state efforts to prevent recognition of a right to self-determination for Indigenous peoples presents an example: states protected their territorial integrity but opened the content of their practice of sovereignty to challenge and change. I explore this argument further in chapters 7 and 8.

The ambivalence of rights does not lead Golder to reject their tactical deployment. Rather, Golder suggests, the critical counterconduct of rights operates according to the principle Foucault articulated in "The Subject and Power": "My point is not that everything is bad, but that everything is dangerous" (Foucault 1982:232).[41] Indigenous advocates' mobilization of rights may pry open spaces that allow groups like the Mopan and Q'eqchi' Maya to achieve deeply held objectives, challenging previous productions of the state, sovereignty, law, and property in Belize. I explore how this challenge plays out in chapters 7 and 8.

## *Intersection of Rights with Market Rationality*

The events in this chapter reveal several conjunctures between the practice of government, in Foucault's sense, and the practice of sovereignty, between markets and rights, as strategies motivated by distinct logics have collided in practice. Indigenous advocates' mobilization of the right to property to secure collective Indigenous rights to lands and territories represents one key point of intersection between rights and markets. Property rights and their scaffolding of violence and law have been deployed historically to dispossess Indigenous peoples of land, in favor of colonizing states or non-Indigenous land claimants. Guarantees for property were enshrined in inter-American treaties, in part, because property was deemed foundational to market exchange. However, because the right to property was thus available in the Inter-American System, while a right to culture was not, Indigenous advocates appropriated that right to construct Indigenous rights to lands and territories through strategic litigation.

Another point of intersection between markets and rights appeared in the IACHR's invocation of the Belizean government's messaging to potential tourists to counter its rejection of Mopan and Q'eqchi' indigeneity in court. For the purpose of promoting Belize as a tourism destination, state actors highlighted the combination of reef, rainforest, and Maya culture. Mundo Maya marketing promoted—and linked—ancient and contemporary forms of "Maya culture" as a comparative advantage, rather than highlighting the violent seventeenth-century dispossession of Chols and Mopans or the subsequent nineteenth-century immigration of Mopan and Q'eqchi'. This intrusion of market rationality into the terrain of rights, engineered by the authors of the IACHR decision, pitted against one another two different sets of actors speaking in the name of the state, pursuing distinct objectives, targeting different audiences, and articulating opposite arguments.

A third point of intersection between markets and rights is that the constitution of property rights through invocations of the right to culture decenters market exchange and the atomistic subjects formed in relation to markets. The use of culture in the Maya argument introduces a logic or ethic that exists in tension with market rationality.

CHAPTER 7

# Advancing the Maya Claim through the Belizean Judicial System

Although the 2004 ruling by the Inter-American Commission on Human Rights (IACHR) in *Maya Indigenous Communities* circulated through subsequent cases in the hemisphere, solidifying a regional jurisprudence on Indigenous rights, the ruling had little immediate impact in Belize. Government leaders initiated talks with representatives of Maya organizations, which quickly stalled. Following this, elected officials performed Belizean sovereignty by ignoring the IACHR decision.

As a result, by mid-2005, the Maya and their international allies were once again preparing for litigation. Two communities, the Q'eqchi'-speaking village of Conejo and the Mopan-speaking village of Santa Cruz, initiated demarcation of the lands they claimed. Village leaders met with leaders of neighboring communities to agree upon and map their shared boundaries and then submitted the maps and agreements to the prime minister with a request for state recognition and titling. State officials did not respond.

Tensions between the Maya and elected officials deepened in April 2006, when the government granted permission to an oil company to conduct seismic testing in the Sarstoon-Temash National Park on Belize's southern border. Earlier, the park's creation, which occurred without consultation with surrounding communities, had dispossessed these villages of some of their lands; now, the government had issued permits for oil exploration without consulting these communities (Stinson 2017).

This chapter traces the trajectory of the Maya land claim through the Belizean judicial system, from the Supreme Court to the Court of Appeal to the court of last resort, the Caribbean Court of Justice (CCJ). My analysis engages the competing legal arguments put forward by the two sides, to the media as well as the courts; the evidence submitted to support those arguments; and the judgments of the courts.

### THE 2007 MAYA LAND RIGHTS CASE

On April 3, 2007, the alcaldes of Conejo and Santa Cruz petitioned the Belize Supreme Court on behalf of their communities, asserting that the government's failure to recognize Maya customary land tenure and adopt measures to secure Maya land rights violated Maya communities' constitutional rights to property, equality, and the equal protection of the law. Belizean attorney Antoinette Moore served as lead local counsel for the Maya, adapting the legal argument presented to the IACHR.[1] James Anaya prepared an accompanying expert report on the rights of Indigenous peoples under international law.

### The Maya Argument: Legal Obligations of Belize

The Maya argument grounded their land claim in the right to property articulated in the Belize constitution, which guarantees to "every person in Belize ... protection from arbitrary deprivation of property."[2] The complaint linked these protections to the constitution's preamble, which declares, "The people of Belize ... require policies of state which protect ... the identity, dignity and social and cultural values of Belizeans, including Belize's Indigenous peoples."[3] The clause recognizing Indigenous peoples had been inserted into the constitution in 2001, following a review of the Belizean political system by a Political Reform Commission. During the review, Maya and Garifuna leaders requested that the constitution explicitly acknowledge the presence of Indigenous groups in Belize. The commission recommended against this request. However, an alliance of Maya and Garifuna organizations jointly criticized the commission's stance in the media, and the legislature subsequently voted to incorporate four new words, "including Belize's Indigenous peoples," into the constitution's preamble.[4]

Although the Maya complaint was grounded in the Belize constitution's guarantees for property and equality, it articulated Belizean law with international law. It emphasized the Inter-American Commission's judgment that the practice of customary tenure by Maya communities in Belize gives rise to property, which is protected by the American Declaration's right to property.[5] The commission, the complaint noted, had defined "the use and enjoyment of the land and its resources" as "integral components of the physical and cultural survival of Indigenous communities and the effective enjoyment of their human rights more broadly."[6] "For the Maya claimants," the petition asserted, "the property rights asserted here are of central importance to their identity, dignity, and social and cultural values," due to "the distinct nature of the right to property as it applies to Indigenous people, whereby the land traditionally used and occupied by these communities plays a central role in their physical, cultural and spiritual vitality."[7]

Reprising the legal argument contained in the IACHR petition, the complaint noted that Belize is party to international treaties that require states to recognize and respect the rights of Indigenous peoples over their lands: the International Convention on Civil and Political Rights (ICCPR), the International Convention on the Elimination of Racial Discrimination (ICERD), and the American Declaration on the Rights and Duties of Man. Further, the complaint asserted, customary international law and general principles of international law "also affirm Indigenous property rights in traditional lands."[8]

Because Belize is a common-law jurisdiction, the complaint also articulated the state's obligations under the common law. Canadian legal scholar Kent McNeil provided an expert report on the common-law jurisprudence on Indigenous claims to lands, which began by explaining, "A feature of common law jurisdictions throughout the world is that legally enforceable rights in land may exist on the basis of longstanding use or occupancy."[9] (Indeed, this provision had provided the legal basis for Britain's recognition of the Baymen's "location" system, as Britain was establishing its own property system in the colony.) Summarizing the common-law jurisprudence on native title, the petition cited the Australian high court's groundbreaking 1992 ruling in *Mabo v. Queensland*, which established that native title under the common law is "grounded in occupation by native people according to their own customary law."[10] *Mabo* concluded, "Native title has its origin in and is given its content by the traditional laws acknowledged by and the traditional customs observed by the Indigenous inhabitants of a territory."[11] Thus, the petition asserted, the common-law doctrine of native title supports the IACHR's determination that the Maya communities of southern Belize have rights to property that "arise from and are defined by" their customary land use practices.[12]

## *The Maya Argument: Existence of Customary Tenure in Maya Communities*

Because both inter-American jurisprudence and common law identify customary tenure practices as the source of Indigenous property in lands, legal representatives for the Maya introduced evidence to demonstrate Maya customary tenure in southern Belize. They drew upon the maps and narrative of the *Maya Atlas*, affidavits from leaders of Conejo and Santa Cruz, and a joint affidavit from the Maya Leaders Alliance (MLA) (an umbrella organization established in 1999 to represent multiple Maya organizations from Toledo in negotiations with the government). Anthropologists Richard Wilk and Liza Grandia, ethnohistorian Grant Jones, and geographer Joel Wainwright provided expert affidavits based on their research in southern Belize.[13]

The Maya petition presented the Alcalde System as the cornerstone of Maya customary land tenure, introducing the colonial legal framework that recognized alcaldes as local governing authorities. Citing Wilk's affidavit, the complaint asserted that the British colonial government "both tolerated and affirmatively protected Maya customary land use," "incorporat[ing] existing Maya village leadership structures and Maya customary law into the administration of the Settlement" and managing the natives "through their own Chiefs and according to their own customs."[14] These policies continued postindependence, despite the Belizean government's imposition of the Village Council System on Maya communities.

Maya affidavits described community autonomy and authority, with the alcalde and members of the village—rather than state actors—granting or refusing newcomers permission to settle and live in their community and use its lands. They explained alcaldes' responsibility for upholding community rules regarding individuals' rights to particular parcels and the use of shared lands, as well as convening collective work parties and resolving conflicts. Citing the affidavits of villagers and anthropologists, the claim asserted that Maya land use patterns are "governed by a system of unwritten customary rules that form part of the social, cultural, and political organization of their communities," via the institutions of the Alcalde System.[15] Men of Conejo and Santa Cruz described the steps they followed to clear and plant their milpas, including offerings to the hills and valleys. "I learned how to plant this way from my parents; they learned from their parents. This is the way planting has always been done," Higinio Teul, from Conejo, explained.[16] Expert affidavits reinforced the sacred nature of Q'eqchi' and Mopan relationships to the places they live, farm, and hunt.

The evidence marshaled by the Maya legal team to demonstrate the existence of customary tenure in Maya communities of southern Belize resonated with the territorializing definition of Indigenous cultures elaborated by Indigenous advocates in international law and jurisprudence. Integrating livelihood practices with Indigenous cosmovisions and asserting a vital relationship between Indigenous peoples and their lands, legal representatives for the Maya positioned them as the collective culture-bearing subjects of Indigenous rights.

The petition noted, "Because of their collective aspect and unique source, Maya customary rights to lands and resources are by nature different from the sorts of property rights routinely protected and respected by government offices and ministries. By failing to accommodate this difference . . . government officials are discriminating against Maya people," by not providing legal and administrative frameworks to enable the Maya to exercise their right to property "fully and equally with other members of the Belizean population."[17]

## *The Government's Response*

The Belizean government was represented by attorney Nicola Cho, legal counsel in the Ministry of Natural Resources. Asserting the sovereignty of the Belizean state, Cho declared that the IACHR decision in favor of the Maya was not relevant to this litigation; instead, this case must focus on the guarantees provided by the Belize constitution, not the American Declaration. Having lost at the IACHR largely on the basis of inter-American and international law, Cho insisted that the case be evaluated solely on common-law principles concerning native title.[18]

Cho invoked the state's interpretation of the common-law doctrine of native title introduced at the IACHR, which insisted that the claimants must prove they are (1) descended from a group that (2) exercised exclusive occupation over (3) the same lands they are claiming (4) at the time colonial sovereignty was imposed. Citing the dominant narrative of Belizean history, Cho asserted that the Mopan and Q'eqchi' could not meet these criteria. Spanish forces had captured and removed a majority of the Maya people who had inhabited southern Belize in precolonial times, she declared, leaving Toledo uninhabited. Though she acknowledged that some Maya had escaped capture by the Spanish and remained in Belize, Cho questioned whether their numbers were sufficient to constitute continued "occupation."[19] Spain's forced removal of the Maya population from southern

Belize defeated requirements three and four, she argued: Mopan and Q'eqchi' did not occupy the same lands they now claimed at the time British sovereignty was imposed. Further, she asserted, the establishment of Garifuna villages along the coast of southern Belize during the early 1800s defeated the requirement of exclusive occupation. Defining Mopan and Q'eqchi' as the descendants of nineteenth-century immigrants from Guatemala, Cho argued that they were not Indigenous to southern Belize and thus had no Indigenous rights to lands.

Cho's account relied on the dominant narrative of Belizean history, which holds that the Spanish "emptied" the territory, and that the Baymen thus established their settlement in an uninhabited territory, which subsequently became a haven for groups fleeing violence and exploitation in neighboring republics.[20] This government-sanctioned version of history, which positions all present-day Belizean ethnic groups as immigrants, has been taught in Belizean schools and is familiar to most Belizean adults. Cho's contention that Mopan and Q'eqchi' are *not* Indigenous to Belize and thus cannot claim Indigenous rights also relies on the official Belizean language ideology, which posits that languages map directly onto cultures to define peoples, whose shared ancestry is assumed. The official narrative of Belizean history projects contemporary language-based ascriptions of identity backward in time across centuries, assuming that current state classification practices have always defined identities in Mesoamerica. Although this assumption is a fallacy, Cho drew on this narrative to argue that the original Maya inhabitants of southern Belize spoke Chol and must have identified as Chols; thus, only Chol-speakers could be Indigenous to southern Belize.

Additionally, Cho casts the Mopan and Q'eqchi' claim to collective lands as "incompatible" with the government's assertion of Belizean sovereignty. "All Mayan villages in Toledo admit a connection to Guatemala. To acknowledge or recognize Indigenous/traditional/native rights for a group who admittedly migrated from Guatemala . . . is incompatible with assertion of sovereignty, given that Guatemala continues to claim half the territory of Belize."[21] The implication was that the Maya were attempting to wrest control over the Toledo District, with the possible aim of transferring that territory to Guatemala. A local newspaper captured Cho's argument in the headline "GOB Lawyer Claims Maya Case Threatens Belize's sovereignty!"[22]

### *The Maya Argument: Evidence for Mopan and Q'eqchi' Indigeneity*

Confronting the government attorney's assertions that the Mopan and Q'eqchi' are not Indigenous to Belize, counsel for the Maya sought to demonstrate Mopan and Q'eqchi' indigeneity. It is significant that the presiding judge, Chief Justice Abdulai Conteh, was not a Belizean native. Born and raised in Sierra Leone, Conteh had earned law degrees from British institutions. He served in the government of Sierra Leone between 1977 and 1992 but fled the country following a coup. Because judges from one common-law jurisdiction may be appointed to serve in another common-law jurisdiction, Conteh was able to win appointment as chief justice of the Belize Supreme Court in 2000. As a non-native, Conteh had not been socialized through the Belizean education system into official narratives of Belizean history and ethnic identities.

To demonstrate Mopan and Q'eqchi' indigeneity, Attorney Moore relied on the *Maya Atlas* and the expert affidavits of anthropologists Grant Jones, Richard Wilk, and Liza Grandia, who agreed that Spanish forces had captured and removed much of the Maya population from southern Belize around the turn of the seventeenth century and that Mopan and Q'eqchi' had migrated into Toledo during the late nineteenth century. However, their testimony presented a more complex rendering of Belizean history.

While the dominant narrative of Belizean history is based on an analysis published in 1930 (Thompson 1930), Jones's affidavit explained that his recent research in the Spanish archives had revealed complex dynamics and relationships across this region that were not previously known or understood. According to Jones's analysis, the principal inhabitants of Toledo from the sixteenth to the eighteenth centuries were "Mayas who spoke the Mayan languages of Chol and Mopan."[23] Many individuals spoke both languages and interacted through trade relations that connected the populations of southern Belize with the Itzaj kingdom of the Peten. Outside the control of Spanish colonial strongholds, Jones described southern Belize as a "zone of refuge" for Maya fleeing Spanish domination.[24] Based on evidence that Spanish troops encountered Q'eqchi'-speakers as far north as central Belize in 1570, Wilk suggested that the region may also have served as a refuge for Q'eqchi' speakers fleeing colonial rule in Guatemala.[25]

After the conquest of the Itzaj kingdom in 1697, Spanish forces removed thousands of Chol-speakers from Peten and southern Belize to the Verapaz region in Guatemala (Jones 1998:242–243). There, Chol speakers intermarried with Q'eqchi'-speaking populations. Thus, Jones asserted, it is an oversimplification to suggest that the Chol became "extinct" following their removal to Verapaz; rather, descendants of Chol-speakers survived as Q'eqchi'-speakers, some of whom retained their original Chol surnames.[26] Further, baptismal registers from the Peten demonstrate that people with Itzaj, Mopan, Chol, and Q'eqchi' surnames later came to live together in communities identified simply as "Mopan" in colonial records, with frequent marriages across lineages or linguistic lines (Jones 1998:522). This complexity cannot be accommodated within official Belizean ideologies concerning ethnic identity.

Beginning in the 1770s, Spanish appropriations of labor and land also drove Q'eqchi'—or Q'eqchi'-Chols—from Verapaz into the Peten where, according to church records, they intermarried with Mopan. As a result, many contemporary Mopan speakers in southern Belize, whose ancestors came from the community of San Luis, Peten, bear Q'eqchi' or Q'eqchi'-Chol names.[27] Summarizing this evidence, Jones explained, "During the process of Spanish invasion and colonization . . . the Toledo area became a frontier zone of refuge, and prior political and cultural distinctions became blurred as intermixing took place" between Chol and Q'eqchi' and between Q'eqchi' and Mopan. Throughout the conquest period, "Maya people from different linguistic groups intermarried and moved back and forth" between territories that only later came to belong to distinct countries.[28] "In all," he concluded, "there is sufficient evidence to support my conclusion that the Mopan and Q'eqchi'-speaking inhabitants of Toledo have a historical and cultural relationship with the lands on which they currently live and work, and with the populations that have historically inhabited them. That relationship grounds their identity as an Indigenous people of the region."[29]

Expert witnesses thus offered more complex versions of history and identity than official state discourses, pointing to migration, multilingualism, and intermarriage across the boundaries the government attorney sought to impose. Further, by invoking the factors that organized affiliations during earlier time periods, including lineage or political and military alignments that created divides among speakers of a single language and united speakers of different languages, expert testimony revealed the artificiality and arbitrariness of the criteria for identity on which government attorneys insisted.

Summarizing the data and analysis presented in the expert affidavits, the Maya petition asserted, "People who are identified as Maya have, for centuries, formed organized societies that have inhabited a vast territory—which includes the Toledo District of southern Belize—long before the arrival of Europeans and the colonial institutions that gave way to the modern State of Belize. Distinct linguistic subgroups and communities have existed and evolved within a system of interrelationships and cultural affiliations among the historical and contemporary Maya people of the Middle American region encompassing Belize." The contemporary Mopan- and Q'eqchi'-speaking people of the Toledo District are "the descendants or relatives of the Maya subgroups that inhabited the territory since precolonial times."[30]

The expert affidavit on native title under the common law also challenged the criteria for indigeneity upon which the government attorney had insisted. Canadian legal scholar Kent McNeil provided an expert report on the common-law jurisprudence concerning Indigenous claims to lands, which explained, "A feature of common law jurisdictions throughout the world is that legally enforceable rights in land may exist on the basis of longstanding use or occupancy."[31] McNeil explained that the common law had recognized current occupation by an Indigenous group as sufficient evidence of an Indigenous community's long-standing relationship with a territory, where conclusive evidence of presovereignty occupation cannot be produced.[32] Further, McNeil asserted, the common-law notion of continuity "does not require the occupation to have been constant nor in the same manner or form historically." Canadian jurisprudence had declared that such an approach "would risk 'perpetuating the historical injustice suffered by Aboriginal peoples at the hands of colonizers,'" including the forced removal of Maya from the region that is now southern Belize by Spanish forces.[33]

## *The Judgment*

Chief Justice Conteh issued his ruling in October 2007. Responding to Cho's assertion that the IACHR ruling was irrelevant to these proceedings, he agreed, "The present proceedings are not a claim to enforce the findings of the Inter-American Commission on Human Rights"; rather, these proceedings concern alleged breaches of the Belize constitution.[34] However, the chief justice continued, the IACHR is the regional body charged with advancing human rights in the region and monitoring Organization of American States (OAS) member states' compliance with their legal obligations to uphold the American Declaration on the Rights and Duties of Man.[35] Although the findings of the commission "may not bind this court," he continued, "I can hardly be oblivious to them, and may even find these, where appropriate and cogent, to be persuasive."[36]

Engaging the state attorney's insistence that the judgment rely on the common law, rather than international law, the chief justice drew on common-law precedents that defined native title as "a question of fact" to be decided by the trial judge based on "the totality of the evidence."[37] After reviewing the extensive body of evidence presented by the claimants, Conteh concluded that the evidence clearly established that contemporary Maya communities in southern Belize occupy areas "that had formed part of the ancestral and historic territory of the Maya people since time immemorial, and certainly since prior to Spanish and later British assertions of sovereignty."[38] His analysis embraced the evidence presented by expert witnesses for the Maya of complex relationships across the language boundaries the government sought to impose.

Further, Conteh determined that Maya customary tenure exists in the Toledo District and that the villages of Conejo and Santa Cruz have "interests" in land based on customary tenure.[39] These interests constitute "property," which is "clearly deserving" of the property protections afforded by the Belize constitution, he concluded, citing the IACHR decision to "fortify" this analysis.[40] Conteh also drew on international law to support his conclusions, noting, "In contemporary international law, the right to property is regarded as including the rights of Indigenous peoples to their traditional lands and natural resources."[41] The defendants, he noted, had not presented any evidence to refute the existence of Maya customary tenure in the Toledo District. Rather, the government had explicitly recognized the rights of the Maya people to lands and resources in southern Belize "based on their long-standing use and occupancy," in signing the Ten Points of Agreement in 2000.[42] He deemed this "an important admission by the defendants sufficient to dispose of this aspect of the case in the claimants' favour."[43]

Although Spanish colonizers removed Maya inhabitants of southern Belize by force, Conteh noted, there is no evidence the Maya of southern Belize ever ceded their lands.[44] Rather, he concluded, "Throughout the unfolding drama regarding the territory, first between Spain and later Guatemala on the one hand, and the British authorities on the other, the Maya people were all the while living on their land. There was some forced removal of some of the Maya people by Spanish authorities from some parts of the land; but the fact remains that they were never wholly removed so as to make the land *terra nullius* rendering it ownerless or unoccupied."[45]

Addressing the question of whether the rights of the Maya had been violated, Conteh determined that although the government failed to protect the Maya people's constitutional right to property, the government's actions did not rise to the level of "arbitrary deprivation" or "compulsory acquisition," the terms used in the constitution's property guarantees.[46] However, he continued, the government had violated the claimants' right to equality and nondiscrimination by failing to provide legal mechanisms by which the Maya could exercise their right to property "fully and equally with other Belizeans."[47]

Finally, Conteh directly engaged the petitioners' claim that Indigenous rights to lands had been incorporated into Customary International Law and General Principles of law. He noted that the UN General Assembly had just approved the long-delayed UN Declaration on the Rights of Indigenous Peoples in September 2007 with an "overwhelming number of 143 states in favour," including Belize; only four states had voted against the declaration, and eleven abstained.[48] Based on this "overwhelming" support, the judge determined, the declaration embodies general principles of international law, with its Article 26 reflecting "the growing consensus and the general principles of international law on Indigenous peoples and their lands and resources."[49] Article 26 accords to Indigenous peoples "the right to own, use, develop and control the lands, territories and resources that they possess by reason of traditional ownership or other traditional occupation or use" and calls upon states to "give legal recognition and protection to these lands, territories and resources . . . with due respect to the customs, traditions and land tenure systems of the Indigenous peoples concerned."[50] Thus, Conteh asserted, "It is my considered view that both customary international law and general principles of international law would require that Belize respect the rights of its Indigenous people to their lands and resources."[51] He acknowledged that declarations by the UN General Assembly are not ordinarily binding on member states; however, he concluded, when such declarations "contain principles of general international law, states are not expected to disregard them."[52]

The chief justice thus determined that the Belizean state was bound by both domestic and international law—including conventions, customary law, and general principles—to respect the rights of the Maya to their lands.[53]

## Responses to the Belize Supreme Court Decision

The Belize Supreme Court decision won international acclaim for its determination that the property provisions of the United Nations Declaration on the Rights of Indigenous Peoples (UNDRIP) embody general principles of international law. International legal scholars called the ruling a "landmark decision" on the binding nature of the UN declaration (Anaya 2009:104; Baldwin and Morel 2011; Barelli 2010; Burger 2011; Daes 2011; Gilbert and Doyle 2011; Stavenhagen 2011; Stefania 2011). The lack of Belizean domestic legislation on Indigenous rights heightened the international significance of the Supreme Court decision: if Belize has obligations to uphold the land rights accorded to Indigenous peoples by the UNDRIP, by virtue of its constitutional guarantees for the right to property, other countries that protect rights to property might be held to the same standards (Baldwin and Morel 2011:124; Medina 2016).

However, despite the acclaim that greeted the Belize Supreme Court decision outside of Belize, Belizeans who embraced official narratives on national history and the assignment of ethnic identities asserted that Conteh simply did not understand Belize.

Leaders of both political parties voiced measured support for the ruling in its immediate aftermath, as national elections approached. As PUP ministers campaigned for re-election, they took no steps to implement the decision, but neither did they appeal it. After the election brought the United Democratic Party (UDP) to power in February 2008, the new administration initiated discussions with Maya organizations regarding implementation of the decision. In March 2008, the Solicitor General issued an order to government ministries and departments directing them "to immediately cease all activities and/or operations" on lands in Toledo until further instructions were issued. However, a month later, government officials insisted that the Supreme Court ruling applied only to Santa Cruz and Conejo. The Solicitor General sent a second memorandum to government ministries and departments informing them that the cease-and-desist order would henceforth apply only to lands used by these villages.[54]

Within two months, in May 2008, a Creole man, Francis Johnston, bulldozed over 2,000 acres of cacao and corn planted by Maya farmers in the village of Golden Stream. Johnston, married to a Maya woman from Golden Stream, claimed that his wife's brother had sold him a lease for these lands. Golden Stream residents requested state intervention to protect the community's land rights, which, they asserted, had been confirmed by both the IACHR and the Supreme Court. State representatives refused. While the conflict in Golden Stream was unfolding, a minister of government announced that lands around the village of San Pedro Colombia would be surveyed and leased, and the Forestry Department issued several new logging permits for areas of Toledo. Confronting aggressive infringements on lands claimed by Maya communities, the village of Golden Stream initiated a complaint in the Supreme Court that was later consolidated into a class action suit on behalf of all Maya communities in Toledo not named in the original case. Although the villages in Stann Creek District participated in the mapping project, they were not explicitly included in this lawsuit.[55]

### 2008 Supreme Court Claim

In June 2008, the Toledo Alcaldes Association (TAA), the Maya Leaders Alliance (MLA), and the alcaldes of twenty-two Maya communities filed the consolidated complaint in the Supreme Court. By this time, debates over whether the MLA should sue the government had transformed the organization from an umbrella group representing several Maya organizations to a group of self-selected leaders whose explicit aim was to support the TAA and its struggle for land rights.

The claimants sought a declaration that Maya customary land tenure exists in the Toledo District, that it gives rise to property protected by the Belize constitution, and that the government's failure to adopt measures to enable the Maya to exercise their right to property "fully and equally with other Belizeans" violated constitutional guarantees for property, nondiscrimination, and equal protection of the law.[56] "The constitutional rights of property and non-discrimination impose an affirmative duty on the government to provide a statutory or administrative mechanism through which Maya land rights can be identified, demarcated, and titled," the claimants argued.[57] Thus, the Maya sought orders for the government to implement measures to protect Maya customary property rights "in accordance with Maya customary laws and land tenure practices, and in consultation with the affected Maya people."[58]

In June 2009, the case was tried before Chief Justice Conteh in the Supreme Court. Attorney Antoinette Moore again represented the claimants. The alcaldes of all villages named in the claim submitted affidavits describing their customary tenure practices. Expert affidavits by anthropologists Rick Wilk, Liza Grandia, and Grant Jones described the history of the Maya presence in Toledo, the connections between current and ancient Maya populations, and the operation of Maya customary land tenure.

The new UDP government contracted a prominent attorney from the private sector, Senior Counsel Lois Young, to lead its defense. Young offered a more vigorous defense than her predecessor, targeting the court of public opinion as well as the Supreme Court. She solicited an affidavit from a prominent Belizean archaeologist that presented the official version of Belizean history, to counter the historical narratives of expert affidavits submitted by the Maya.

### Market Subjects versus Rights-Bearing Subjects

In the run-up to the trial, the Maya leaders of the Toledo Cacao Growers Association (TCGA) publicly announced their opposition to communal land tenure. Chairman of the Toledo Cacao Growers Association Justino Peck submitted an affidavit in support of the government's case, asserting that cacao farmers, who numbered more than 1,000, sought individual ownership of lands.[59] In a television news interview, TCGA manager Armando Choco explained that cacao farmers preferred individual land titles, which they could use to secure credit, and asked the government of Belize to "do all in its power to refrain from granting communal land ownership to Maya villages in the Toledo District."[60] "For farmers," Choco explained, communal land "would mean they would have to go back and live the lifestyle of our ancestors, forty to fifty years or even more years ago." Farmers are not willing to sacrifice all the struggles they have endured to make a better life, he continued, so "it's important for them to have some sort of documentation for their land. And the best system for them is through the government system."[61]

On the day of the Supreme Court trial, some 250 Maya cacao farmers traveled by bus to Belize City to demonstrate against communal land holdings in front of the Supreme Court Building, waving signs that asserted, "We want to live a better life. Communal is not the way!!"[62] Maya supporters of the land claim also traveled to Belize City to demonstrate in front of the Supreme Court, turning out in larger numbers than the demonstrators who favored individual titles.[63]

At a rally in Toledo in support of the Maya land claim, Cristina Coc of the Maya Leaders Alliance countered Choco's assertions by noting that the elected alcaldes, not the TCGA, represent the Maya communities in Toledo, and a large majority of the Toledo Alcaldes Association had authorized the MLA to bring the lawsuit.[64] Another MLA spokesperson, Greg Ch'oc, pointed to involvement by UDP operatives and elected representatives in mobilizing the TCGA to oppose communal lands.[65] Questioning whether the TCGA really spoke for all cacao farmers, Ch'oc asked cacao growers at the rally to raise their hands. As hands went up, he challenged the TCGA leaders to publicly demonstrate the support they claimed to enjoy from their members.[66] A cacao farmer and TCGA member present at the rally, Alfonso Cal, addressed the crowd, identifying himself as one of the farmers in Golden Stream whose crops had been bulldozed. He rejected the TCGA manager's pronouncements: "The protection that the lawsuit is asking from the Supreme Court, it will not harm the cacao farmers or take away their plantation. In fact, by securing Maya land rights it will allow Mayan farmers to plant without fear of losing their plantation like I did."[67]

Although MLA spokespersons cast the move by the TCGA as part of a UDP strategy to mobilize opposition to the Maya land claim, this can also be interpreted as a strategy to mobilize market subjects against Indigenous rights-bearing subjects, market-rational farmers seeking access to credit against communities' broader cultural and livelihood goals.

### Sovereignty in the Court of Public Opinion

Beyond the Supreme Court, the arguments of the claimants and the defense played out in the court of public opinion via interviews with local print and television reporters. Media coverage of the trial focused on disputes over the history of southern Belize. Attorney Lois Young argued, "It would be very very easy if you could jump up and say, 'I have been here from time immemorial, and this piece of land is mine.'" But, she insisted, the common law requires that groups claiming native title must *prove* their descent from the original inhabitants of the lands being claimed. The Maya, she declared, had failed to do this.[68]

Further, Young warned, the Maya case constituted a threat to Belizean sovereignty: "Toledo is the biggest district. It's a huge district. Can you imagine that you have the government not in control of the land in the Toledo District? Because that's what it basically amounts to!"[69] Again, the attorney representing the government suggested that Maya collective ownership of lands in Toledo would prevent the Belizean government from exercising sovereignty over the district. This claim elided distinctions—and the relationship—between property and sovereignty and suggested that Maya collective ownership of lands might lead to secession.

Young's warning that the Maya land claim threatened Belizean sovereignty referenced a concern of extreme importance to Belizeans, but it was also deeply ironic. The Guatemalan president had recognized Belize in 1991, but a subsequent Guatemalan government had reasserted its claim to Belize in 1994 (Shoman 2018:280–289). In 2001, conflict between Guatemalan and Belizean militaries ratcheted up, when Guatemalan armed forces kidnapped four Belize Defense Force (BDF) soldiers patrolling the western border, marched them westward into Guatemala, and charged them with illegal entry and possession of firearms. The Guatemalan army detained the BDF soldiers for a week before releasing them in response to international protests (Shoman 2011:285).

Later in the 2000s, two conservation nongovernmental organizations (NGOs), Friends of Conservation and Development and Ya'axché Conservation Trust, became comanagers of extensive protected areas along the western border of Belize. As the conservation NGOs began to patrol, they discovered significant incursions by Guatemalan civilians across the western border to illegally extract resources from Belizean territory. NGO leaders convened frequent press conferences to denounce Guatemalans' extraction of timber, ornamental xate leaves, wildlife, gold, and ancient Mayan artifacts from Belizean protected areas.[70] These press conferences garnered front-page newspaper headlines.

Patrols by conservation NGOs also led to violent confrontations with Guatemalan poachers, who sometimes fired on rangers. The NGOs sought backup from the Belize Defense Force, responsible for securing Belizean borders, and the police, responsible for arresting persons who violate Belizean environmental laws. As joint NGO-BDF-police patrols began, numerous violent incidents occurred in the border region in the late 2000s. Guatemalan loggers and xate harvesters fired on patrols, and BDF soldiers fired back.[71] The increasingly violent confrontations along the border spurred OAS-facilitated negotiations between Belizean and Guatemalan governments that resulted in an agreement in December 2008 that laid out a process for submitting Guatemala's claim to the International Court of Justice (ICJ) for adjudication.

As debate raged in Belize about the advantages or risks of submitting the Guatemalan claim to the ICJ, Guatemalan incursions into western Belize continued. In 2009, a group of armed Guatemalans encircled a joint military patrol of BDF and Guatemalan forces and held the soldiers of both countries prisoner, demanding information about a man from their village who had been arrested in Belize weeks earlier.[72] In March 2010, Friends of Conservation and Development (FCD) reported the discovery of thirty-one Guatemalans living inside the Chiquibul National Park, including many who had been there for years.[73] The director of FCD complained that the number of squatters was increasing.

Along the southern boundary between Belize and Guatemala, the Guatemalan military conducted increasingly belligerent maneuvers, preventing Belizeans from transiting waters claimed by Belize. Heightened public anger over incursions by Guatemalan civilians and growing aggression by the Guatemalan military shaped the context in which Attorney Young asserted that the Maya claim posed a threat to Belizean sovereignty over southern Belize. At the same time, news coverage of intrusions by Guatemalan soldiers and civilians made it clear to Belizeans that their government was not effectively exercising sovereignty along Belizean borders. While the Belizean government sought to "protect" Belizean territorial sovereignty from what Young cast as a "Maya threat," it was failing to protect Belizean territorial sovereignty from Guatemalan aggression.

## 2010 Supreme Court Decision

A year passed before the Supreme Court issued a decision in the case. On June 28, 2010, Chief Justice Conteh affirmed his earlier ruling and asserted the state's obligation to protect the constitutional rights of the Maya.[74] He explicitly stated that the decision applied to all Maya communities in Toledo. He noted, additionally, that it was "reasonable to extend the existence of Maya customary land tenure to the five Maya villages in the Stann Creek District."[75] However, because the claimants had not advanced this argument, he did not include these communities.

Conteh determined that the Maya legal team had provided compelling evidence of "historical, ancestral, and cultural continuity and links between the original inhabitants of what is now Toledo District and the present claimants, which entitled the contemporary Mopan and Q'eqchi' to claim customary rights and interests in land in the region.[76] The chief justice also reaffirmed that Maya customary tenure exists in all Maya villages in Toledo District and that it gives rise to property that is protected by the Belize constitution. Affirming the government's obligation "to adopt affirmative measures to identify and protect the rights of the claimants based on Maya customary tenure," he ordered the state to consult with the Maya people to develop the legislative or administrative measures required to protect Maya property rights and to cease infringing those rights while protective measures were being developed.[77]

The prime minister announced that the status quo would remain in Toledo while the government appealed the decision. In March 2011, the Maya Lands case was taken up by the appeals court, a panel of three judges, one from Belize, one from Jamaica, and one from Dominica.

## The Court of Appeal

Before the Court of Appeal, the state's attorney repeated that in order for Mopan and Q'eqchi' to claim Indigenous rights, it was necessary for them to prove that they are the direct descendants of the Manche Chol who occupied the Toledo District in 1540, when Spain asserted sovereignty over the area. Thus far, she declared, they had failed to do this.[78]

Recasting the Maya claim as "a land problem" common to "all races" in Belize, Young argued, "No group should be given special privileges or rights. This is all about obtaining a piece of land in order to better yourself economically. Nothing is wrong with that, but other groups in Belize would also like to have that." Therefore, she continued, "This is a matter that must be addressed by the Belizean society as whole, led by the government. This is a matter that would require a nationwide consultation process." Other groups "have to be taken into account."[79]

On behalf of the Maya, Attorney Moore noted that three judgments, including two by the Supreme Court of Belize and one by the IACHR, had recognized Maya rights to lands based on their practice of customary tenure. The Supreme Court's 2007 *Maya Land Rights* judgment, which the government had not appealed, remained in effect. Because the Belize constitution offers protections for property, she asserted, it must protect the property that arises out of Maya customary tenure practices. Failure to protect such property is discriminatory and violates constitutional guarantees of nondiscrimination and equal protection of the law. Thus, the government has an affirmative duty to develop the legislative or administrative means to protect Maya customary title. Further, she argued, "a test which requires proof by present-day Maya of genealogical descent from the pre-1540 occupants of southern Belize is unreasonable and unrealistic."[80] Indeed, Moore noted, the government itself had acknowledged in the Ten Points of Agreement in 2000 that the long-standing use and occupation of lands by the Maya of southern Belize had given rise to rights over those lands and resources.

### *Appeals Court Decision*

In July 2013, a two-judge majority in the appeals court upheld Maya rights to the lands they have traditionally used. The decision by the court's two non-Belizean judges deeply engaged the common law to arrive at the determination that reason is the cornerstone of common law, and the Belizean government's demand that the Mopan and Q'eqchi' prove their direct descent from the sixteenth-century Chols who had inhabited the Toledo District was unreasonable.

The majority decision, written by Judge Morrison of Jamaica, reviewed relevant language from the Belize constitution, the 2007 Supreme Court decision, and the inter-American jurisprudence. Morrison concluded that Conteh was correct to consider Belize's obligations under international treaties and its responsibilities in relation to general principles of international law.[81]

Then, responding to the government's insistence that the case be decided based on common-law criteria for native title, Morrison carefully considered the common-law cases most relevant to the claim. He deemed the *Mabo* decision from Australia especially significant, because it had brought to bear on the common law the "powerful influence" of the ICCPR. "The common law does not necessarily conform with international law," Morrison wrote, "but international law is a legitimate and important influence on the development of the common law, especially when international law declares the existence of universal human rights."[82] *Mabo* had determined that "native title has its origin in and is given its content by the traditional laws acknowledged by and the traditional customs observed by the Indigenous inhabitants of a territory." Therefore, "native title, though recognized *by* the common law, is not an institution *of* the common law and is not alienable by the common law."[83]

In response to the government's assertion that Mopan and Q'eqchi' claimants must prove direct descent from the very same Chols who had been captured and removed from the lands that now constitute the Toledo District, Morrison quoted another Australian case, *Mason v. Tritton*. That case determined, "In the nature of Aboriginal society, their many deprivations and disadvantages following European settlement of Australia and the limited record keeping of the earliest days, it is next to impossible to expect that Aboriginal Australians will ever be able to prove, by record details, their precise genealogy back to the time before 1788. *In these circumstances, it would be unreasonable and unrealistic for the common law of Australia to demand such proof for the establishment of a claim to native title. The common law, being the creation of reason, typically rejects unrealistic and unreasonable principles.*"[84]

Further, Morrison cited the *Delgamuukw* decision from Canada, which allowed that present occupation could serve as proof of presovereignty occupation, providing there is "continuity" between present and presovereignty occupation.[85] However, he noted, "There is no need to establish 'an unbroken chain of continuity' . . . between present and prior occupation," as disruptions may have occurred as a result of colonization.[86] Thus, "*to impose the requirement of continuity too strictly would risk . . . perpetuating the historical injustice suffered by aboriginal people at the hands of colonizers who failed to respect aboriginal rights to land.*"[87]

Concluding that the common law provides the flexibility necessary to give effect to both the "letter and spirit" of laws that affirm the rights of Indigenous peoples, Morrison thus rejected the government's contention that the Mopan and Q'eqchi' must prove their direct descent from the Maya who inhabited southern Belize in 1540. It would be "wholly 'unrealistic and unreasonable' for the common law of Belize, a member of the Inter-American System and an adherent to a number of international instruments designed to afford special protection to the rights of Indigenous peoples, to adopt such a restrictive test," he determined.[88] "Precisely because of the history of forced migrations among the Maya . . . the adoption of too strict a test for the ascertainment of Indigenous title" might "perpetuate the historical injustice suffered by Indigenous people at the hands of colonizers."[89]

Noting that a shared feature of the common law and international rights instruments is that Indigenous peoples' rights have been held to derive from their longstanding use and occupancy of traditional lands, in accordance with their traditional customary laws and practices, Morrison accepted Conteh's finding that on the strength of the evidence, "there were historical, ancestral, social and cultural links between the original inhabitants of what is today Toledo District and the claimants" and that Maya customary land tenure exists in the villages of Toledo.[90] In accepting Conteh's assessment of the evidence regarding centuries of migration, intermarriage, and shared practices across linguistically distinct groups in the region to which Toledo District belongs, Morrison also rejects the Belizean government's vision of culture and identity as grounded in—and bounded by—language, as well as the underlying assumption that language, culture, and descent neatly map onto one another.

However, Morrison determined that the government had not deprived the Maya of their property.[91] Further, because legal processes to vindicate their rights were available to the Maya, the appeals court found that the government had not violated their right to protection of the law. If there was no violation of rights, no remedies for violations could be prescribed.[92] On this reasoning, the appeals court rejected Conteh's injunction requiring the state to develop legal and administrative mechanisms to recognize and protect Maya customary tenure. Judge Alleyne, a native of Dominica, joined this decision to constitute a majority. Judge Sosa, the lone Belizean judge to hear the Maya lands claim, vehemently dissented.

## Caribbean Court of Justice

The appeals court judgment was satisfactory to neither side. The attorney general rejected its finding in favor of Mopan and Q'eqchi' land rights, while the Maya Leaders Alliance and TAA rejected its reversal of Conteh's order that the government develop and implement mechanisms to protect the property rights of Maya communities. Thus, both sides appealed the appeals court ruling to the Caribbean Court of Justice, which serves as Belize's court of last resort, the final legal authority to which a decision can be appealed.

In April 2015, on the eve of a CCJ ruling, the government of Belize signed a consent order that affirmed that "Maya customary land tenure exists in the Maya villages of the Toledo District and gives rise to collective and individual property rights within the meaning of sections 3(d) and 17 of the Belize Constitution." The government committed to adopt measures to identify and protect the rights of the Maya arising from their customary tenure, in consultation with the Maya and in accordance with Maya customary laws and land tenure practices.[93] Until such measures were in place, the government agreed to "cease and abstain from any acts" by state actors or third parties acting with state acquiescence "that might adversely affect the value, use or enjoyment of the lands that are used and occupied by the Maya villages, without the informed consent of the communities."[94] The consent order also reaffirmed state territorial sovereignty, asserting, "The constitutional authority of the Government over all lands in Belize is not affected by this order."[95]

The CCJ retained jurisdiction to oversee state compliance with the consent order and committed to deciding the remaining issue in the case, the Maya claim for damages based on the land seizure in Golden Stream. In October 2015, the CCJ issued its judgment. It declared that the government of Belize had a duty "to recognize Maya customary land tenure and the land rights following therefrom" and "establish the legal mechanisms necessary to clarify and protect these rights" in Belizean law.[96] The state's failure to meet this obligation had denied the Maya the protection of the law, the court determined, reversing the conclusion of the appeals court.

The CCJ ordered the Belizean state to establish a fund of BZ$300,000 as a first step toward compliance with its obligation to protect Maya customary land tenure. This order represented a "reparation" in recognition of the government's contravention of the customary land tenure rights of the Maya people in southern Belize and "a form of redress for the centuries of oppression endured by the Maya people since the arrival of the European colonizers."[97] However, noting that some legal scholars cast reparations as a recognition of Indigenous sovereignty, the CCJ asserted, "Our award in this case is not to be taken as encouraging or providing implicit support for Maya communities to operate as a state within the state of Belize. As the Consent Order clearly recognizes . . . the constitutional authority of the Government of Belize over all lands in Belize is not affected by that order and, we would add, by this award."[98]

## Analysis

If rights claimants never have "mastery" over the law and rights, this series of cases also calls into question the state's mastery over the law and rights. In this case, those who acted on behalf of a sovereign Belizean state, bound only by rules to which it has consented, confronted responsibilities that derive from a complex system of legal pluralism, in which multiple legal systems operate in the space of the nation-state. Attorneys for the state sought to limit state obligations to those imposed by the Belize constitution and the common law. Judges determined that the Belizean state, as an OAS member and party to the ICCPR and ICERD, is also subject to obligations defined by international human rights law and the inter-American jurisprudence on Indigenous rights. In addition, a series of judges recognized yet another source of legal obligation for Belizean state actors: Maya customary tenure practices, which produce Maya collective property in lands. The judges thus cast the sovereign Belizean state as a bearer of responsibilities to Maya communities as collective legal subjects.

Jonas Bens describes indigeneity as "a paradoxical formation . . . in which the Indigenous must appear as both part of the state and as dissociated from it" (Bens 2020:2). "The task of an Indigenous rights claim," he suggests, "is to invoke the rule of law of the national legal system in order to call for the suspension of that very system, thereby opening up a space for the Indigenous community's own legal system" (Bens 2020:17–18). In Belize, Maya customary tenure has long functioned as both *a part of* state governance and *apart from* state governance. In one sense, Maya customary tenure represents a refusal (Simpson 2014) of the state property system: Maya communities have appropriated the lands they require to sustain themselves without asking for state permission and without regard for state actors' claims to these lands as state property. In another sense, colonial officials, unable to exercise direct rule over southern Belize, sanctioned the Alcalde System as a form of indirect colonial rule over Maya communities, and political leaders in independent Belize have continued to recognize the Alcalde System. The demand by the courts that the Belizean state engage the Maya as a collective legal subject extends this both/and relationship.

In the context of intensified Guatemalan aggression, lawyers speaking for the government repeatedly argued that Maya collective property threatened Belizean sovereignty and territorial integrity. However, in the shadow of the Guatemalan claim, Maya leaders carefully positioned their rights to collectively held lands within the context of Belizean state sovereignty. Likewise, the judicial decisions in the Maya lands cases acknowledged that the Belizean state retained sovereignty over all lands within Belizean territory; however, at the same time, these decisions remake Belizean state sovereignty. Citizens' rights had "renewed" absolutist forms of sovereignty in the eighteenth century, producing a new form of sovereignty constrained by the rights of the governed, the individual bearers of citizens' rights. Human rights further constrained sovereignty in the twentieth century, by holding states accountable to the broader community of states for their treatment of the individual bearers of human rights. Indigenous rights renovate sovereignty once again by requiring the state to recognize Indigenous peoples as collective political subjects. The judicial decisions require the state to recognize Indigenous customary tenure practices as the source of Indigenous collective property, to protect that property in the same way it protects property created through the state's own property system, and to negotiate with the Maya how the state system and Maya customary tenure practices will engage one another. This disrupts the circular dynamic by which the production of property as a recognized claim reauthorizes the state as authorizer.

States' rejection of Indigenous self-determination protects the territorial integrity of existing states. However, their acceptance of territorializing visions of Indigenous cultures requires revisions to the practice of sovereignty itself. The CCJ affirmed the sovereignty of the Belizean state over all Belizean lands and rejected the possibility that the Maya could constitute a "state within a state." However, explicitly recognizing the legal pluralism that exists in Belize, the courts ordered state actors to negotiate with representatives of the Maya to determine the interface between the Belizean legal system and Maya customary tenure practices. As Jeremy Webber (2000) points out, judges in common-law jurisdictions cannot themselves decide how non-Indigenous and Indigenous legal orders should engage one another. The common-law doctrine of native title accords to judges the authority to rule only on the existence of customary tenure; its content lies outside the purview of the common law. Indigenous title is "recognized but not created by the common law," and while the common law requires respect for Indigenous systems of land tenure, "it does not absorb them" (Webber 2000:62, 70–71). Indigenous title is therefore about "relations between societies and systems of law rather than the simple vindication of property rights," and the consequence of Indigenous title is the need to negotiate the interface between non-Indigenous and Indigenous legal orders (Tully 2000:56; Webber 2000:70–71, 85).

The requirement to negotiate how Indigenous and state legal systems will engage one another marks a distinction between Belize as a common-law country and plurinational or multicultural states such as Bolivia, Ecuador, or Colombia. The new constitutions that established these countries as plurinational or multicultural accorded authority to the state to approve or disapprove proposed Indigenous governance procedures (Arteaga Bohrt 2017; Jackson 2007, 2019; Postero 2017; Sieder and Vivero 2017) or to identify "common principles" on which Indigenous and state legal systems should agree (Cervone and Cucuri 2017:125). In Belize, state actors, bound by the common law, lack the legal authority to judge the content of Indigenous legal systems. The next chapter examines the strategies deployed by Maya and state leaders in the course of negotiating the interface between state and Indigenous legal and property systems.

CHAPTER 8

# Negotiating the Interface of Maya Customary Tenure and Belizean Law

The Belizean Maya emerged victorious from nearly twenty years of litigation, with the Caribbean Court of Justice (CCJ) consent order affirming the Belizean state's obligation to recognize and protect Maya collective property in lands and negotiate with the Maya the relationship between the Maya customary tenure system and the law of the encompassing Belizean state. (See photos 7 and 8 from the celebration of this victory). These negotiations became the new front in the struggle over Maya Indigenous rights to lands.

Studies of the aftermath of Indigenous legal victories in land rights cases from across Latin America suggest that it is often easier to win litigation than it is to "win" the implementation of judicial decisions (Correia 2018a, 2018b, 2019; Wainwright and Bryan 2009). Reliance on the law and rights to claim lands may reinforce the power of the state as the guarantor of rights, with the power to choose—or refuse—to enforce those rights. However, recognizing "the state" as performative, with risks involved in each effort to perform its existence, complicates "the power of the state." I analyze the strategies and tactics deployed by both state actors and Maya communities to "win" the implementation, as well as their effects.

Individuals acting in the name of the Belizean state have pursued three principal tactics to strengthen the state's hand in negotiating—or preventing—implementation of the consent order. These tactics support an overarching strategy of extending control of the state property system over lands in Toledo, sustaining the possibility for the state to govern lands in Toledo District *for* or *through* the market. Early on, state actors sought to discredit Maya customary tenure practices, casting them as discriminatory against Black Belizeans and a threat to Belizean sovereignty in an apparent effort to elicit opposition to Maya land rights from Afro-Belizean Creoles and Garifuna. Political leaders also stalled implementation, sustaining the possibility of nonimplementation. This tactic reinforces the power of the state as the entity that can choose—or refuse—to enforce rights. Delay also extends state options for leases, concessions, or state appropriation of the lands

Photo 7. Maya Leaders Alliance spokesperson Cristina Coc with alcaldes at celebration of Maya legal victory in Indian Creek, April 2015. Credit: Tony Rath, Naturalight Productions.

Photo 8. Antoinette Moore, attorney for the Maya, addressing audience at celebration of Maya legal victory in Indian Creek, April 2015. Credit: Tony Rath, Naturalight Productions.

claimed by the Maya and exacerbates uncertainty about rights-claiming in Maya communities that have been waiting for tenure security since litigation began in 1997. State actors have also sought to divide Maya individuals and communities against one another.

However, as state actors have sought to discredit, delay, and divide, Mopan and Q'eqchi' have pursued a "critical conduct of rights." The Toledo Alcaldes Association (TAA), the Maya Leaders Alliance (MLA), and the Julian Cho Society (JCS) have collaborated to sustain and strengthen the Alcalde System and their customary tenure practices, including supporting the Toledo Alcaldes Association as the collective body that enables alcaldes to deliberate issues and priorities across communities. Together, the TAA and JCS also engaged communities in a collective visioning process to imagine the future they want to build on the foundation of their collective lands. Maya leaders have also continued to deploy Belizean courts against the executive branch of the Belizean government, turning to the CCJ to push the executive to comply with its legal obligations and to the lower courts to lodge new complaints against executive branch actions. Maya leaders and their communities have also advanced the steps in the implementation process that are under their control, demarcating their lands and drafting proposed language for a Free, Prior, and Informed Consent (FPIC) protocol and for legislation to govern the relationship between Maya customary tenure and state property systems. Overall, the Maya have sought to sustain possibilities for Maya individuals and communities to determine the lives and livelihoods they desire.

## Sustaining the Alcalde System and Maya Customary Tenure Practices

The decision to pursue litigation through Belizean and inter-American judicial systems removed the focal point of Maya struggles for lands from Maya communities to spaces that were physically and conceptually distant. Litigation was an opaque process, involving long stretches of time with no discernible action, punctuated occasionally by trials conducted primarily through written submissions, followed by the dramatic delivery of judgments, and then appeals that precluded implementation of those judgments. Most Maya had no involvement with the legal proceedings. Leaders, including spokespersons for the Maya Leaders Alliance and the alcaldes who sued, collaborated with legal counsel to prepare and submit brief affidavits, but none testified in court.

An additional distancing factor involved lawyers' translation of Mopan and Q'eqchi' concepts and institutions into nationally and internationally recognizable legal terms. For example, in litigation, lawyers representing Maya communities centered "Maya customary tenure" as the source of Maya collective property. This involved translating "the Alcalde System," already a summarizing translation created during the colonial period, to represent sets of linked practices and institutions for which Mopan and Q'eqchi' languages had their own terms. However, the practices and institutions that lawyers translated as "the Maya customary tenure system" became the through line connecting legal theory with alcaldes' affidavits and litigation with daily events in Maya communities.

While lawyers positioned Maya customary tenure as the source of Maya property in lands in their legal petitions, Maya communities relied on Alcalde System institutions to manage their lands and relationships, and Maya organizations including the TAA, the Julian Cho Society, and the Maya Leaders Alliance supported and defended these practices. For example, the Julian Cho Society made it its mission to support alcaldes and the Alcalde System. On market days in Punta Gorda, when buses make their way from the villages to the district town, the JCS office was usually busy, as alcaldes arrived to seek information, discuss challenges that had emerged from within or outside of their communities, and explore how other alcaldes and communities had responded to similar circumstances.

The Toledo Alcaldes Association also played a significant role in sustaining and strengthening the institution of the alcalde. A significant motivation for the alcaldes who founded the TAA in 1992 was to center the Alcalde System in governance processes in southern Belize, an objective the organization has pursued for three decades. The TAA has supported individual alcaldes while working collectively to enable alcaldes and the communities they represent to share information, strategize, deliberate, and act in concert to meet shared challenges. The TAA membership comprises all first and second alcaldes, selected by their communities. The alcaldes represent the views of their respective communities in deliberations at TAA assemblies; they also convey the content of discussions held and decisions taken at TAA assemblies to residents of their villages.

Even before the legal cases concluded, the TAA, supported by the Maya Leaders Alliance, had developed a Maya Consultation Framework to stipulate how Maya communities expected government actors and other external agencies to engage them. The framework insisted that approaches to communities go through the alcaldes, "the traditional representatives of each Maya village . . . elected in accordance with Maya customary practices," who serve as "the appointed representative[s] of the will of the villagers" as expressed through the Village Meeting, "the fundamental authority and primary decision-making body" of Maya villages. The Maya Consultation Framework stipulated that government or private-sector organizations that proposed actions that would impact Maya communities would have to respect the lengthy processes by which communities arrive at decisions through the Village Meeting. For proposed activities that would affect a single community, the approach would engage that community's alcalde; for a proposal that would affect multiple communities, the approach would need to engage the TAA, which the framework designated as "the central authority and representative body of the Maya people as a whole" and "the arbiter and defender of Mayan customary law and practices."[1]

After the consent order was signed, the TAA continued to place alcaldes and the institutions that constitute the Alcalde System at the center of the implementation process: the TAA demanded that implementation of the consent order conform to the Maya Consultation Framework and proposed that the framework be adopted as the government's Free, Prior, and Informed Consent protocol. The TAA also formed a steering committee from among its members to coordinate representation of Maya communities in negotiations with the government to implement the order.

Beyond the context of negotiations with the Belizean government to implement the consent order, the TAA and the Maya Leaders Alliance also engaged communities to articulate a shared vision for the future they would build on the foundation of communal lands. "We are asking ourselves what we really want to achieve," MLA spokesperson Cristina Coc explained. Alcaldes and village council chairs from Maya villages in Toledo, along with their deputies, were invited to participate. Each community also selected five additional representatives: two women, two young people, and one elder. Representatives from communities near one another collaborated in workshops that considered three questions: Who are we? What are our greatest strengths and challenges? What is our vision for the future? Working in small groups that matched elders with elders, youth with youth, and so on, participants drew their responses on large sheets of paper. Each group presented their drawings and thoughts to the gathering as a whole for consideration and discussion, and a team of TAA and MLA members identified the recurring themes and wove them into a collective vision for the future. Throughout the visioning process, the practices and values that had been translated into English and legal terms for litigation could be engaged without translation, and the narrowly conceptualized "property" of Belizean law and litigation was treated more expansively as *cho'och*, "the land."

One of the key terms that recurred across these workshops was *raal cho'och*, a Q'eqchi' phrase participants translated as "people of the land," people "who live on the land, depend on the land and work and care for the land" (MLA and TAA 2019:10, 14). Living as raal cho'och involves "a web of reciprocal and interdependent relationships"—not only with the land but also "with each other and other beings with whom we share the land"—which form "the basis of our practices of community" (MLA and TAA 2019:19–20). Community emerged as another key term, with participants identifying institutions central to the Alcalde System, especially the Village Meeting, as the means through which the community comes into being: "It is in joining our words and thoughts . . . that we become community" (MLA and TAA 2019:22, 29).

The futures that the participants imagined prioritized these reciprocal and interdependent relationships, grounded in institutions and practices controlled by the communities. Although their drawings included many forms of engagement with markets, from cash crops to tourism to an airline, they centered relationships with lands and with one another. "We envision a future in which we have a prosperous economy that has a goal of achieving the collective wellbeing of our lands and people; that is defined and directed by our own people, which is rooted in our values while being open to new ideas" (MLA and TAA 2019:45). However, recognizing that Maya communities' traditional forms of governance and communality have been "under constant threat," the vision document asserted the imperative of sustaining Maya communities' practices and institutions for governing themselves: "We understand that if we are to exist as Maya Q'eqchi' and

Mopan, our leadership must be strong and respond to the needs of our communities. For our leadership to remain strong, it must be entrusted to the people of each of our villages, and not anyone else" (MLA and TAA 2019:29).

In response to Wendy Brown's (2004) concern that the pursuit of rights strategies may limit people's ability to imagine other forms of struggle that offer greater potential for dismantling the structures that reproduce inequality, I understand the visioning process undertaken by Maya communities as an effort to imagine the structures that participants wish to inhabit. Glenn Coulthard has called for Indigenous peoples to engage in "individual and collective self-fashioning" that constructs "radical alternatives to the structural and subjective dimensions of colonial power" (Coulthard 2014:18, 48–49). The visioning process conducted in Maya communities of southern Belize is an example of such "self-fashioning." James Tully defines the activities capable of grounding such alternatives as "practices of freedom." Although practices of freedom occasionally manifest in "spectacular public displays of resistance," Tully suggests that they most often involve "quotidian acts of protecting, recovering, gathering together, keeping, revitalizing, teaching and adapting" forms of indigenous life (Tully 2000:59). Maya customary tenure practices, which ground this vision and bring communities into being through relationships of respect, are precisely the kinds of quotidian acts Tully highlights as practices of freedom.

At the same time, the vision generated through this participatory process not only incorporates radical alternatives to the structures and subjectivities of colonial power, for which Coulthard advocates; the vision also engages some of the structural and subjective dimensions of colonial power. The future imagined by participants in the visioning process is described as "rooted in our culture" but "open to the world." "We do not see our culture as something to be frozen and preserved. The many achievements of our ancestors and contemporary communities are the result of learning and change," the vision document explains. "At the same time, we refuse to see our culture as an obstacle to our future. We therefore envision a future in which we continue to be rooted as we imagine and create new paths. We envision a space in which we define who we are and determine the speed and direction of change" (MLA and TAA 2019:47).

Thus, this vision is not simply a rejection of existing structures or an effort to dismantle those structures; rather, it is an effort to sustain and defend an alternative set of structures and subjectivities from which Maya individuals may choose whether and how fully to engage "the market" and the market rationalities that structure Belizean politics, economy, and society. These alternative structures and subjectivities also represent a refuge upon which individuals can rely as a hedge against the vicissitudes of the market, a refuge that makes market engagement less dangerous. This objective represents the version of self-determination that Maya participants articulated in the process of imagining their desired futures.

The village of Maya Centre offers a case in point. After losing access to lands that could support rainy-season cultivation of corn, their dietary staple, households in the community were forced to rely on exchanges with tourists or wage labor to meet their needs, or they planted citrus on the water-logged lands they were allocated by the state. In its reliance on cash economies, the village became a model of the form of development the Belizean state sought to impose on Maya communities. However, when the global COVID-19 pandemic shut down tourism for two years in 2020 and 2021 and a virus from Asia decimated their citrus orchards, villagers struggled to sustain their households. Relying heavily on food distributed by the government during the pandemic, those who had access to parcels for dry-season corn cultivation or lands that could support less desirable food crops than corn considered themselves fortunate. Until the pandemic passed and tourism returned, access to lands—of any quality—was critical to their survival.

This experience of vulnerability was not unusual; in southern Belize, all economic booms have eventually gone bust (Wilk 2006). Elders thus asserted the importance of communities retaining their lands. However, as Maya leaders and the communities they represented labored to sustain their lands and strengthen the Alcalde System, state actors continued to attack those institutions.

### Criminalizing Maya Customary Tenure? The Santa Cruz Incident and Guatemalan Aggression

On June 22, 2015, two months after the consent order was signed, news broke of an incident that had occurred two days earlier in the village of Santa Cruz, Toledo. Images of an Afro-Belizean man, handcuffed and tied with a rope by the village's Alcalde System Police, appeared on social media and national news broadcasts. The Creole man in the photographs, Rupert Myles, claimed his treatment was motivated by racial animus against Black Belizeans. The title of one news report, "Citizen's Arrest in Santa Cruz: Was It Racially Motivated?" reflected the tenor of public debate concerning the incident.[2]

United Democratic Party (UDP) prime minister Dean Barrow immediately denounced the actions of Santa Cruz villagers as "outrageous" and "indefensible." He called for an investigation to determine whether village leaders should be held criminally liable for "what they did to that gentleman." Then, pivoting from Myles to the CCJ consent order, Barrow asserted,

> The consent judgment merely recognizes that [the Maya] are entitled to certain rights. The rights, the nature of the rights is not spelled out. We have agreed we will set up some sort of a commission, we will hear from everybody, all parties in Toledo and elsewhere before we can come to a decision as to what their rights ought to be. In the meantime, for them to do something like this, they talk about human rights, what about that man's human rights? What about his rights as a Belizean? I don't know how on earth they can ever justify this. In my view, they have lost whatever moral high ground that they ever had.[3]

Santa Cruz leaders, backed by the MLA and TAA, soon shared with the media a more complicated backstory for the viral images. In 2014, the Alcalde explained, Mr. Myles had constructed a house on top of a mound at the ancient Maya site of

Uxbenka, adjacent to Santa Cruz Village and within lands claimed by the community. The Archaeology Department, the government unit responsible for the nation's archaeological heritage, was in the process of declaring the site an archaeological reserve and had negotiated an agreement with Santa Cruz Village to refrain from building on or farming lands that would lie inside the future reserve. Myles, whose common-law wife was a Maya woman from Santa Cruz, had appropriated the land on which he built his house without permission from the village. This violated the rules of Maya customary tenure, which require individuals who seek to join a village and access its lands to request—and receive—permission from the alcalde, after the whole community has considered the request. The Alcalde of Santa Cruz had repeatedly asked Myles to remove his house from the site. He had summoned Myles to Village Meetings, but Myles had not appeared. Further, Myles had fired a weapon in the village on multiple occasions, which villagers interpreted as an effort to intimidate them. Thus, Pablo Mis of the Maya Leaders Alliance asserted, the incident had "nothing to do with race. It has to do with a person that thinks they can bully the villagers and disregard village rules."[4]

Myles had also violated the laws of Belize, which prohibit building on, damaging, or destroying ancient Maya sites. Santa Cruz officials had reported Myles's actions to the Archaeology Department and to the police in the district town of Punta Gorda. Neither had taken action to enforce Belizean law.

Subsequently, Myles bulldozed a driveway up the ancient mound, further damaging the structure. The Alcalde again summoned him to a Village Meeting. Village leaders, aware that Myles had a gun, contacted the police in Punta Gorda to request a police presence at the meeting, but the police had not responded.

Myles appeared at this meeting but behaved disrespectfully, speaking out of turn and slamming his fist on the table where the Alcalde was seated before attempting to leave. Concerned that Myles might retrieve his gun, the Alcalde ordered his assistants to restrain Myles. After a brief struggle, they handcuffed him and tied a rope to the cuffs to prevent him from leaving the meeting. Then, village leaders negotiated an agreement with Myles that gave him two more weeks to dismantle his house.[5] The Alcalde again contacted the police in Punta Gorda, asking them to come to Santa Cruz to take Myles into custody. However, the police replied that "they did not have fuel, they did not have a vehicle to be able to move."[6]

In an interview aired on the national news, the People's United Party legislator who represented western Toledo District, Oscar Requeña, supported the account of Santa Cruz leaders and accused the prime minister of sowing racial animosity "to divide this country and tear it apart." He reminded the prime minister that the Alcalde System is "enshrined in our constitution as a form of local government" and that "the Alcalde *has* the authority to arrest within the community." "An appropriate response by state authorities could have averted this entire situation," he concluded.[7]

Four days later, four truckloads of police officers, now in possession of both vehicles and fuel to operate them, arrived in Santa Cruz at 3:30 A.M. In a dramatic performance of state sovereignty, they burst into homes in a predawn raid and arrested eleven villagers. The Superintendent of Police in Punta Gorda attributed the operation to instructions "from higher up."[8] Police arrested Cristina Coc of the Maya Leaders Alliance in Punta Gorda on the same day. They arrested the Santa Cruz Alcalde a day later. In what Odile Hoffman (2021:181) characterizes as an effort to criminalize the practice of Maya customary tenure, the Director of Public Prosecutions charged the Santa Cruz villagers with unlawful imprisonment and common assault. Two were also charged with aggravated assault. Cristina Coc was charged with conspiracy to commit unlawful imprisonment.[9]

Interviewed again on the evening news, the UDP prime minister cast Maya customary tenure practices as a challenge to Belizean sovereignty and a threat to law and order. The CCJ consent order, he asserted, "did not supersede the Constitution and laws of this country. It did not transfer sovereignty over any part of government territory to any ethnic group. It did not create a state within a state. It did not set up a separate Maya nation in Belize. And it did not give anyone the right to use force to vindicate any claim they might have to land."[10] The consent order, he repeated, recognized only that "Maya Belizeans have certain rights over certain land in the Toledo District." However, "the precise nature of those rights must be defined and legislated by government in partnership with the Maya and after consultation with all Belizeans."[11]

Across Belize, the events in Santa Cruz generated debate. An article headlined "Racial Discrimination or Mayan Justice?" noted, "Since there is no police presence in many of those villages, the Alcalde—who has the right to judge disputes over land and crop damage—would be called to settle a dispute . . . and in minor cases, the Alcalde has the authority to try and punish offenders." Yet critics argued that the Alcalde System "is exploited to racially discriminate against Belizeans of other ethnicities who venture to take up residence within those Indigenous communities."[12] This was Mr. Myles's claim.[13]

As Belizeans debated the significance of the Santa Cruz incident, information emerged that suggested United Democratic Party involvement in the event. For example, Myles had arrived at the Village Meeting in the vehicle of a man who had been working for years on behalf of the UDP to garner support in Maya communities for private land titles and oil exploration.[14] The editor of the *Amandala* newspaper concluded that Maya leaders had "walked into a trap." "In Belize today, as we fight to consolidate our nationhood and sovereignty, the worst thing that could happen to us is now happening to us: division between African and Maya Belizeans. At this newspaper, we do not believe that such a crisis as the present one is accidental: we believe that this has been carefully and cleverly orchestrated. The question you have to ask yourself is who stands to benefit from this."[15] If the government planned to consult with "all Belizeans" to determine the content of Maya land rights, stoking antagonism toward the Maya by Afro-Belizean Creole and Garifuna would make it easier to limit those rights.

Speaking for the Belizean state, Prime Minister Barrow continued to frame Maya communal lands and the Alcalde System as threats to Belizean sovereignty and "law and order," although Maya leaders had repeatedly declared their support for the Belizean state's sovereignty over southern Belize in the context of Guatemala's claim to Belizean territory.[16] In fact, the Santa Cruz alcalde had called for a performance of state sovereignty, when he requested that the police remove Mr. Myles from Uxbenka, whose occupation and destruction were prohibited by Belizean law.

In July 2015, the Director of Archaeology finally announced that he was preparing an eviction order and charges against Myles "for destruction of a Maya monument, in contravention of Belizean law."[17] However, Myles was never charged.[18]

UDP leaders had used a confrontation between a Creole man and a Maya community to discredit Maya customary tenure practices as racially discriminatory, a threat to law and order, and damaging to Belizean territorial sovereignty. However, Belizean media pointed out the contradiction between the state's "law and order" rhetoric vis-à-vis Santa Cruz leaders and its failure to charge Myles for destroying a national monument in violation of Belizean law.[19] Further, in June 2016, the Director of Public Prosecutions dropped all charges against the Santa Cruz leaders and Cristina Coc, citing a lack of evidence.[20] The criminalization of Maya customary tenure had failed.

A lawyer representing the Santa Cruz leaders highlighted another contradictory juxtaposition, comparing the state's dramatic show of force vis-à-vis Santa Cruz villagers with the government's nonresponse to Guatemalan civilian and military incursions into southern Belize. Speaking to the Belizean press, the lawyer noted that Belizean security forces never mobilized predawn raids to "go to the border and get the Guatemalans" who illegally occupied or harvested resources from Belizean lands.[21] In fact, the prime minister's assertions that Maya customary tenure threatened Belizean sovereignty were made in the context of increasingly belligerent Guatemalan incursions into Belizean territory.

Conservation nongovernmental organizations (NGOs) patrolling protected areas along Belize's western border had encountered rampant extraction of Belizean resources by Guatemalan civilians, which the NGOs reported to the Belizean press.[22] On multiple occasions, Guatemalan civilians had fired on joint NGO–Belize Defense Force patrols.[23] In 2014, Guatemalans illegally harvesting in the Caracol Archaeological Reserve shot and killed a Tourism Police Special Constable on duty at midday at Belize's largest Maya site and an important tourist attraction six miles east of the Belize-Guatemalan border.[24] Belizeans were outraged.

Further, following the 2008 agreement between Guatemalan and Belizean governments to submit Guatemala's claim to the International Court of Justice, Guatemalan military aggression had surged along the southern border.[25] In response to increased Guatemalan belligerence in the south, a group of civilians organized the Belize Territorial Volunteers (BTV) in 2012 to mark and monitor the southern and southwestern borders.[26] BTV members transited Belizean land and sea territories in the south, planting Belizean flags and singing the national anthem with the explicit aim of performing sovereignty over Belizean territory (see photo 9). In February 2015, the Guatemalan military intercepted a

Photo 9. Belize Territorial Volunteers on trip to the Sarstoon River. Credit: Wil Maheia, PGTV.

group of thirty-seven Belizeans traveling by boat on the Sarstoon River, forced them to a Guatemalan port, and held them prisoner overnight before releasing them.[27] Three months later, Guatemalan naval officers confronted members of the Belize Coast Guard on Sarstoon Island, claimed by Belize, and demanded that the coast guard leave the island. The Belizean prime minister ordered the coast guard to stand down.[28]

Angered by Guatemala's repeated aggression and the lack of response by the Belize Defense Force, the BTV announced plans to travel to Sarstoon Island in August 2015. The Minister of Foreign Affairs called the BTV plans "imprudent and potentially dangerous" and warned that the BDF would not protect them.[29] As the BTV's small flotilla entered the mouth of the Sarstoon River, Guatemalan navy vessels in Belizean waters blocked their passage, while Belizean military vessels anchored some distance away. Although the Guatemalans prevented the largest BTV boat from reaching Sarstoon Island, four smaller boats evaded the Guatemalan vessels to complete a triumphant circuit of the island in a dramatic performance of Belizean territorial sovereignty, carried on the evening news.[30] In response to the entry of Guatemalan military vessels into Belizean waters during this confrontation, the prime minister of Belize announced that his government had sent an "extremely strong" note of protest to Guatemala.[31] However, the Belizean press reported, Guatemala responded, "We do not recognize Belize's borders!"[32]

In the context of these incursions into Belizean territory by the Guatemalan military and armed Guatemalan civilians, the prime minister had chosen to focus on Maya customary tenure and Maya communal lands as threats to Belizean sovereignty, forcefully performing sovereignty by arresting Santa Cruz leaders, rather than confronting the Guatemalan military.

### Reinforcing "State Power"? The Executive versus the Courts

Following the signing of the consent order in April 2015, the CCJ convened periodic compliance hearings to oversee its implementation. Despite this oversight, Belizean elected leaders and political appointees delayed every step required of them. For example, the government took no action to implement the ruling during 2015. In 2016, as the first compliance hearing approached, the attorney general finally appointed a Maya Land Rights Commission (MLRC), chaired by former cabinet minister Lisel Alamilla. Alamilla announced that the MLRC would consult with all ethnic groups regarding how to implement the consent order, echoing the prime minister's assertion that all Belizeans must be consulted in defining Maya land rights.[33] Ignoring the steering committee established by the TAA to represent Maya communities collectively in negotiations, the MLRC engaged village council chairpersons in both Maya and non-Maya communities in Toledo, prioritizing the state's Village Council System over the Alcalde System.

When the TAA sent its president, Alfonso Cal, to a commission meeting to demand that the MLRC negotiate with the TAA steering committee, Alamilla called the police, who arrived promptly to remove Mr. Cal.[34] The Maya then turned to the CCJ, which ordered the MLRC to engage the TAA and MLA, as signatories to the consent order and complainants in the litigation that had produced the order.

Similarly, at a 2017 compliance hearing, the attorney representing the Maya complained that the government was in "flagrant violation" of the consent order's requirement that it prevent infringement on lands used by Maya villages.[35] In response, the CCJ ordered the government to establish procedures to address land disputes during the implementation process. The government failed to comply, resulting in repeated admonitions at subsequent compliance hearings. When the government finally submitted a proposal for a dispute resolution mechanism in 2018, the attorney representing the TAA and MLA pointed out that the government had failed to seek Maya feedback on the plan. The presiding CCJ judge reprimanded the government again and demanded that the MLRC consult with the TAA and MLA to revise the proposal. "I insist that we get some sort of results, as we cannot continue in the way that we have continued up to now," the judge admonished.[36] However, the government delayed creation of a dispute resolution process for two full years.

While the government stalled creation of a mechanism to address land conflicts during the implementation process, the CCJ directed the Maya to take their complaints to the lower courts. In response, the alcalde of Santa Cruz filed suit against the government for its failure to remove Mr. Myles from lands claimed by the village, and Jalacte Village and two of its members filed a second complaint against the Ministers of Agriculture and Works and the Attorney General for appropriating lands claimed by Jalacte in the process of paving a road from the Southern Highway west to the Guatemalan border. Claiming these lands as state property, the ministries had seized them without the consent of villagers and without compensation. In the Santa Cruz case, Supreme Court justice Michelle Arana determined that it was not possible to say whether the lands in question belonged to the village of Santa Cruz, because demarcation of Santa Cruz lands had not been completed and confirmed by both parties; further, Myles had finally left the village. The justice dismissed the case, rewarding the government for its delay in demarcating Santa Cruz lands.[37] However, in the Jalacte case, village residents testified that they held and managed the lands appropriated by the government ministries through Maya customary tenure practices, and Justice Arana determined that the ministries had violated the property protections of the Belize constitution, as well as the 2010 Supreme Court order and the CCJ consent order. She awarded the village of Jalacte and the individual claimants BZ$6.3 million in compensation, a sum that shocked political leaders.[38] In this instance, Maya claimants successfully used the courts to advance their land rights and punish the government for disregarding those rights, although the government is appealing the ruling.

In an additional example of foot-dragging, the MLRC ignored the CCJ order to negotiate with the TAA and MLA to develop a work plan to implement Maya land rights.[39] When the government failed to meet the original December 2017 deadline, the presiding CCJ justice expressed exasperation. Demanding that the government move faster to implement the consent order, he imposed a new deadline in March 2018.[40] The government submitted a plan by this deadline, but attorneys for the Maya advised the judge that the MLRC had not adequately engaged the Maya in its development. The judge ordered the commission to consult further with the TAA and MLA and report at the next compliance hearing how it had incorporated Maya input into the work plan.[41] In December 2018, more than three and a half years after the consent order, the Maya Land Rights Commission, the Toledo Alcaldes Association, and the Maya Leaders Alliance finally signed a work plan.

That plan committed the commission to develop and adopt a Free, Prior, and Informed Consent protocol to ensure Maya participation in decision making, using the Maya Consultation Framework as a starting point for negotiations (TMLRC et al. 2018). It specified that the Maya themselves would delimit the outer boundaries of Maya lands and territories. Third-party rights and interests within these lands would then be identified, and the MLA and TAA would consult with affected Maya communities to determine whether or not they would accept their continued occupation. The plan stipulated that Maya villages would be titled as separate entities, rather than in the aggregate. This reflected state actors' priority to avoid a single title for all Maya lands, rendering Maya communal lands more property-like and less territory-like, but it also aligned with the Maya priority of community control via the Alcalde System. The agreement also committed the MLRC to work with the MLA and TAA to draft legislation to implement Maya land rights and identify amendments to existing laws that would need to accompany the new legislation.

None of these actions have happened as specified in the plan or according to its timeline. Although the COVID-19 pandemic certainly slowed progress, and Alcalde System practices require potentially lengthy deliberations, government delay has played a significant role in extending the timeline. As this book goes to press, nearly a decade after the consent order was signed, neither land demarcation and titling nor the required legislation has been completed.

However, Maya communities continued their de facto control over most of the lands they claimed, and the TAA and MLA worked independently of the government to help communities demarcate their lands and prepare language for legislation to enshrine their rights in Belizean law. In response to the government's delay in implementing the consent order, MLA spokesperson Cristina Coc explained, "Implementation is us doing the things we are doing right now, engaging the communities. That way, when the government comes around, we will have a basis to talk."

With a grant from the Tenure Facility, an international financial mechanism based in Sweden with a mission to secure land and forest rights for Indigenous Peoples and local communities, the Julian Cho Society collaborated with the TAA to develop and apply procedures for demarcating and harmonizing village boundaries in communities seeking communal titles for village lands. By 2023, twenty-five communities had committed to communal land titles. One community had completed agreements with all neighboring villages regarding their shared boundaries, and eighteen additional villages had completed boundary agreements with at least one neighbor. With a second grant to continue this work, Maya communities are advancing toward the goal of preparing all the documentation required for titling. The TAA and MLA also drafted a Land Tenure Policy, which they submitted to the government as a starting point for negotiations over legislation. Meanwhile, the CCJ has pushed, chided, and admonished the Government of Belize to live up to the commitments to which it agreed in the consent order.

While state tactics to delay implementation of the consent order held open the possibility that the order would never be implemented, the Maya used the courts to demand actions from the executive branch. At compliance hearings with the CCJ, attorneys for the Maya repeatedly called out state actors for failing to comply with the consent order, and CCJ justices continually demanded action from the MLRC, even as they repeatedly extended their deadlines. Implementation of the consent order thus pitted the Belizean judicial system against the executive branch of the Belizean state. By using the courts—both the CCJ and the lower courts—to force the government to comply with its obligations, the Maya have achieved some advances, without yet accomplishing full implementation of the consent order. However, the Maya have also countered the state's delaying tactics by taking implementation into their own hands to the greatest degree possible.

## Divide and Rule?
### *Alcaldes versus Village Councils*

The government's strategy of delay provided additional time for state actors to pursue divide-and-rule tactics that pit Maya against Maya. During the UDP administration of Prime Minister Barrow, the MLRC had sidelined alcaldes, engaging village council chairs instead. However, the CCJ had ordered the commission to negotiate with the TAA and MLA as partners in implementation.

After November 2020 elections brought to power a Peoples United Party (PUP) government, Prime Minister John Briceño created new state structures to address Maya land rights. Briceño established a Ministry of Indigenous Peoples Affairs for the first time and appointed Greg Ch'oc to the newly created position of Commissioner of Indigenous Peoples' Affairs. In previous decades, Ch'oc had played key roles in the Maya movement in Belize. He led the Kekchi Council of Belize and served as a spokesperson for the Maya Leaders Alliance. He had also founded and directed the Sarstoon-Temash Institute for Indigenous Management (SATIIM), an NGO that comanaged the Sarstoon-Temash National Park. In that role, Ch'oc had pursued litigation against the government to prevent seismic testing for petroleum in the park. Later, Ch'oc had left Belize to complete a law degree. He had recently returned with his degree in hand. Now, as commissioner of Indigenous peoples' affairs, he would represent the government in negotiations with the Maya.

The new PUP minister of Indigenous peoples' affairs, Dolores Baldermos, repeatedly asserted the PUP's intention to accelerate implementation of the consent order. However, acceleration has been achieved by minimizing negotiations with the Maya. An attorney representing the Maya protested to the CCJ that the Briceño administration had developed a Free, Prior, and Informed Consent protocol and submitted it to the CCJ as the "final" version, without consulting the MLA and TAA. The Maya rejected multiple provisions in the protocol, including a shift from seeking Maya communities' "consent" to merely "consulting" Maya communities. Further, although the Maya Consultation Framework developed by the Toledo Alcaldes Association required outsiders to engage Maya villages through their alcaldes, the government's FPIC protocol required notification of both the alcalde and the village council chair regarding any proposed actions that might affect a community. This would elevate the Village Council System to a role equal to the Alcalde System, a move the TAA and MLA rejected. In lodging a complaint with the CCJ, MLA spokesperson Cristina Coc asserted, "Both the past administration and this new administration seem to think that an FPIC Protocol should not include the traditional governance system of the Maya community. Of course, that is contrary to self-determination and the process by which Indigenous communities are afforded the rights to determine their own representation."[42]

In addition to complaints lodged with the CCJ, the Toledo Alcaldes Association has devised other strategies to counter government efforts to divide Alcalde System and Village Council System leaders. For example, the TAA began to invite village council chairs and deputies to TAA assemblies to inform them of initiatives the alcaldes were developing and foster collaborations between the two sets of leaders. As a result, when government officials engage only village council leadership, those leaders often inform the alcaldes and invite their participation.

Further, while elected political officials have refused to recognize alcaldes as the primary representatives of their communities, a number of government departments have done exactly that. The Lands Department, the Forestry Department, the Belize Defense Force, and the police have all recently negotiated with the TAA to establish procedures that assign new responsibilities to alcaldes. For example, negotiations between Forestry and the TAA resulted in the transfer of authority to grant permits for villagers to extract logs to build houses from the Forestry Department to the village alcalde. As part of this agreement, the alcalde will notify the BDF, so that patrols will be able to recognize authorized versus unauthorized timber cutting.

### TAA versus NGOs

Since his appointment as commissioner of Indigenous peoples' affairs, Ch'oc has argued that the TAA is not a part of Maya customary tenure practices. The Alcalde System, he asserts, exists only at the village level, so the TAA cannot form part of that system. Instead, Ch'oc declared, as an "association," the TAA is like an NGO. Thus, he reasoned, if the TAA is allowed to play a role in decision-making in relation to lands, NGOs such as SATIIM, the Kekchi Council of Belize, and the Toledo Maya Cultural Council should play equivalent roles in decision-making.[43] Ch'oc's argument ignored the fact that the TAA was created by alcaldes acting on behalf of their communities to coordinate initiatives that extend across villages and has operated in this role—with communities' support—across several decades. The argument also ignores the differences in structure and dynamics between the TAA and Maya NGOs: no NGO has a similarly representative and responsive structure vis-à-vis Maya communities.

The TAA and MLA rejected this stance and complained to the CCJ, which reiterated that the government must negotiate with the Toledo Alcaldes Association and the Maya Leaders Alliance, because they were the claimants in the litigation that resulted in the consent order.[44] A larger issue is at stake, however: according to the common law, Ch'oc has no legal authority to judge the content of Maya customary tenure in his capacity as the government's commissioner for Indigenous peoples' affairs. Under the common law, Indigenous customary tenure is not subsumed within the common law and cannot be dictated by state actors. This is the very reason the courts demanded *negotiations* between state actors and Maya leaders to determine the interface of the state legal system and the Maya customary tenure system. Insofar as Ch'oc may be a member of a Maya community, he would have authority to express his opinions within the context of that community's decision-making. However, as the state's commissioner of Indigenous peoples' affairs, he has no authority to define the content of Maya customary tenure practices.

### Communal versus Individual Titles

Additionally, the divide that became publicly visible during litigation—between Maya who want communal lands managed through customary tenure practices and Maya who prefer private property through the state land tenure system—persists. For decades, development project personnel and political party representatives promoted private landholdings as the key to tenure security and access to credit, distributing leases or titles to individuals in many villages. These practices generated tensions between those with private parcels and those who rely only on communal lands. Administrations of both political parties have leveraged those tensions to undermine collective tenure and cultivate support for individual tenure.

However, recognizing divisions between supporters of collective titles and supporters of private titles, the TAA determined that all communities would make their own decisions to either participate in collective land demarcation and titling or operate within the state property system. This honored the principle of community self-governance that characterizes the Alcalde System. To date, twenty-five communities have decided to participate in the demarcation and titling of communal lands. Communities with the largest number of private leases have not opted to participate, either preferring private titles or waiting to see how the communal tenure process will play out.

## Analysis

Eight years after the CCJ consent order was signed, neither party has definitively "won" the implementation process. Each of the two sides has pursued tactics that support its own strategies and attempt to thwart the strategies of the other. The government of Belize has strategized to bring "the market" to bear on as much land and as many people as possible, resisting Maya land rights in defense of the state property system and its orientation toward rule through the market. On the other hand, the TAA and MLA have worked to secure collective tenure over their traditional lands and sustain the Alcalde System, seeking to hold open multiple possibilities for balancing market and nonmarket forms of governance, livelihoods, and relationships.

If rights reinforce the power of the state as the entity that enforces—or strategically fails to enforce—rights, the Belizean state has used this power effectively: the consent order has not yet been implemented. However, the state has not "won." Elected officials struggle to perform "the sovereign Belizean state," beset by challenges from within and without. Guatemalan military forces and civilians aggressively infringe on Belizean territory, while Belizean political leaders send letters of protest to their Guatemalan counterparts. In response, the activism of the Belize Territorial Volunteers represents a rebuke of the Belizean government as well as a challenge to the Guatemalan military. Further, the judicial branch of government itself has thwarted the delaying tactics of the executive branch. In compliance hearing after compliance hearing, CCJ justices have admonished the executive to comply with the consent order. While the lower courts have produced both wins and losses for political leaders, the executive's loss in the Jalacte case came at a significant price. The Belizean state is thus divided against itself, with the executive branch seeking ways to avoid complying with what the judicial branch has declared are its constitutional obligations.

On the other hand, if the state is divided against itself, Maya communities are not unitary, either. Distinct subjectivities—homo economicus versus the collective culture-bearing subject of Indigenous rights—coexist within Mopan and Q'eqchi' individuals and Maya communities as well as between them. Members of Maya communities have deliberated and debated among themselves how to balance, reconcile, or choose between these competing subjectivities and the distinct futures they offer. Relative to Indigenous peoples who have lost control over their lands, Maya communities in Toledo enjoy two critical advantages: they retain control of much of the lands they have traditionally used, and they continue to manage their relationships with these lands and with one another through their own procedures and principles, without relying on the Belizean state. The strength of the Alcalde System at the core of Maya customary tenure is crucial to their struggles to sustain their communal lands and define their own futures, and Maya leaders and communities have successfully defended these practices.

# Conclusion

This book began by offering a narrow definition of neoliberal government as rule through "the market," distinguishing neoliberal government from the practice of sovereignty, and positioning the production of rights as a strategy to limit the power of the sovereign. The assertion that markets, states and their sovereignties, and rights are all objects that must be constructed was key to an analysis that explored their production in Belize. Further, throughout the events narrated in this book, sovereignty imposed in the name of the state through the use or threat of force, rights claims that attempt to constrain state power, and government through the market appear as "disparate logics" that nevertheless "overlap, intersect, lean on each other, challenge each other, and struggle with each other" (Foucault 2008:313). I conclude with an analysis of these intersections and their significance.

## Sovereignty and Markets

In southern Belize, state actors have often performed sovereignty in the service of "government through the market": the sovereign governs *for* the market to facilitate the operation of government *through* the market. Conservation NGOs played on government ministers' market rationalities to persuade them to protect the Cockscomb, promising that a jaguar sanctuary would attract ecotourists, expanding and diversifying the Belizean economy. In response, cabinet ministers performed sovereignty in declaring a wildlife sanctuary in the Cockscomb, evicting the community of Quam Bank and restricting access to subsistence resources for other communities near the sanctuary. The Ministry of Natural Resources immediately devolved management of the sanctuary to the Belize Audubon Society, whose U.S. conservation NGO allies conducted the conduct of government ministers by offering to fund ecotourism infrastructure. Subsequently, the implementation of ecotourism delegated the conduct of conduct to "the market." Cabinet ministers' exercise of sovereignty to govern *for* the market secured the conditions in which the Cockscomb's forests, state officials themselves, communities on the

Cockscomb's perimeter, and even Audubon Society staff could be governed *through* the market. Subjection to market rationalities has thus been the fundamental centerpiece of neoliberal environmental government in Belize. To the degree that these diverse actors were—or became—subjects of interest, they came to conduct their own conduct through the application of market rationality, considering the anticipated leisure expenditures of international ecotourists, whose preferences were collected and aggregated by experts to constitute "the market." Thus, when Maya Centre residents, motivated by both market and rights subjectivities, blocked tourists' access to the sanctuary, the Forestry Department head threatened to exercise sovereign power once again, to govern *for* the market by reopening the sanctuary's tropical nature to tourists. Meanwhile, BAS leaders continued the strategy of governing villagers *through* the market, engaging villagers' market subjectivities—expanded with the creation of the sanctuary, which enclosed resources on which they had depended for subsistence—by offering greater access to ecotourism revenues to win their renewed support for the sanctuary.

Similarly, over decades of development projects in Toledo, elected officials, government department heads, and development project administrators governed *for* the market, pursuing strategies to incorporate both land and people into markets. In fact, actors who performed "the state" in Toledo District seem to have prioritized governing for the market over other forms of sovereign intervention, such as national defense (against Guatemala) or law enforcement (against Mr. Myles). Some Maya farmers who received private parcels of land now reject communal lands, prioritizing the market rationalities that have "gotten a hold on them." Others, animated by rights- and culture-bearing subjectivities, advocate for communal lands.

## Rights and Sovereignty

The relationship between sovereignty and rights is paradoxical: even as rights challenge or limit the sovereign power of the state, they also reinforce state power, insofar as they rely on the state for their enforcement. However, this "both/and" relationship between rights and sovereignty is complicated by recognition of the state as an object to be constructed rather than a given, which renders the state and state power potentially more precarious than critiques of rights have recognized. If rights *claimants* never occupy "a simple position of mastery" with respect to the law and rights (Golder 2015), the Maya lands cases call into question the degree of mastery over the law and rights exercised by the actors who perform the state. Acknowledging the challenges confronting both parties, my analysis assessed the effects of the strategies and tactics state agents deployed to constrain Indigenous people's options as well as Indigenous leaders' strategies to expand Maya communities' possibilities.

Both inter-American and Belizean judicial bodies repeatedly rejected the arguments advanced by attorneys for the government, ruling in favor of the Maya. Attorneys speaking for the Belizean state acknowledged the obligations of the

Belizean government to the Belize constitution and the common law, but they sought to define those obligations in ways that supported political leaders' contention that the Mopan and Q'eqchi' are not Indigenous peoples. However, guided by international law (ILO 169), historical evidence provided by expert witnesses, and legal scholars' interpretations of the common-law doctrine of native title, judges rejected the state's argument on the criteria for Indigeneity as "unreasonable." Indeed, the more emphatically attorneys for the Belizean government insisted on their criteria for Indigeneity and their version of history, the more unreasonable these appeared to judges.

Judges in both inter-American and Belizean systems also determined that the Belizean state is subject to obligations defined by international and inter-American human rights law and the inter-American jurisprudence on Indigenous rights, despite the efforts of government attorneys to subordinate these sources of law to the Belize constitution and the common law. In addition, judges in Belizean courts recognized yet another source of legal obligation for Belizean state actors: Maya customary tenure practices. The Belizean courts concurred with the Inter-American Commission on Human Rights that Maya communities' own customary practices for managing communal lands and relations among community members are the source of Maya collective property, rather than the state property system. The courts have insisted that the Belizean state accept Maya customary tenure practices as the source of Maya collective property and, as sovereign, recognize and protect those practices and the communal property to which they give rise.

Judges ordered the sovereign Belizean state to engage Maya communities as collective legal subjects and to *negotiate* with representatives of the Maya the interface between the Belizean legal system and Maya customary law, between state and Maya land tenure systems. Thus, despite state foot-dragging, Mopan and Q'eqchi' pursuit of Indigenous rights to lands challenges—and is reshaping—the production of the state, sovereignty, law, and property in Belize. Rather than asserting sovereignty for themselves, Mopan and Q'eqchi' land claims are recasting the options available to state actors to perform sovereignty.

These outcomes demonstrate that the state does not enjoy mastery over the law and rights in the process of adjudication: the courts found arguments articulated by attorneys for the Maya more compelling than the arguments advanced by lawyers representing the government. Neither does the state—either the executive or the judicial branch—exercise mastery over the implementation phase of litigation: the courts make demands on the executive but struggle to enforce compliance; the executive resists, delays, and maneuvers but is continually rebuked by judges demanding that political leaders comply with their constitutional obligations.

## The Right to Property and the Right to Culture in Relation to Neoliberal Government and Sovereignty

The creation and defense of property emerged as a critical point of intersection across markets, sovereignty, and rights. The production of property is a principal means of producing the state, its territory, and its sovereignty; by authorizing the creation of property, the state affirms its existence and its power. Although neoliberal government subordinates "the state" to "the market," state guarantees for property are nonetheless deemed essential to the operation of the market. However, the inter-American jurisprudence on Indigenous rights to lands also built on the right to property, deployed by Indigenous peoples to secure control over their collectively held lands with the objective of keeping them out of land markets. In the Maya lands cases, the courts determined that constitutional guarantees for property rights also protect indigenous collective property. However, by identifying the practice of Maya customary tenure, rather than the law of the state, as the source of Maya collective property, judges interrupted the recursive authorization of the state as authorizer of property and disrupted a significant mechanism for the co-construction of state, sovereignty, and territory.

The critical conduct of rights by Indigenous advocates internationally and by Q'eqchi' and Mopan communities in Belize has generated additional creative, disruptive possibilities. Both internationally and in Belize, the production of collective Indigenous rights to property via the right to culture challenges both sovereignty and rule through the market. UN and OAS member states rejected Indigenous demands for self-determination, with the aim of protecting the territorial integrity of existing states. However, those states accepted Indigenous activists' territorializing vision of Indigenous cultures, elaborated in the process of drafting declarations, applying human rights conventions, and arguing court cases. This acceptance resulted in a jurisprudence on Indigenous rights that positions Indigenous peoples as collective political subjects with rights to collectively held lands, who challenge the sovereign state from within the national territory. These collective political subjects have produced their own property through the practice of their own cultures, outside the state property system. Now, judges are requiring the state to recognize and accommodate both Indigenous communal property and the customary tenure system that has produced it.

The territorializing vision of Indigenous culture on which Indigenous rights to land were constructed also challenges efforts to rule through the market. This vision of Indigenous cultures decenters the market and its atomistic market-rational subjects. Indigenous cultures, as defined by Indigenous advocates in international law, and Maya customary tenure practices, as defined in Belize, introduce a distinct logic or ethic that exists in significant tension with market rationality. Maya customary tenure practices accord priority to subsistence security and center nonmarket relationships. Collective land rights and the practice of Maya customary tenure sustain possibilities for both lives and livelihoods outside of market relations. They offer protection for Maya individuals and communities from the vulnerabilities associated with participation in markets, and they prevent Maya lands—and to some extent Maya labor—from becoming commodities. Further, the customary tenure practices that produce Maya communal property also embed Q'eqchi' and Mopan individuals within a "web of reciprocal and interdependent relationships" with the land, with members of their communities, and with other beings with whom they share the land (MLA and TAA 2019:19). These relationships of respect and conviviality are the basis for Mopan and Q'eqchi' practices of community.

Nonetheless, the incompatible, disparate rationalities of markets and Indigenous rights do not prevent Maya individuals and communities from engaging, even embracing, both. In the past, communities' management of collectively held lands through the Alcalde System has not prevented individual control of parcels of land or engagement with markets and market rationalities through the cultivation of cash crops. Maya customary tenure itself has allowed individuals to hold parcels across time. Moreover, decades of attempts by cabinet ministers, area representatives, and development project staff to privatize Maya reservation lands has resulted in a patchwork of individually held leases across Maya lands, many of them held by Maya. At the same time, leaseholders typically continue to rely on access to their communities' collectively held lands to meet their households' needs. Thus, the culture-bearing subjects of Indigenous rights are not only rights- and culture-bearing subjects. They are also, at the same time, market-rational subjects of interest. And vice versa.

The fault line that sets atomized market subjects apart from and against the collective culture-bearing subjects of Indigenous rights does not only run between individuals and communities; that fault line also runs *through* individuals and communities. Individuals become homo economicus to the degree—*but only to the degree*—that market rationality "gets a hold" on them (Foucault 2008:253), and Mopan and Q'eqchi' farmers have long been market subjects, to a degree. However, the "practices of freedom" manifested through Maya customary tenure practices open spaces beyond the market, sustaining possibilities for "being otherwise," and perhaps constraining the degree to which market rationality gets a hold on Mopan and Q'eqchi' people.

To extend the metaphor, such faults both separate and connect, break apart and fuse together, simultaneously. The continuous pressure exerted in opposing directions along these fault lines generates tensions that are unlikely to be resolved once and for all. Rather, these tensions generate opposing possibilities that will require persistent struggle, negotiation, and creativity, within and between individuals, families, and communities and between communities and state actors. The theoretical framework offered by this book—focusing on the intersections among practices of neoliberal government through the market, state sovereignty, and Indigenous rights-claiming—illuminates the tensions and challenges that Q'eqchi' and Mopan navigate, as they attempt to sustain multiple options for individuals and communities to balance market and rights subjectivities. It bears repeating that the power of Indigenous peoples to determine for themselves how to balance market engagements with relations of respect is a critical aspect of self-determination.

These same tensions—between market and nonmarket rationalities, between autonomy and engagement with state institutions—characterize Indigenous struggles across Latin America. Further, states throughout Latin American confront tensions between the imperative to perform and expand sovereignty and incitements to govern through the market. This is the case whether or not they also must respond to rights demands from their Indigenous citizens. Thus, I argue, the theoretical framework developed and applied in this analysis—focusing on the intersections of neoliberal government through the market, efforts to perform state sovereignty, and Indigenous rights-claiming—offers insights that can illuminate the interplay between the strategies and dilemmas that shape both Indigenous mobilization and state responses across the region.

# Glossary of Non-English Terms

**alcalde.** Spanish; traditional leader of Maya communities in southern Belize, selected by the community.

**cho'och.** Q'eqchi'; the land.

**encomienda.** Spanish; a mechanism that allocated the right to extract forced labor from native peoples to Spanish colonizers.

**milpa.** Spanish/Nahuatl; rainy-season corn plot cleared and cultivated through a form of swidden agriculture, which typically includes a range of additional cultivated species as well.

**milpero.** Spanish; swidden farmer.

**Mundo Maya.** Spanish; Maya World.

**naleb'.** Q'eqchi'; respect as action, a way of living and being in relation to others.

**raal cho'och.** Q'eqchi'; people of the land.

**reducciones.** Spanish; literally, reductions; towns created during the colonial period by capturing and concentrating Indigenous people to facilitate colonial control.

**repartimiento.** Spanish; forced labor contracts imposed on Indigenous communities to meet the labor needs of colonial elites.

**tzik.** Mopan; respect

**Tzuultaq'a.** Q'eqchi'; literally, hills and valleys; refers to the nonhuman persons recognized as keepers of the hills and valleys.

**Witz-hok.** Mopan; literally, hills and valleys; refers to the nonhuman persons recognized as keepers of the hills and valleys.

# Notes

### CHAPTER 1 — COMPETING RATIONALITIES OF RULE

1. Grounded in Marxist political economy, this strand of analysis begins with the second contradiction of capitalism: capitalism inevitably tends to destroy the ecological base on which its reproduction depends, leading to both ecological and accumulation crises (O'Connor 1998). From this theoretical vantage point, conservation organizations should logically oppose capitalism, because it is inherently destructive of the environment (Buscher et al. 2012:6; Igoe and Brockington 2007:433).

2. This second strand of analysis sometimes reified capitalism as a coherent object with a singular logic that causes things to happen or even an agent pursuing strategic interests, suggesting that "conservation and capitalism are remaking the world in partnership" (Brockington, Duffy, and Igoe 2008:15). This reification of "capitalism" as an agent obscures the actions of actual agents who govern for the market (Mitchell 2002:246, 303).

3. This was Foucault's response to critics who took issue with his focus on nonstate practices of discipline and rule.

4. Although some scholars have viewed natural rights as self-evident facts (Donnelly 2003), anthropologists have interrogated the production of rights, casting "natural rights" as a social construction rather than accepting their "naturalness" at face value (Merry 1996; Niezen 2003; Riles 2000).

5. My approach thus contrasts with Robert Fletcher's use of the more general meaning of the term (Fletcher 2010).

6. Foucault asserts that the theory of the price-value relationship constructs "the market" as an object that reveals "something like a truth." The "natural mechanisms of the market" generate a "standard of truth which enables us to discern which governmental practices are correct and which are erroneous." The market constitutes a "site of veridiction." Political economy thus "pointed out to government where it had to go to find the principle of truth of its own governmental practice" (Foucault 2008:32).

7. Through the invisible hand, political economy "steals away" from the sovereign "precisely that which is emerging as the essential element of a society's life, namely economic processes" (Foucault 2008:282). Homo economicus says to the sovereign, "You must not." But "he does not say: You must not, because I have rights." Rather, homo economicus tells the sovereign, "You must not because you cannot.... You cannot because you do not know, and you do not know because you cannot know" (Foucault 2008:283). The invisibility

of "the totality of the economic process" means that there can be "no sovereign in economics" (Foucault 2008:283).

8. Though Foucault distinguished between German and American versions of neoliberalism in the late twentieth century, he identified connections between them: both were reactions to Keynesianism; both rejected state intervention in the economy; and people and theories passed between them (Foucault 2008:79). My analysis focuses on themes common to both, which derive from their common origin in liberalism.

9. The market depends for its "truth" on homo economicus's free pursuit of interests, while the social contract requires the subject of right to relinquish some rights to the state (Foucault 2008:271–274, 278). Thus, Foucault concludes, the market and the social contract function in exactly opposite ways, and the subject of interest and the subject of right are governed by "incommensurable" logics (Foucault 2008:274, 276).

### CHAPTER 2 — HISTORIES OF BELIZE

1. One sign of this control was the lack of fortifications around settlements in this region, compared with the fortifications Cortés found in other regions, whose inhabitants sought to repel Itzaj attacks (Jones 1998:38). Further, the Itzaj leader informed Cortés that, prior to his arrival, he had received news about Spanish activities along the Caribbean coast, from "vassals" who worked cacao orchards nearer to the coast and merchants who traveled between the Itzaj capital and the coast (Jones 1998:35).

2. Spanish strategy for controlling the labor of Indigenous people included "reducing" scattered Indigenous communities into larger towns (*reducciones*), where they could be more closely supervised by colonial officials and clergy.

3. This evidence takes the form of the legend that accompanied a map that has been lost. Produced in the early 1700s, the legend refers to "a native 'province'" in the southern coastal plain of Belize, where a member of the old Itzaj ruling family ruled over Mopan and Chols (Jones 1998:418).

4. When the colonial government exerted its claim to all lands between the Hondo and the Sarstoon that were not already in private hands, most of these lands lay south of the Sibun. Further, in the latter half of the 1800s, a logging interest with extensive holdings in the south went bankrupt and forfeited these properties to the Crown (Wainwright 2007:47–48).

5. This dominant narrative has not taken notice of evidence that both Guatemala and Britain sought to perform sovereignty in southern Belize before 1859. Dr. Angel Cal, a Belizean historian, has discussed these efforts in several venues, including a morning television show (*Wake Up Belize!* Channel 5, October 9, 2018; https://www.youtube.com/watch?v=ym4G78Alk2g, accessed 3/8/20). The evidence Dr. Cal has brought to light also indicates a Maya presence in southern Belize during the first half of the nineteenth century, which contradicts the dominant historical narrative in Belize.

6. As a result of the language determinacy of this model of ethnicity, language shift across generations from Yucatec to Spanish in the north led many to adopt Spanish/Mestizo identities (Brockmann 1977, 1985; Medina 1997).

### CHAPTER 3 — NGO GOVERNMENT OF THE STATE

1. Prior to this time, a Tourism Bureau existed, but its activity was limited to collection of the hotel tax.

2. This includes broadleaf forest, pine forest, and mangrove swamps (Barry 1992:130). Official data on forest cover have been criticized by environmental consultants as inaccurate and inflated (Hartshorn et al. 1984:93); however, subsequent assessments, utilizing new techniques to increase accuracy, asserted similar numbers (Jacobs and Castañeda 1998:v, 12).

3. At the time, the Wildlife Conservation Society was called Wildlife Conservation International, based at the Bronx Zoo. Its name changed later. For clarity, I use its current name throughout.

4. Launched as a branch of the Florida Audubon Society, the BAS became independent in 1973 (Waight and Lumb 1999:1).

5. Belize has a Westminster model of government. The small size of its legislative branch means that a majority of ruling party area representatives are assigned ministerial portfolios. There are few "backbenchers." As a result, most policies are set by the cabinet, which can typically impose its collective will in the legislature to confirm cabinet policy decisions.

6. In 1987, the UDP government issued a letter reiterating, "The Belize Audubon Society as a body, is authorized to work along with the Forestry Department of the Government of Belize in the management and protection of any of the designated areas specified by the Minister" (Waight and Lumb 1999:33).

7. "Loosely Speaking," *Beacon*, March 3, 1987.

8. "US$25,000 for Cockscomb from the World Wildlife Foundation (WWF-US) to assist in the development and management of the CBWS!" *Belize Audubon Society Newsletter*, Vol. 19, No. 8, October 1987.

9. "US$120,000 from WWF-US," *Belize Audubon Society Newsletter*, Vol. 22, No. 2, 1990.

10. "WWF-US visit to Belize," *Belize Audubon Society Newsletter*, Vol. 19, No. 11, 1988.

11. "Address by the Deputy Prime Minister and Minister of Natural Resources," *Belize Times*, November 18, 1990.

12. This portrayal of the "Maya World" is a manifestation of what Quetzil Castañeda (1997) has described as the self-interested construction of "the Maya" and "Maya Culture" over the last century through interactions among archaeologists, who produce and interpret ancient Mayan cities as ruins *and* tourist attractions; state officials, who seek to capitalize on "the Maya" for their own political or economic ends; tourism marketers and entrepreneurs, who deploy stylized narratives and images to promote "the Maya," based on their perceptions of what tourists want; and tourists, who travel to consume the Maya otherness that marketing materials construct.

While the Mundo Maya brochure portrays "the Maya" as "possessors" of the Maya World, both Maya and scholars have criticized the Mundo Maya apparatus for excluding Maya themselves from project planning and from most of the benefits of tourism to the Maya World (Brown 1999; van den Berghe 1995).

13. "PACT Passed into Law," *Belize Audubon Society Newsletter*, Vol. 28, No. 1, 1996.

14. Highlighting the state's prioritization of economic diversification and expansion, not ecotourism or sustainable tourism per se, the state also began to court cruise lines to tap into another segment of the tourism market. This also required relatively little state expenditure on infrastructure, because cruise lines themselves would pay for the development of port facilities to accommodate cruise passengers, as long as they could control access to that infrastructure. Cruise tourism grew from 0.2 percent of total tourism in 1988 to 72 percent of total tourist arrivals in 2008 (BTB 1998, 2008). The tensions between ecotourism and cruise tourism strategies are obvious and unresolved. The state's pursuit of both types of tourism reflects its prioritization of income generation and emphasizes that protected areas must generate tourism revenues to maintain government support.

CHAPTER 4 — GOVERNING THROUGH THE MARKET

1. "Tropical forests and Their Conservation Published, a CBWS Education Manual," *Belize Audubon Society Newsletter*, Vol. 26, No. 1, 1994.

2. Michael Cepek warns that the analytic of governmentality "risks overestimating the grip that governmental rationalities have on governmental agents themselves" (Cepek

2011:512). The scientists engaged in the project Cepek studied were able to see past their commitments to scientific knowledge and methods to recognize Cofan perspectives and priorities. However, the Audubon Society's embrace of ecotourism as a strategy to fund protected areas conservation rendered the BAS itself materially subject to markets for tropical nature.

### CHAPTER 5 — CONTESTED HISTORIES AND HISTORIES OF CONTESTATION IN SOUTHERN BELIZE

1. Anthropological analyses from previous decades have used a range of terms for these beings or forces—deities, gods, spirits—that reflect the terms used in the field of anthropology during the times these analyses were produced (see Wilk 1997). Accordingly, Stinson's (2017) designation of the Tzuultaq'a as other-than-human persons reflects contemporary anthropological approaches.

2. "Esquivel Fires 860!" *Amandala*, December 24, 1995, 1.

3. Petition to IACHR (August 7, 1998), para. 36.

4. All mappers were men. On the gendered nature of this mapping project, see Wainwright and Bryan (2009). For a critique of the overall premises of the project, see also Wainwright (2007).

5. Petition to IACHR (August 7, 1998), para. 75.

### CHAPTER 6 — THE PRODUCTION OF INDIGENOUS RIGHTS

1. Foreshadowing conflicts to come, however, the 1960 declaration also contained language whose purpose was to limit the exercise of this right for peoples who would be deemed "internal colonies." Its Article 6 proclaimed any disruption of the territorial integrity of an existing country "incompatible with the purposes and principles of the Charter of the United Nations." This introduced the qualification that only colonies separated from the colonizing country by "blue" or "salt" water qualified for independent statehood; as "internal colonies," indigenous peoples would be blocked from exercising this right.

2. UNDRIP, https://www.un.org/development/desa/indigenouspeoples/wp-content/uploads/sites/19/2018/11/UNDRIP_E_web.pdf, accessed March 7, 2020.

3. UNDRIP, https://www.un.org/development/desa/indigenouspeoples/wp-content/uploads/sites/19/2018/11/UNDRIP_E_web.pdf, accessed March 7, 2020.

4. Karen Engle suggests that Latin American states did not forcefully challenge the assertion of self-determination in the UN Declaration, because they did not see it as a threat to themselves; indigenous groups in Latin America were not making such claims. When the UNDRIP was finally passed by the UN General Assembly in 2007, all but one Latin American state voted in favor; Colombia abstained (Engle 2010:48).

5. In fact, a key concession that finally allowed the UNDRIP to be brought to a vote in the UN General Assembly in 2007 was the addition of Article 46, which constrained Article 3's affirmation of indigenous peoples' right to self-determination, stating that the declaration should not be "construed as authorizing or encouraging any action which would dismember or impair, totally or in part, the territorial integrity" of existing states (Engle 2010:5).

6. A majority of Latin American countries ratified ILO 169: Bolivia, Colombia, Paraguay, Costa Rica, Peru, Honduras, Guatemala, and Ecuador ratified the convention during the 1990s; Argentina, Brazil, Venezuela, Chile, and Nicaragua ratified during the 2000s (ILO n.d.).

7. Indigenous advocates were able to use the ICCPR to pursue indigenous rights, because its Optional Protocol permits nonstate parties to bring claims against states that have ratified the protocol.

8. Although the ICCPR also enshrines the right of "peoples" to "self-determination," the HRC did not apply this right to indigenous peoples. Instead, the General Comment affirmed that the right to culture is not meant to threaten the sovereignty and territorial integrity of a state party (UN HRC 1994).

9. Those countries are Argentina, Barbados, Bolivia, Brazil, Chile, Colombia, Costa Rica, Dominican Republic, Ecuador, El Salvador, Guatemala, Haiti, Honduras, Mexico, Nicaragua, Panama, Paraguay, Peru, Suriname, and Uruguay.

10. American Declaration on the Rights and Duties of Man (1948), https://www.cidh.oas.org/basicos/english/basic2.american%20declaration.htm.

11. American Declaration on the Rights and Duties of Man (1948), https://www.cidh.oas.org/basicos/english/basic2.american%20declaration.htm.

12. *Awas Tingni v. Nicaragua*, Inter-A. Ct. H.R. (Ser. C) No. 79 [2001], para. 145 (hereafter, cited as *Awas Tingni*).

13. *Awas Tingni*, para. 146.

14. *Awas Tingni*, para. 146.

15. *Awas Tingni*, para. 149, emphasis added.

16. *Awas Tingni*, para. 164.

17. *Maya Indigenous Communities of Toledo District v. Belize*, Case No. 12.053 (Belize), Inter-Am C.H.R. Report No. 40/04, October 12, 2004, OAS Doc. OEA/Ser. L/V/II.122, Doc. 5 rev. 1 (2005), para. 8 (hereafter, cited as *Maya Indigenous Communities*).

18. Petition to the IACHR, para. 117.

19. Petition to the IACHR, para. 92.

20. Petition to the IACHR, para. 101–106.

21. Petition to the IACHR, para. 109.

22. *Maya Indigenous Communities*, para. 21; Petition to IACHR, para 12.

23. Petition to IACHR, para 12.

24. Petition to IACHR, para. 18–19.

25. *Maya Indigenous Communities*, para. 24.

26. Petition to IACHR, para. 27.

27. *Maya Indigenous Communities*, para. 73.

28. *Maya Indigenous Communities*, para. 93.

29. *Maya Indigenous Communities*, para. 93, citing www.belize.gov.bz.

30. *Maya Indigenous Communities*, n. 80.

31. *Maya Indigenous Communities*, para. 86–88.

32. *Maya Indigenous Communities*, para. 117, emphasis added.

33. *Maya Indigenous Communities*, para. 124.

34. *Maya Indigenous Communities*, para. 127.

35. *Maya Indigenous Communities*, para. 125.

36. *Maya Indigenous Communities*, para. 129.

37. *Maya Indigenous Communities*, para. 193, 194.

38. *Maya Indigenous Communities*, para. 197.

39. Beyond the scope of this study, a range of discourses had shaped what judges were "willing and able to hear," from the centuries-old trope of the "noble savage" (Bens 2020:20, 111) to the more recent figure of the "ecological Indian" (Conklin and Graham 1995; Ramos 1994). Beth Conklin and Laura Graham (1995) and Jonas Bens (2020) critique these discourses as dangerous and limiting for indigenous peoples.

40. Their efforts offer an example of "subaltern cosmopolitan legalities," forms of legal innovation by marginalized groups that link locally grounded orders to international legal orders (Santos and Rodriguez-Garavito Arenas 2005:2–3).

41. Foucault continues, "The ethico-political choice we have to make every day is to determine which is the main danger" (Foucault 1982:232).

### CHAPTER 7 — ADVANCING THE MAYA CLAIM THROUGH THE BELIZEAN JUDICIAL SYSTEM

1. Students in the Indigenous Peoples Law and Policy Program at the University of Arizona's Rogers College of Law, where James Anaya was then appointed, collaborated in drafting the brief, based on the IACHR petition (Anaya 2008).

2. Belize Constitution, Section 3(d) and Article 17(1), cited in *Cal et al. v. Attorney General* (Claims Nos. 171 and 172 of 2007); Belize S. Ct. Judgment of 18 October 2007, Appendix B: para. 3 (hereafter, cited as *Maya Land Rights*).

3. Skeleton argument of claimants, para. 55.

4. "Indigenous Peoples Demand Special Mention in the Belize Constitution," *Amandala*, January 30, 2000, 6; "The Indigenous People of Belize: Joint Communique," *Amandala*, February 6, 2000, 4B.

5. Skeleton argument of claimants, para. 54, citing *Maya Indigenous Communities*, paras. 127, 131.

6. Skeleton argument of claimants, para. 31.

7. Skeleton argument of claimants, para. 56, citing *Maya Indigenous Communities*, para. 155.

8. Skeleton argument of the claimants, para. 67.

9. Skeleton argument of claimants, Appendix C, para. 1.

10. Skeleton argument of claimants, para. 71.

11. Skeleton argument of claimants, paras. 33–34, citing *Mabo v. Queensland II*, (1992) 175 C.L.R. 1, paras. 58, 61, vol. 2, Tab 14.

12. Skeleton argument of claimants, Appendix C, paras. 5–6.

13. Because of the copious amount of evidence submitted in written form, the chief justice did not allow oral testimony that would repeat written submissions. Thus, only three witnesses gave oral testimony for the claimants. Greg Ch'oc represented the Maya Leaders Alliance. S. James Anaya spoke on the obligations of the Belizean state in relation to international law. Richard Wilk, anthropologist, also provided oral testimony, because the government's lawyer had introduced into evidence an article published by him (Grandia 2009).

14. Skeleton argument of claimants, para. 16; Second Affidavit of Richard R. Wilk, para. 62.

15. Skeleton argument of claimants, paras. 18–19.

16. Affidavit of Higinio Teul, para. 8.

17. Skeleton argument of claimants, paras. 104, 113, 117.

18. Defendant's Skeleton Argument and Submissions, 11.

19. Defendant's Skeleton Argument and Submissions.

20. Casting Belizean territory as "empty" resonates with "terra nullius" justifications of colonial conquest. The expansion of rights regimes since the 1960s has eroded the acceptability of these arguments.

21. Defendant's Skeleton Argument and Submissions, 17.

22. "GOB Lawyer Claims Maya Case Threatens Belize's Sovereignty!," *Amandala*, June 22, 2007.

23. Second affidavit of Grant Jones, para. 8.

24. Second affidavit of Grant Jones, para. 8.

25. First affidavit of Richard R. Wilk, para. 12.

26. First affidavit of Grant Jones, para. 53.

27. First affidavit of Grant Jones, paras. 59–60.
28. First affidavit of Grant Jones, para. 63.
29. First affidavit of Grant Jones, para. 65.
30. Skeleton argument of claimants, para. 8.
31. Skeleton argument of claimants, Appendix C, para. 1.
32. Skeleton argument of claimants, Appendix C: Protection of Indigenous Customary Property Rights by the Common Law, para. 13.
33. Skeleton argument of claimants, Appendix C: Protection of Indigenous Customary Property Rights by the Common Law, para. 14, citing *R. v. Cote* [1996] 3 S.C.R. 139 (Can), para. 53 (Lamer CJ) [vol. 3, tab 13].
34. *Maya Land Rights*, para. 21.
35. *Maya Land Rights*, paras. 21–22.
36. *Maya Land Rights*, paras. 21–22.
37. *Maya Land Rights*, para. 66.
38. *Maya Land Rights*, para 62.
39. *Maya Land Rights*, paras. 40, 51–59.
40. *Maya Land Rights*, paras. 42, 101.
41. *Maya Land Rights*, para. 120.
42. *Maya Land Rights*, paras. 43, 45.
43. *Maya Land Rights*, paras. 43, 45, 48.
44. *Maya Land Rights*, para. 80.
45. *Maya Land Rights*, para. 79.
46. *Maya Land Rights*, paras. 109–110.
47. *Maya Land Rights*, para. 113.
48. A key concession by indigenous representatives had allowed the UNDRIP to be brought to a vote in the UN General Assembly in 2007. Article 3, which affirmed indigenous peoples' right of self-determination, had been constrained by the addition of Article 46, which provides that the declaration should not be "construed as authorizing or encouraging any action which would dismember or impair totally or in part, the territorial integrity or political unity of sovereign and independent States" (Engle 2010:5).
49. *Maya Land Rights*, para. 132; Medina 2016.
50. *Maya Land Rights*, para. 131.
51. *Maya Land Rights*, para. 127.
52. *Maya Land Rights*, para. 131.
53. *Maya Land Rights*, para. 134.
54. SGF/40/01/08(23), cited in *MLA et al. v. Attorney General et al.*, para. 60.
55. The government had never sanctioned the use of the Alcalde System in Stann Creek District, and the Alcalde System was central to the current claim and previous rulings regarding Maya Customary Tenure.
56. *MLA et al. v. Attorney General et al.*, para. 19.
57. *MLA et al. v. Attorney General et al.*, para. 19.
58. *MLA et al. v. Attorney General et al.*, para. 20.
59. *Court of Appeal Judgment*, para. 129.
60. "Toledo Cacao Growers Demanding Private Titles," Channel 7 News, Belize, February 17, 2009; "TCGA Opposes Communal Land Rights Suit," Channel 5 News, Belize, February 18, 2009.
61. "TCGA Opposes Communal Land Rights Suit," Channel 5 News, Belize, February 18, 2009.
62. "Mayans Battle in Battlefield Park," Channel 7 News, Belize, June 10, 2009.

63. "Mayans Battle in Battlefield Park."
64. "TCGA Distances Itself from Maya Leaders Alliance," Channel 5 News, Belize, February 17, 2009.
65. "... And Claim Cacao Growers Are Trying to Create a Rift among Them," Channel 5 News, Belize, February 19, 2009.
66. "... And Claim Cacao Growers."
67. "... And Claim Cacao Growers."
68. "Archaeologist Speaks on Behalf of Mayas in Court," Channel 5 News, Belize, www.channel5belize.com/archive_detail_story.php?story_id=24362.
69. "Archaeologist Speaks."
70. "Guatemalan Xateros and Loggers Rape Columbia River Forest Reserve," *Amandala*, June 8, 2008, 1–2; "Belize Foreign Affairs Calls on OAS to Investigate Armed Confrontation with Illegal Guatemalan Loggers," *Amandala*, September 7, 2008, 3; "Guat Loggers, Xateros Fire on BDF, Forest Rangers in Toledo!," *Amandala*, September 7, 2008, 1, 2; "The Slow Rape of Belize," *Amandala*, December 28, 2008, 1, 2, 25; "Guat Milperos, Xateros, Loggers Punk Belize," *Amandala*, March 29, 2009, 22, 23; "Xateros Loot Archaeological Artifacts from Western Border to Belmopan: Dr. Awe," *Amandala*, April 18, 2010, 29.
71. "Belize Foreign Affairs Calls on OAS to Investigate Armed Confrontation with Illegal Guatemalan Loggers," *Amandala*, September 7, 2008, 3; "Guat Loggers, Xateros Fire on BDF," 1, 2.
72. "Guat Villagers Belligerent near Caracol," *Amandala*, January 11, 2009, 1, 4.
73. "Guat Squatters inside Belize's Chiquibul National Park," *Amandala*, April 4, 2010, 1, 4.
74. *MLA et al. v. Attorney General et al.*, para. 74.
75. *MLA et al. v. Attorney General et al.*, para. 79.
76. *MLA et al. v. Attorney General et al.*, paras. 92, 101.
77. *MLA et al. v. Attorney General et al.*, para. 126.
78. *Court of Appeal Judgment*, para. 188.
79. "The Government versus the Maya Leaders Alliance," Channel 7 News, Belize, March 21, 2011.
80. *Court of Appeal Judgment*, para. 190.
81. *Court of Appeal Judgment*, paras. 274, 276.
82. *Court of Appeal Judgment*, para. 215.
83. *Court of Appeal Judgment*, paras. 64–65, emphasis added.
84. *Court of Appeal Judgment*, para. 218, citing *Mason v. Tritton*, emphasis added.
85. *Court of Appeal Judgment*, para. 222.
86. *Court of Appeal Judgment*, para. 223, citing *Delgamuukw v. British Columbia* [1997] 3 S.C.R. 1010.
87. *Court of Appeal Judgment*, para. 223, citing *Delgamuukw v. British Columbia* [1997] 3 S.C.R. 1010; emphasis added.
88. *Court of Appeal Judgment*, paras. 270, 283.
89. *Court of Appeal Judgment*, paras. 153, 284.
90. *Court of Appeal Judgment*, paras. 291, 296.
91. *Court of Appeal Judgment*, para. 311.
92. *Court of Appeal Judgment*, para. 320.
93. CCJ consent order.
94. CCJ consent order.
95. CCJ consent order.
96. CCJ Appeal, para. 59.

NOTES TO PAGES 138–150

97. CCJ Appeal, para. 75.
98. CCJ Appeal, para. 78.

CHAPTER 8 — NEGOTIATING THE INTERFACE OF MAYA CUSTOMARY TENURE AND BELIZEAN LAW

1. Toledo Alcaldes Association and Maya Leaders Alliance, Maya Consultation Framework, June 13, 2014; in author's possession.
2. "Citizen's Arrest in Santa Cruz; Was It Racially Motivated?," Channel 5 News, Belize, June 22, 2015, http://edition.channel5belize.com/archives/115156.
3. "PM Barrow—It is Indefensible and Won't be Countenanced," Channel 5 News, Belize, June 22, 2015, http://edition.channel5belize.com/archives/115151.
4. "Maya Leaders Alliance Says Villager Was Trespassing on Sacred Grounds," Channel 5 News, Belize, June 22, 2015, http://edition.channel5belize.com/archives/115153.
5. "Maya Leaders Alliance Says Villager Was Trespassing"; "Santa Cruz Villagers Meet with Maya Leaders Alliance Post Rupert Myles Incident," Channel 5 News, Belize, June 23, 2015, http://edition.channel5belize.com/archives/115222.
6. "Was Rupert Myles Aggressive in Santa Cruz?," Channel 5 News, Belize, June 26, 2015, http://edition.channel5belize.com/archives/115364.
7. "Was Rupert Myles Aggressive in Santa Cruz?"
8. Kareem Clarke, "GOB Raids Santa Cruz Maya!," *Amandala*, June 28, 2015, 1, 55.
9. Clarke, "GOB Raids Santa Cruz Maya!," 1, 55.
10. "PM Reiterates: No Alcalde System Can Supersede Laws of Belize," Channel 5 News, Belize, June 26, 2015, http://edition.channel5belize.com/archives/115391.
11. "PM Reiterates."
12. Kareem Clark. "Racial Discrimination or Mayan Justice?," *Amandala*, June 28, 2015, 1, 54.
13. "Santa Cruz: Unlawful Imprisonment, Predawn Raid, Mass Arraignment," Channel 5 News, Belize, June 25, 2015, http://edition.channel5belize.com/archives/115299).
14. G. Michael Reid, "A Wicked Agenda," *Belize Times*, July 4, 2015, http://www.belizetimes.bz/?p=23803.
15. Editorial, "A Belizean Crisis in Toledo," *Amandala*, June 28, 2015, 5.
16. "PM Maintains Position on Rupert Myles' Unlawful Arrest," Channel 5 News, Belize, June 29, 2015, http://edition.channel5belize.com/archives/115439; "Maya Peoples' Declaration on Guatemala's Unfounded Claim to Belize," *Amandala*, December 14, 2008, 21.
17. "Charges to Be Brought against Rupert Myles for Desecrating Uxbenka," Channel 5 News, Belize, July 24, 2015, http://edition.channel5belize.com/archives/116634; "PM Barrow Says Force Cannot Be Used to Evict Rupert Myles," Channel 5 News, Belize, September 29, 2015, http://edition.channel5belize.com/archives/119406.
18. "Santa Cruz Thirteen Back in Court . . . Uxbenka Denuding Continues," Channel 5 News, Belize, September 29, 2015, http://edition.channel5belize.com/archives/119410; "Uchbenka Executive Weighs in on Myles," Channel 5 News, Belize, July 28, 2015, http://edition.channel5belize.com/archives/116785.
19. "PM Barrow Says Force Cannot Be Used."
20. "Santa Cruz 13 Vindicated," Channel 5 News, Belize, December 17, 2015, http://edition.channel5belize.com/archives/122634.
21. "Mayas Were Detained in Pre-Dawn Raid," Channel 5 News, Belize, June 24, 2015, http://edition.channel5belize.com/archives/115260.
22. "Guats' Armed Plunder of Our Natural Resources Escalates," *Amandala*, August 5, 2012, 1, 4; "Belize Loses $23 Mil to Illegal Logging: FCD," *Amandala*, September 30, 2012, 1, 4;

"Illegal Xate Harvesting by Guatemalans 'an Acute Problem,'" *Amandala*, December 9, 2012, 1, 2; "46 Illegal Clearings and 9 Illegal Settlements Reported in Chiquibul," *Amandala*, March 17, 2013, 46; "$60 Mil Lost due to Illegal Logging by Guats over 174 Square Miles of Belize," *Amandala*, December 20, 2015, 1, 54, 55; "Guatemalans Continue the Destruction of Chiquibul Forest Reserve," *Amandala*, April 24, 2016, 2, 54; "Flyover Reveals 35 Active Incursion Points in Chiquibul," *Amandala*, January 29, 2017, 13–14; "Upsurge in Illegal Cattle Ranching by Guatemalans in Western Belize," *Amandala*, August 11, 2017, 15; "Belize Officials' Response to Guat Cattle Ranching in Chiquibul 'Very Weak,'" *Amandala*, January 19, 2019, 1, 4; "Guats Stealing Gold in Chiquibul!," *Amandala*, May 6, 2012, 1, 4; "Grave Concerns over Gold Panning by Guatemalans in Chiquibul," *Amandala*, March 3, 2017, 7; "Guats Planting Weed in Belizean Territory and Shooting at Belizean Soldiers," *Amandala*, March 13, 2016, 4.

23. "BDF, Guat Loggers in Chiquibul Gunfight!!," *Amandala*, July 17, 2011, 1; "BDF Soldier Shot in Chiquibul by Suspected Guatemalans," *Amandala*, April 3, 2016, 2, 55; "Guatemalans Open Fire on BDF Again, Says GOB Report," *Amandala*, September 9, 2016, 3–4.

24. "Belize Police Murdered at Caracol!," *Amandala*, September 28, 2014, 1, 54.

25. An *Amandala* article documents Guatemalan aggression increasing significantly from 2006 ("Guatemala Has Increased Militarization at the Sarstoon," *Amandala*, March 20, 2016, 2, 4, 54).

26. "Belize Territorial Volunteers Begin Monitoring Belize-Guat Border in April," *Amandala*, April 1, 2012, 2.

27. "Aggression and Emergency," *Amandala*, March 8, 2015, 27.

28. "Guat Gunboat Runs onto Glovers Reef," *Amandala*, June 14, 2015, 1, 55.

29. "Guatemala Threatens; GOB Trembles; BTV Stands Firm," *Amandala*, February 28, 2016, 3, B.

30. "He Went to Sarstoon and Came Back a National Hero," *Amandala*, August 23, 2015, 3.

31. "PM Barrow Sends 'Extremely Strong Protest Note' to Guatemala," *Amandala*, August 23, 2015, 1, 4.

32. "'We Do Not Recognize Belize's Borders!,'" *Amandala*, September 13, 2015, 1, 55.

33. "Mayan Land Rights Commission Named," Channel 5 News, Belize, January 12, 2016, https://edition.channel5belize.com/archives/123630; "Toledo Maya Land Rights Commission Gives Update," Channel 5 News, Belize, June 14, 2016, https://edition.channel5belize.com/archives/130513.

34. "Toledo Alcaldes vs. Lisel Alamilla," Channel 7 News, Belize, May 16, 2016, www.7newsbelize.com/sstory.php?nid=36333&frmsrch=1; Adele Ramos, "Toledo Maya and GOB at Odds over Land Rights Consultations," *Amandala*, May 21, 2016, https://amandala.com.bz/news/toledo-maya-gob-odds-land-rights-consultations/.

35. "Maya Say GOB in 'Flagrant Violation' of CCJ Order," *Amandala*, October 28, 2017, https://amandala.com.bz/news/maya-gob-flagrant-violation-ccj-order.

36. Glenn Tillett, "Caribbean Court of Justice 'Exasperated' with GOB's Delay in Implementing Maya Court Order," *Amandala*, February 24, 2018, https://amandala.com.bz/news/caribbean-court-justice-exasperated-gobs-delay-implementing-maya-court-order/; "GOB and Mayas Back before CCJ," Channel 7 News, July 30, 2018; Rowland A. Parks, "CCJ Holds Compliance Report Hearing Regarding Mayan Land Rights," *Amandala*, August 1, 2018, https://amandala.com.bz/news/ccj-holds-compliance-report-hearingn-mayan-land-rights/.

37. "Will Maya Leaders Alliance Appeal Rupert Myles Case?," Channel 7 News, Belize, October 30, 2019, https://www.7newsbelize.com/printstory.php?func=print&id=50833.

38. "Jalacte Village Emerges Victorious in Land Rights Claim against G.O.B.," Channel 5 News, Belize, June 17, 2021, https://edition.channel5belize.com/archives/220192; *Jalacte (Jose Ical and Estevan Caal) v. Attorney General et al.* [Claim No. 190 of 2016], Belize S. Ct. Judgment of June 16, 2021. The minister of Indigenous peoples' affairs has indicated the government's intention to appeal this judgment, on grounds of the size of the monetary award and unspecified "legal issues" ("Minister of Indigenous Peoples' Affairs Confirms Appeal of Jalacte Compensation Case," Breaking Belize News, July 8, 2021).

39. Micah Goodin. "CCJ Orders Barrow Administration to Get Serious about Respecting Maya Rights," *Amandala*, October 30, 2017, https://amandala.com.bz/news/ccj-orders-barrow-administration-respecting-maya-rights/.

40. Tillett, "Caribbean Court of Justice 'Exasperated.'"

41. "Maya Leaders Call for Joint Work Plan on Maya Land Rights Order," Breaking News Belize, August 2, 2018, https://www.breakingbelizenews.com/2018/08/02/maya-leaders-call-for-joint-work-plan-on-maya-land-rights-order.

42. "Free, Prior, and Informed Consent," Channel 5 News, Belize, June 18, 2021, https://edition.channel5belize.com/archives/220262.

43. "Traditional Alcaldes Represent Maya Communities," Channel 5 News, Belize, June 18, 2021, https://edition.channel5belize.com/archives/220260.

44. "Traditional Alcaldes Represent Maya Communities."

# Bibliography

Abrams, Philip. 1988. "Notes on the Difficulty of Studying the State." *Journal of Historical Sociology* 1, no. 1: 58–89.
Abu-Lughod, Lila. 1991. "Writing against Culture." In *Recapturing Anthropology: Working in the Present*, edited by Richard Fox, 137–150. Santa Fe: School of American Research Press.
Agrawal, Arun. 2005. *Environmentality*. Durham, NC: Duke University Press.
Alexander, P. 1985. Belize: Sectoral Development Plan: Tourism, 1986–1987.
Alfonso, Tatiana. 2019. "Landscapes of Property: Socio-Legal Perspectives from Latin America." In *Routledge Handbook of Law and Society in Latin America*, edited by Rachel Sieder, Karina Ansolabehere, and Tatiana Alfonso, 404–419. New York: Routledge.
American Declaration on the Rights and Duties of Man. 1948. https://www.cidh.oas.org/bsicos/english/basic2.american%20declaration.htm, accessed July 13, 2023.
American Declaration on the Rights of Indigenous Peoples (ADRIP). 2016. Organization of American States. https://www.oas.org/en/sare/documents/DecAmIND.pdf, accessed July 13, 2023.
Anaya, S. James. 1991. "The Capacity of International Law to Advance Ethnic or Nationality Rights Claims." *Human Rights Quarterly* 13: 403–411.
———. 1998. "Maya Aboriginal Land and Resource Rights and the Conflict over Logging in Southern Belize." *Yale Human Rights and Development Law Journal* 1, no. 1: 17–35.
———. 2004. *Indigenous Peoples in International Law*. 2nd ed. Oxford: Oxford University Press.
———. 2008. "Reparations for Neglect of Indigenous Land Rights at the Intersection of Domestic and International Law—The Maya Cases in the Supreme Court of Belize." In *Reparations for Indigenous Peoples: International and Comparative Perspectives*, edited by Federico Lenzerini, 567. Oxford: Oxford University Press.
———. 2009. *International Human Rights and Indigenous Peoples*. New York: Wolters Kluwer.
Anaya, S. James, and Claudio Grossman. 2002. "The Case of Awas Tingni v. Nicaragua." *Arizona Journal of International and Comparative Law* 19: 1–16.
Arteaga Bohrt, Ana Cecilia. 2017. "'Let Us Walk Together': Chachawarmi Complementarity and Indigenous Autonomies in Bolivia." In *Demanding Justice and Security: Indigenous Women and Legal Pluralities in Latin America*, edited by Rachel Sieder, 150–172. New Brunswick, NJ: Rutgers University Press.

Aukerman, Robert, and Glenn Haas. 1992. *Revenue Generation Strategy for Protected Areas of Belize*. Belize: Ministry of Natural Resources, WWF-US, USAID.

Baines, Kristina. 2016. *Embodying Ecological Heritage in a Maya Community: Health, Happiness, and Identity*. New York: Lexington Books.

Baldwin, Clive, and Cynthia Morel. 2011. "Using the United Nations Declaration on the Rights of Indigenous Peoples in Litigation." In *Reflections on the UN Declaration on the Rights of Indigenous Peoples*, edited by Stephen Allen and Alexandra Xanthaki, 121–143. Portland, OR: Hart.

Barelli, Mauro. 2010. "The Interplay between Global and Regional Human Rights Systems in the Construction of the Indigenous Rights Regime." *Human Rights Quarterly* 32: 951–997.

Barrera, Leticia, and Sergio Latorre. 2019. "Ethnography, Bureaucracy, and Legal Knowledge in Latin American State Institutions: Law's Material and Technical Dimensions." In *Routledge Handbook of Law and Society in Latin America*, edited by Rachel Sieder, Karina Ansolabehere, and Tatiana Alfonso, 95–110. New York: Routledge.

Barry, Tom. 1992. *Inside Belize*. Albuquerque, NM: Inter-Hemispheric Education Resource Center.

Bartolome, Miguel Alberto, Guillermo Bonfil Batalla, Victor Daniel Bonilla, Gonzalo Castillo Cardenas, Miguel Chase Sardi, George Grunberg, Nelly Arvelo de Jimenez, Esteban Emilio Mosonyi, Darcy Ribeiro, Scott S. Robinson, and Stefano Varese. 1973. "The Declaration of Barbados: For the Liberation of the Indians." *Current Anthropology* 14, no. 3: 267–270.

*Belize and the Barrier Reef Cayes: Profile*. N.d. Brochure.

Belize Tourism Board (BTB). N.d. "The Beginnings of Tourism in Belize." www.belizetourism.org/belize-tourism/history.html, accessed September 16, 2009 (no longer available).

———. 1993. Tourism towards 2000, Tourism Marketing Summit, April 20, 1993.

———. 1998. Travel and Tourism Statistics. Belize City, Belize.

———. 2006. Travel and Tourism Statistics. Belize City, Belize.

———. 2008. Travel and Tourism Statistics. Belize City, Belize.

Bens, Jonas. 2020. *The Indigenous Paradox: Rights, Sovereignty, and Culture in the Americas*. Philadelphia: University of Pennsylvania Press.

Berl-Cawtran Consortium. 1984. *Tourism Development, 1984–1990: Strategy and Action Plan*. Report Commissioned by UN Development Program.

Bhandar, Brenna. 2018. *Colonial Lives of Property: Law, Land, and Racial Regimes of Ownership*. Durham, NC: Duke University Press.

Blomley, Nicholas. 2014. "Making Space for Property." *Annals of the Association of American Geographers* 104, no. 6: 1291–1306.

Bolland, O. Nigel. 1977. "The Maya and the Colonization of Belize in the Nineteenth Century." In *Anthropology and History in Yucatán*, edited by Grant Jones, 69–102. Austin: University of Texas Press.

———. 1987. "Race, Ethnicity, and National Integration in Belize." In *Belize: Ethnicity and Development*. Belize City, Belize: Society for the Promotion of Education and Research.

———. 1988. *Colonialism and Resistance in Belize: Essays in Historical Sociology*. Belize: Cubola/SPEAR/ISER.

Bolland, O. Nigel, and Assad Shoman. 1977. *Land in Belize 1765–1871*. Kingston: Institute of Social and Economic Research, UWI.

Boo, Elizabeth. 1990. *Ecotourism: The Potentials and Pitfalls*. Washington, DC: World Wildlife Fund.

Boyle, Alan, and Christine Chinkin. 2007. *The Making of International Law*. Oxford: Oxford University Press.

Bricker, Victoria. 1981. *The Indian Christ, the Indian King: The Historical Substrate of Maya Myth and Ritual*. Austin: University of Texas Press.

Brockington, Dan, and Rosaleen Duffy. 2010. "Capitalism and Conservation." *Antipode* 42, no. 3: 469–484.

Brockington, Dan, Rosaleen Duffy, and Jim Igoe. 2008. *Nature Unbound: Conservation, Capitalism and the Future of Protected Areas*. London: Earthscan.

Brockington, Dan, and Elizabeth Scholfield. 2010. "The Conservationist Mode of Production and Conservation NGOs in sub-Saharan Africa." *Antipode* 42, no. 3: 551–575.

Brockmann, Thomas C. 1977. "Ethnic and Racial Relations in Northern Belize." *Ethnicity* 4: 246–262.

———. 1985. "Ethnic Participation in Orange Walk Economic Development." *Ethnic Groups* 6: 187–208.

Brown, Denise Fay. 1999. "Mayas and Tourists in the Maya World." *Human Organization* 58, no. 3: 295–304.

Brown, Wendy. 2002. "Suffering the Paradoxes of Rights." In *Left Legalism/Left Critique*, edited by Wendy Brown, 420–434. Durham, NC: Duke University Press.

———. 2004. "'The Most We Can Hope For . . .': Human Rights and the Politics of Fatalism." *South Atlantic Quarterly* 103, no. 2/3: 451–463.

Bryant, Raymond. 2002. "Non-governmental Organizations and Governmentality." *Political Studies* 50: 268–292.

Brysk, Alison. 2000. *From Tribal Village to Global Village: Indian Rights and International Relations in Latin America*. Palo Alto, CA: Stanford University Press.

Burger, Julian. 2011. "The UN Declaration on the Rights of Indigenous Peoples: From Advocacy to Implementation." In *Reflections on the UN Declaration on the Rights of Indigenous Peoples*, edited by Stephen Allen and Alejandra Xanthaki, 41–59. Portland, OR: Hart.

Buscher, Bram, and Wolfram Dressler. 2012. "Commodity Conservation." *Geoforum* 43: 367–376.

Buscher, Bram, Sian Sullivan, Katja Neves, Jim Igoe, and Dan Brockington. 2012. "Towards a Synthesized Critique of Neoliberal Biodiversity Conservation." *Capitalism, Nature, Socialism* 23, no. 2: 4–30.

Butler, Judith. 1990. *Gender Trouble: Feminism and the Subversion of Identity*. New York: Routledge.

———. 1997. *The Psychic Life of Power: Theories of Subjection*. Palo Alto, CA: Stanford University Press.

Byers, Michael. 1999. *Custom, Power and the Power of Rules: International Relations and Customary International Law*. New York: Cambridge University Press.

Cal, Angel. 1991. "Rural Society and Economic Development: British Mercantile Capital in Nineteenth-Century Belize." PhD diss., University of Arizona.

Campbell, Jeremy. 2015. *Conjuring Property: Speculation and Environmental Futures in the Brazilian Amazon*. Seattle: University of Washington Press.

Cañas Bottos, Lorenzo. 2015. "Assemblages of Sovereignty and Anti-Sovereignty Effects on the Irish Border." *Focaal* 71: 86–99.

Caribbean Tourism Research and Development Centre (CTRDC). 1985a. *PMS Country Report: Belize*.

———. 1985b. *Tourism Action Plan for Belize*.

Carlsen, Robert. 1997. *The War for the Heart and Soul of a Highland Maya Town*. Austin: University of Texas Press.

Castañeda, Quetzil. 1997. *In the Museum of Maya Culture: Touring Chichen Itzá*. Minneapolis: University of Minnesota.

Castree, Noel. 2007. "Neoliberalising Nature." *Environment and Planning A* 40: 131–152.
Ceballos-Lascurain, Hector. 1987. "Estudio de Prefactibilidad Socioeconomica del Turismo Ecologico y Anteprojecto Arquitectonico y Urbanistico del Centro de Turismo Ecologico de Sian Ka'an, Quintana Roo." Study made for SEDUE, Mexico.
Central Statistical Office (CSO). 2001. "Population Census 2000: Major Findings." Belmopan, Belize: Ministry of Budget Management.
Cepek, Michael. 2011. "Foucault in the Forest: Questioning Environmentality in Amazonia." *American Ethnologist* 38, no. 3: 501–515.
Cervone, Emma, and Cristina Cucuri. 2017. "Gender Inequality, Indigenous Justice, and the Intercultural State: The Case of Chimborazo, Ecuador." In *Demanding Justice and Security: Indigenous Women and Legal Pluralities in Latin America*, edited by Rachel Sieder, 120–149. New Brunswick, NJ: Rutgers University Press.
Conklin, Beth, and Laura Graham. 1995. "The Shifting Middle Ground: Amazonian Indians and Eco-Politics." *American Anthropologist* 97, no. 4: 695–710.
Corntassel, Jeff J., and Thomas H. Primeau. 1995. "Indigenous 'Sovereignty' and International Law: Revised Strategies for Pursuing Self-Determination." *Human Rights Quarterly* 17, no. 2: 343–365.
Correia, Joel E. 2018a. "Adjudication and Its Aftereffects in Three Inter-American Court Cases Brought against Paraguay: Indigenous Land Rights." *Erasmus Law Review* 11: 43–56.
———. 2018b. "Indigenous Rights at a Crossroads: Territorial Struggles, the Inter-American Court of Human Rights, and Legal Geographies of Liminality." *Geoforum* 97: 73–83.
———. 2019. "Unsettling Territory: Indigenous Mobilizations, the Territorial Turn, and the Limits of Land Rights in the Paraguay-Brazil Borderlands." *Journal of Latin American Geography* 18, no. 1: 11–37.
Coulthard, Glenn. 2014. *Red Skin, White Masks: Rejecting the Colonial Politics of Recognition*. Minneapolis: University of Minnesota Press.
Cowan, Jane K. 2006. "Culture and Rights after *Culture and Rights*." *American Anthropologist* 108, no. 1: 9–24.
Daes, Erica-Irene. 2000. "The Spirit and Letter of the Right to Self-Determination of Indigenous Peoples: Reflections on the Making of the United Nations Draft Declaration." In *Operationalizing the Right of Indigenous Peoples to Self-Determination*, edited by Pekka Aidio and Martin Scheinin, 67–83. Turko/Abo: Abo Akademi University.
———. 2001. "Striving for Self-Determination for Indigenous Peoples." In *Pursuit of the Right to Self-Determination: Collected Papers and Proceedings of the Fist International Conference on the Right to Self-Determination and the United Nations*, edited by Yussuf Naim Kly and Diana Kly, 50–62. Atlanta: Clarity.
———. 2011. "The UN Declaration on the Rights of Indigenous Peoples: Background and Appraisal." In *Reflections on the UN Declaration on the Rights of Indigenous Peoples*, edited by Stephen Allen and Alejandra Xanthaki, 11–40. Portland, OR: Hart.
Dannenmaier, Eric. 2008. "Beyond Indigenous Property Rights: Exploring the Emergence of a Distinctive Connection Doctrine." *Washington University Law Review* 86, no. 1: 53–110.
Danziger, Eve. 2001. *Relatively Speaking: Language, Thought and Kinship among the Mopan Maya*. Oxford: Oxford University Press.
Das, Veena, and Deborah Poole. 2004. "State and Its Margins: Comparative Ethnographies." In *Anthropology in the Margins of the State*, edited by Veena Das and Deborah Poole, 3–34. Santa Fe: School of American Research.
Dean, Mitchell. 1999. *Governmentality: Power and Rule in Modern Society*. London: Sage Publications.

de la Peña, Guillermo. 2005. "Social and Cultural Policies toward Indigenous Peoples: Perspectives from Latin America." *Annual Review of Anthropology* 34: 717–739.

Department of the Environment (DOE). 1992. *Belize National Report to the UN Conference on Environment and Development*. Belmopan: Ministry of Tourism and Environment.

Dobson, Narda. 1973. *A History of Belize*. Kingston: Longman Caribbean.

Donnelly, Jack. 2003. *Universal Human Rights in Theory and Practice*. 2nd ed. Ithaca, NY: Cornell University Press.

Downey, Sean. 2010. "Can Properties of Labor-Exchange Networks Explain the Resilience of Swidden Agriculture?" *Ecology and Society* 15, no. 4: 15.

Downie, J. 1959. *An Economic Policy for British Honduras*. Belize City: Government Printer.

Elden, Stuart. 2009. *Terror and Territory: The Spatial Extent of Sovereignty*. Minneapolis: University of Minnesota Press.

———. 2013. *The Birth of Territory*. Chicago: University of Chicago Press.

Emmons, Katherine M., Robert H. Horwich, James Kamstra, Ernesto Saqui, James Beveridge, Timothy McCarthy, Jan Meerman, Scott C. Silver, Ignacio Pop, Fred Koontz, Emiliano Pop, Hermelindo Saqui, Linde Ostro, Pedro Pixabaj, Dorothy Beveridge, and Judy Lumb. 1996. *Cockscomb Basin Wildlife Sanctuary*. Caye Caulker, Belize: Producciones de la Hamaca.

Engle, Karen. 2010. *The Elusive Promise of Indigenous Development: Rights, Culture, Strategy*. Durham, NC: Duke University Press.

Ferguson, James. 2009. "The Uses of Neoliberalism." *Antipode* 41, no. 1: 166–184.

Ferguson, James, and Akhil Gupta. 2002. "Spatializing States." *American Ethnologist* 29, no. 4: 981–1002.

Fischer, Edward. 1999. "Cultural Logic and Maya Identity: Rethinking Constructivism and Essentialism." *Current Anthropology* 40, no. 4: 473–499.

———. 2009. "Introduction." In *Indigenous Peeples, Civil Society, and the Neo-liberal State in Latin America*, edited by Edward F. Fischer, 1–18. New York: Berghahn Books.

Fletcher, Robert. 2010. "Neoliberal Environmentality: Towards a Poststructuralist Political Ecology of the Conservation Debate." *Conservation and Society* 8, no. 3: 171–181.

Foucault, Michel. 1977. *Discipline and Punish: The Birth of the Prison*. New York: Pantheon Books.

———. 1982. "Afterward: The Subject and Power." In *Michel Foucault: Beyond Structuralism and Hermeneutics*, edited by Hubert Dreyfus and Paul Rabinow, 208–226. Chicago: University of Chicago Press.

———. 2007. *Security, Territory, Population: Lectures at the Collège de France, 1977–78*. New York: Palgrave Macmillan.

———. 2008. *The Birth of Biopolitics: Lectures at the Collège de France, 1978–79*. New York: Palgrave Macmillan.

Gargarella, Roberto. 2019. "Latin America's Contribution to Constitutionalism." In *Routledge Handbook of Law and Society in Latin America*, edited by Rachel Sieder, Karina Ansolabehere, and Tatiana Alfonso, 25–36. New York: Routledge.

Gilbert, Jeremie, and Cathal Doyle. 2011. "A New Dawn over the Land: Shedding Light on Collective Ownership and Consent." In *Reflections on the UN Declaration on the Rights of Indigenous Peoples*, edited by Stephen Allen and Alejandra Xanthaki, 289–328. Portland, OR: Hart.

Golder, Ben. 2015. *Foucault and the Politics of Rights*. Palo Alto, CA: Stanford University Press.

Goldman, Michael. 2005. *Imperial Nature: The World Bank and Struggles for Social Justice in the Age of Globalization*. New Haven, CT: Yale University Press.

Gonzalez, Nancie. 1988. *Sojourners of the Caribbean: Ethnogenesis and Ethnohistory of the Garifuna*. Chicago: University of Illinois Press.

Goodale, Mark. 2007. "Locating Rights, Envisioning Law between the Global and the Local." In *The Practice of Human Rights: Tracking Law between the Global and the Local*, edited by Mark Goodale and Sally Engle Merry, 1–38. Cambridge: Cambridge University Press.

———. 2019. *A Revolution in Fragments: Traversing Scales of Justice, Ideology, and Practice in Bolivia*. Durham, NC: Duke University Press.

Gordon, Colin. 1991. "Governmental Rationality." In *The Foucault Effect: Studies in Governmentality: With Two Lectures by and an Interview with Michel Foucault*, edited by Graham Burchell, Colin Gordon, and Peter Miller, 1–51. Chicago: University of Chicago Press.

Government Information Service (GIS). 1973. "Visit to Proposed Reserve at Crooked Tree Lagoon." *New Belize*, June. Belize National Archives.

———. 1982. "New Thrust for Tourism." *New Belize*, vol. 16, no. 8. Belmopan. Belize National Archives.

———. 1985. "Tourism: More than Sea and Sun." *New Belize*, February, 6–7. Belize National Archives.

Grandia, Liza. 2004. *The Wealth Report: Q'eqchi' Traditional Knowledge and Natural Resource Management in the Sarstoon-Temash National Park*. Punta Gorda, Belize: SATIIM.

———. 2009. "Milpa Matters." In *Waging War, Making Peace: Reparations and Human Rights*, edited by Barbara Rose Johnston and Susan Slyomovics, 153–182. Walnut Creek, CA: Left Coast.

Grant, Cedric. 1976. *The Making of Modern Belize: Politics, Society, and British Colonialism in Central America*. Cambridge: Cambridge University Press.

Great Belize Productions. 1988. *Jaguars of the Cockscomb*. Belize City, Belize. Accessed in National Archives.

Gregory, James R. 1976. "The Modification of an Interethnic Boundary in Belize." *American Ethnologist* 3, no. 4: 683–708.

———. 1984. *The Mopan: Culture and Ethnicity in a Changing Belizean Community*. University of Missouri Monographs in Anthropology #7, Columbia: Department of Anthropology, University of Missouri.

Hale, Charles R. 2002. "Does Multiculturalism Menace? Governance, Cultural Rights and the Politics of Identity in Guatemala." *Journal of Latin American Studies* 34: 485–524.

Hansen, Thomas Blom, and Finn Stepputat. 2001. "Introduction: State of Imagination." In *States of Imagination: Ethnographic Explorations of the Postcolonial State*, edited by Thomas Blom Hansen and Finn Stepputat, 1–40. Durham, NC: Duke University Press.

———. 2006. "Sovereignty Revisited." *Annual Review of Anthropology* 35: 295–315.

Hartshorn, Gary, Lou Nicolait, Lynne Hartshorn, George Bevier, Richard Brightman, Jeronimo Cal, Agripino Cawich, William Davidson, Random DuBois, Charles Dyer, Janet Gibson, William Hawley, Jeffrey Leonard, Robert Nicolait, Dora Weyer, Hayward White, and Charles Wright. 1984. *Belize: Country Environmental Profile*. San Jose: Trejos Hns Sucs. S.A.

Hartwick, Elaine, and Richard Peet. 2003. "Neoliberalism and Nature." *Annals of the American Academy of Political and Social Science* 590: 188–203.

Harvey, David. 2005. *A Brief History of Neoliberalism*. Oxford: Oxford University Press.

Hilbink, Lisa, and Janice Gallagher. 2019. "State and Law in Latin America: A Critical Assessment." In *Routledge Handbook of Law and Society in Latin America*, edited by Rachel Sieder, Karina Ansolabehere, and Tatiana Alfonso, 37–50. New York: Routledge.

Hoffman, Odile. 2014. *British Honduras: The Invention of a Colonial Territory. Mapping and Spatial Knowledge in the 19th Century*. Benque Viejo, Belize: Cubola Productions and the Institut de recherché pour le developpement.
———. 2021. *Property and Territory: Origins of a Colonial Order in Belize in the 19th and 20th Centuries*. Benque Viejo, Belize: Cubola Productions.
Howard, Michael C. 1977. "Political Change in a Mayan Village in Southern Belize." *Katunob* 10.
Huneeus, Alexandra, Javier Couso, and Rachel Sieder. 2010. "Cultures of Legality: Judicialization and Political Activism in Contemporary Latin America." In *Cultures of Legality: Judicialization and Political Activism in Latin America*, edited by Javier A. Couso, Alexandra Huneeus, and Rachel Sieder, 3–21. New York: Cambridge University Press.
Igoe, Jim, and Dan Brockington. 2007. "Neoliberal Conservation." *Conservation and Society* 5, no. 4: 432–449.
Igoe, Jim, Katja Neves, and Dan Brockington. 2010. "Theorising the Convergence of Biodiversity Conservation and Capitalist Expansion." *Antipode* 42, no. 3: 486–512.
Inter-American Commission on Human Rights (IACHR). 2000. *The Human Rights Situation of the Indigenous People in the Americas*. OEA/Ser.L/V/II.108 Doc. 62, 20 October 2000.
———. 2010. *Indigenous and Tribal Peoples' Rights over Their Ancestral Lands and Natural Resources: Norms and Jurisprudence of the Inter-American Human Rights System*. OEA/Ser. L/V/II. Doc. 56/09.
Interdepartmental Committee on Maya Welfare (ICMW). 1941. *Report of the Interdepartmental committee on Maya Welfare*. Belize City: Government of British Honduras.
International Convention on Civil and Political Rights (ICCPR). 1966. https://www.ohchr.org/en/professionalinterest/pages/ccpr.aspx, accessed March 7, 2020.
International Convention on the Elimination of all Forms of Racial Discrimination (ICERD). 1965. https://www.ohchr.org/en/instruments-mechanisms/instruments/international-convention-elimination-all-forms-racial, accessed July 13, 2023.
International Labor Organization Convention no. 169 of 1989, Indigenous and Tribal Peoples Convention (ILO 169). https://www.ilo.org/dyn/normlex/en/f?p=NORMLEXPUB:12100:0::NO::P12100_ILO_CODE:C169, accessed March 7, 2020.
International Labor Organization. N.d. Ratifications of C169—Indigenous and Tribal Peoples Convention, 1989 (No. 169). http://www.ilo.org/dyn/normlex/en/f?p=NORMLEXPUB:11300:0::NO::P11300_INSTRUMENT_ID:312314, accessed November 17, 2023.
International Work Group for Indigenous Affairs (IWGIA). 1984. "Belize: Mopan and Kektchi Indians Fight for their Culture." *IWGIA Newsletter* 37: 19–21.
Jackson, Jean. 2007. "Rights to Indigenous Culture in Colombia." In *The Practice of Human Rights: Tracking Law Between the Global and the Local*, edited by Mark Goodale and Sally Engle Merry, 204–241. Cambridge: Cambridge University Press.
———. 2019. *Managing Multiculturalism: Indigeneity and the Struggle for Rights in Colombia*. Palo Alto, CA: Stanford University Press.
Jackson, Jean E., and Kay B. Warren. 2005. "Indigenous Movements in Latin America, 1992-2004: Controversies, Ironies, New Directions." *Annual Review of Anthropology* 34: 549–573.
Jacobs, Noel, and Anselmo Castañeda, eds. 1998. *National Biodiversity Strategy*. National Biodiversity Committee, Ministry of Natural Resources and the Environment. Belmopan, Belize.
Johnson, Melissa. 1998. "Nature and Progress in Rural Creole Belize: Rethinking Sustainable Development." Unpublished PhD diss., University of Michigan.

———. 2015. "Creolized Conservation: A Belizean Creole Community Encounters a Wildlife Sanctuary." *Anthropological Quarterly* 88, no. 1: 67–95.
———. 2019. *Becoming Creole: Nature and Race in Belize*. New Brunswick, NJ: Rutgers University Press.
Jones, Grant. 1998. *The Conquest of the Last Maya Kingdom*. Palo Alto, CA: Stanford University Press.
Judd, Karen. 1989. "Cultural Synthesis or Ethnic Struggle? Creolization in Belize." *Cimarron* 2, no. 1: 103–118.
Kahn, Hillary. 2006. *Seeing and Being Seen: The Q'eqchi' Maya of Livingston, Guatemala and Beyond*. Austin: University of Texas Press.
Keck, Margaret, and Kathryn Sikkink. 1998. *Activists beyond Borders: Advocacy Networks in International Politics*. Ithaca, NY: Cornell University Press.
Keenan, Sarah. 2010. "Subversive Property: Reshaping Malleable Spaces of Belonging." *Social and Legal Studies* 19, no. 4: 423–439.
King, R. B., I. C. Baillie, J. R. Dunsmore, R. J. Grimble, M. S. Johnson, J. B. Williams, and A.C.S. Wright. 1989. *Land Resource Assessment of Stann Creek District, Belize*. Overseas Development Natural Resources Institute Bulletin No. 19. Chatham, UK.
King, R. B., J. H. Prat, M. P. Warner, and S. A. Zisman. 1993. *Agricultural Development Prospects in Belize*. Chatham, UK: Natural Resources Institute.
Koskenniemi, Martti. 2000. "General Principles." In *Sources of International Law*, edited by Martti Koskenniemi, 359–402. Burlington, VT: Ashgate.
Kwan, Pia, Paul Eagles, and Amber Gebhardt. 2010. "Ecolodge Patrons' Characteristics and Motivations: A Study of Belize." *Journal of Ecotourism* 9, no. 1: 1–20.
Lemke, Thomas. 2001. "The Birth of Bio-Politics." *Economy and Society* 30, no. 2: 190–207.
Li, Tania. 2005. "Engaging Simplifications: Community-Based Natural Resource Management, Market Processes, and State Agendas in Upland Southeast Asia." In *Communities and Conservation: Histories and Politics of Community-Based Natural Resource Management*, edited by J. Peter Brosius, Anna Lowenhaupt Tsing, and Charles Zerner, 427–457. Walnut Creek, CA: Altamira.
Lindberg, Kreg, and Jeremy Enriquez. 1994. *An Analysis of Ecotourism's Contribution to Conservation and Development in Belize*. World Wildlife Fund (United States).
Lindner, Keith W. 2012. "The Struggle for the Sierra: Sovereignty, Property, and Rights in the San Luis Valley." *Political Geography* 33: 11–20.
Liverman, Diana, and Silvina Vilas. 2006. "Neoliberalism and the Environment in Latin America." *Annual Review of Environmental Resources* 31: 327–363.
Loperena, Christopher A. 2020. "Adjudicating Indigeneity: Anthropological Testimony in the Inter-American Court of Human Rights." *American Anthropologist* 122, no. 3: 595–605.
Lund, Christian. 2016. "Rule and Rupture: State Formation through the Production of Property and Citizenship." *Development and Change* 47, no. 6: 1199–1228.
Mahmood, Saba. 2005. *Politics of Piety: The Islamic Revival and the Feminist Subject*. Princeton, NJ: Princeton University Press.
Martinez, Juan Carlos. 2017. "The State in Waiting: State-ness Disputes in Indigenous Territories." *Journal of Latin American and Caribbean Anthropology* 22, no. 1: 68–84.
Maya Leaders Alliance (MLA) and Toledo Alcalde Association (TAA). 2019. *The Future We Dream*. Punta Gorda, Belize.
McAfee, Kathleen. 1999. "Selling Nature to Save It? Biodiversity and the Rise of Green Developmentalism." *Environment and Planning D: Society and Space* 17, no. 2: 133–154.
McClusky, Laura. 2001. *"Here, Our Culture Is Hard": Stories of Domestic Violence from a Maya Community in Belize*. Austin: University of Texas Press.

Medina, Laurie Kroshus. 1997. "Defining Difference, Forging Unity: The Co-construction of Race, Ethnicity, and Nation in Belize." *Ethnic and Racial Studies* 20, no. 4: 757–780.

———. 2004. *Negotiating Economic Development: Identity Formation and Collective Action in Belize*. Tucson: University of Arizona Press.

———. 2005. "Ecotourism and Certification: Confronting the Principles and Pragmatics of Socially Responsible Tourism." *Journal of Sustainable Tourism* 13, no. 3: 281–295.

———. 2012. "The Uses of Ecotourism: Articulating Conservation and Development Agendas in Belize." In *Global Tourism: Cultural Heritage and Economic Encounters*, edited by Sarah M. Lyon and E. Christian Wells, 227–250. Society for Economic Anthropology (SEA) Monographs #30. Lanham, MD: Altamira.

———. 2016. "The Production of Indigenous Land Rights: Judicial Decisions Across National, Regional, and Global Scales." *Political and Legal Anthropology Review* 39, no. S1: 139–153.

Merry, Sally Engle. 1992. "Anthropology, Law, and Transnational Processes." *Annual Review of Anthropology*, 21, no. 1: 357–377.

———. 1994. "Legal Pluralism." *Law and Society Review* 22, no. 8: 8.

———. 1996. "Legal Vernacularization and ka ho'okolokolonui kanaka maoli, the People's International Tribunal, Hawai'i 1993." *PoLAR: Political and Legal Anthropology Review* 19, no. 1: 67–82.

———. 2006a. "Anthropology and International Law." *Annual Review of Anthropology* 35: 99–116.

———. 2006b. *Human Rights and Gender Violence: Translating International Law into Local Justice*. Chicago: University of Chicago Press.

Mesh, Timoteo R. 2017. "Alcaldes of Toledo, Belize: Their Genealogy, Contestation, and Aspirations." PhD diss., University of Florida.

Ministry of Tourism and the Environment. 1991. *Integrated Tourism Policy and Strategy Statement*. Belmopan, Belize.

Mitchell, Timothy. 1991. "The Limits of the State." *American Political Science Review* 85, no. 1: 77–96.

———. 2002. *Rule of Experts: Egypt, Techno-politics, Modernity*. Berkeley: University of California Press.

Moberg, Mark. 1997. *Myths of Ethnicity and Nation: Immigration, Work, and Identity in the Belize Banana Industry*. Knoxville: University of Tennessee Press.

Mora, Mariana. 2017. *Kuxlejal Politics: Indigenous Autonomy, Race, and Decolonizing Research in Zapatista Communities*. Austin: University of Texas Press.

Morgan, Murna. 1990. "The Tourism Industry in Belize" (draft). Belize Archives Department, M.C. 2734.

Moyn, Samuel. 2010. *The Last Utopia: Human Rights in History*. Cambridge, MA: Harvard University Press.

Muehlebach, Andrea. 2001. "'Making Place' at the United Nations: Indigenous Cultural Politics at the U.N. Working Group on Indigenous Populations." *Cultural Anthropology* 16, no. 3: 415–448.

———. 2003. "What Self in Self-Determination? Notes from the Frontiers of Transnational Indigenous Activism." *Identities: Global Studies in Culture and Power* 10: 241–268.

Mundo Maya Organization (MMO). N.d. "Land of Discoveries: Maya World, Where Man, Nature, and Time are One." Marketing Brochure, in author's possession.

Nadasdy, Paul. 2017. *Sovereignty's Entailments: First Nation State Formation in the Yukon*. Toronto: University of Toronto Press.

Niezen, Ronald. 2003. *The Origins of Indigenism: Human Rights and the Politics of Identity*. Berkeley: University of California Press.

Neumann, Roderick. 1998. *Imposing Wilderness: Struggles over Livelihood and Nature Preservation in Africa*. Berkeley: University of California Press.

———. 2001. "Disciplining Peasants in Tanzania." In *Violent Environments*, edited by Nancy Peluso and Michael Watts, 305–327. Ithaca, NY: Cornell University Press.

O'Connor, James. 1998. *Natural Causes: Essays in Ecological Marxism*. New York: Guilford.

Osborn, Anne. 1982. *Socio-anthropological Aspects of Development in Southern Belize*. Punta Gorda, Belize: Toledo Rural Development Project.

Palacio, Vincent, and Stephen McKool. 1997. "Identifying Ecotourists in Belize through Benefit Segmentation: A Preliminary Analysis." *Journal of Sustainable Tourism* 5, no. 3: 234–243.

Petition to the Inter-American Commission on Human Rights (IACHR) submitted by the Toledo Maya Cultural Council on behalf of Maya Indigenous Communities of the Toledo District against Belize. August 7, 1998. Attorneys for the Petitioner: S. James Anaya, Deborah Schaaf, Steven Tullberg. [Previously available at http://www.law.arizona.edu/iplp/outreach/maya_belize/documents/BelizePetition.pdf; no longer posted to that site.]

Picq, Manuela Lavinas. 2018. *Vernacular Sovereignties: Indigenous Women Challenging World Politics*. Tucson: University of Arizona Press.

Postero, Nancy Grey. 2007. *Now We Are Citizens: Indigenous Politics in Postmulticultural Bolivia*. Palo Alto, CA: Stanford University Press.

———. 2017. *The Indigenous State: Race, Politics, and Performance in Plurinational Bolivia*. Berkeley: University of California Press.

Postero, Nancy Grey, and Leon Zamosc. 2004. "Indigenous Movements and the Indian Question in Latin America." In *The Struggle for Indigenous Rights in Latin America*, edited by Nancy Grey Postero and Leon Zamosc, 1–31. Brighton: Sussex Academic Press.

Povinelli, Elizabeth. 2002. *The Cunning of Recognition: Indigenous Alterities and the Making of Australian Multiculturalism*. Durham, NC: Duke University Press.

Programme for Belize and InterAmerican Development Bank. 1995. *Towards a National Protected Areas Systems Plan for Belize*. Belmopan, Belize: NARMAP.

Rabinowitz, Alan. 2000. *Jaguar: One Man's Struggle to Establish the World's First Jaguar Preserve*. Washington, DC: Island Press.

Ramos, Alcida Rita. 1994. "The Hyperreal Indian." *Critique of Anthropology* 14, no. 2: 153–171.

———. 1998. *Indigenism: Ethnic Politics in Brazil*. Madison: University of Wisconsin Press.

Reed, Nelson. 1964. *The Caste War of Yucatan*. Stanford, CA: Stanford University Press.

Richardson, Robert. 2007. "Economic Development in Belize." In *Taking Stock: Belize at 25 Years of Independence*, edited by Barbara Balboni and Joseph O. Palacio, 21–45. Benque, Belize: Cubola.

Riles, Annelise. 2000. *The Network Inside Out*. Ann Arbor: University of Michigan Press.

Rodriguez-Garavito, Cesar, and Luis Carlos Arenas. 2005. "Indigenous Rights, Transnational Activism, and Legal Mobilization: The Struggle of the U'wa People in Colombia." In *Law and Globalization from Below: Towards a Cosmopolitan Legality*, edited by Boaventura de Sousa Santos and Cesar Rodriguez-Garavito, 241–266. Cambridge: Cambridge University Press.

Rodriguez-Piñero, Luis. 2011. "The Inter-American System and the UN Declaration on the Rights of Indigenous Peoples: Mutual Reinforcement." In *Reflections on the UN Declaration on the Rights of Indigenous Peoples*, edited by Stephen Allen and Alejandra Xanthaki, 457–483. Portland, OR: Hart.

Sahlins, Marshall. 1999. "What Is Anthropological Enlightenment? Some Lessons of the Twentieth Century." *Annual Review of Anthropology* 28: i–xxiii.

Santos, Boaventura de Sousa. 2002. *Toward a New Legal Common Sense: Law, Globalization, and Emancipation*. London: Butterworths/LexisNexis.

Santos, Boaventura de Sousa, and Cesar Rodriguez-Garavito, eds. 2005. *Law and Globalization from Below: Towards a Cosmopolitan Legality*. Cambridge: Cambridge University Press.

Saqui, Pio. 2012. "Mopan Maya Science: Traditional Ecological Knowledge and Its Transmission among Mopan Maya Milpa Communities of Belize." PhD diss., University of Florida.

Sawyer, Suzana. 2004. *Crude Chronicles: Indigenous Politics, Multinational Oil, and Neoliberalism in Ecuador*. Palo Alto, CA: Stanford University Press.

Schroeder, Richard. 2005. "Community, Forestry, and Conditionality in The Gambia." In *Communities and Conservation*, edited by J. Peter Brosius, Anna Lowenhaupt Tsing, and Charles Zerner, 207–229. Walnut Creek, CA: Altamira.

Scott, James C. 1976. *The Moral Economy of the Peasant: Rebellion and Subsistence in Southeast Asia*. New Haven, CT: Yale University Press.

Shelton, Dinah. 2013. "The Inter-American Human Rights Law of Indigenous Peoples." *University of Hawai'i Law Review* 35, no. 2: 937–982.

Shoman, Assad. 1994. *Thirteen Chapters of a History of Belize*. Belize City: Angelus.

———. 2010. *Belize's Independence and Decolonization in Latin America: Guatemala, Britain, and the UN*. New York: Palgrave Macmillan.

———. 2011. *A History of Belize in 13 Chapters*. 2nd edition. Belize City: Angelus.

———. 2018. *Guatemala's Claim to Belize: The Definitive History* (International Edition). Belize City: Image Factory Art Foundation.

Sieder, Rachel, ed. 2002. *Multiculturalism in Latin America: Indigenous Rights, Diversity, and Democracy*. New York: Palgrave Macmillan.

———. 2011a. "Contested Sovereignties: Indigenous Law, Violence, and State Effects in Postwar Guatemala." *Critique of Anthropology* 3, no. 3: 161–184.

———. 2011b. "'Emancipation' or 'Regulation'? Law, Globalization and Indigenous Peoples' Rights in Post-war Guatemala." *Economy and Society* 40, no. 2: 239–265.

Sieder, Rachel, and Anna Barrera Vivero. 2017. "Legalizing Indigenous Self-Determination: Autonomy and Buen Vivir in Latin America." *Journal of Latin American and Caribbean Anthropology* 22, no. 1: 9–26.

Sieder, Rachel, Line Schjolden, and Alan Angell. 2005. "Introduction." In *The Judicialization of Politics in Latin America*, edited by Rachel Sieder, Line Schjolden, and Alan Angell, 1–20. New York: Palgrave Macmillan.

Simpson, Audra. 2014. *Mohawk Interruptus: Political Life across the Borders of Settler States*. Durham, NC: Duke University Press.

Slater, Candace. 2003. *In Search of the Rain Forest*. Durham, NC: Duke University Press.

Speed, Shannon. 2008. *Rights in Rebellion: Indigenous Struggles and Human Rights in Chiapas*. Palo Alto, CA: Stanford University Press.

Speed, Shannon, and Xochitl Leyva Solano. 2008. "Introduction: Human Rights in the Maya Region." In *Human Rights in the Maya Region: Global Politics, Cultural Contentions, and Moral Engagements*, edited by Pedro Pitarch, Shannon Speed, and Xochitl Leyva Solano, 1–23. Durham, NC: Duke University Press.

Stamatopoulou, Elsa. 2011. "Taking Cultural Rights Seriously: The Vision of the UN Declaration on the Rights of Indigenous Peoples." In *Reflections on the UN Declaration on the Rights of Indigenous Peoples*, edited by Stephen Allen and Alejandra Xanthaki, 387–412. Portland, OR: Hart.

Statistical Institute of Belize. 2013. *Belize Population and Housing Census 2010 Country Report*. Belmopan: Statistical Institute of Belize.

Stavenhagen, Rodolfo. 2008. "Cultural Rights and Human Rights: A Social Science Perspective." In *Human Rights in the Maya Region: Global Politics, Cultural Contentions, and Moral Engagements*, edited by Pedro Pitarch, Shannon Speed, and Xochitl Leyva Solano, 27–50. Durham, NC: Duke University Press.

———. 2011. "Making the Declaration on the Rights of Indigenous Peoples Work: The Challenge Ahead." In *Reflections on the UN Declaration on the Rights of Indigenous Peoples*, edited by Stephen Allen and Alejandra Xanthaki, 147–169. Portland, OR: Hart.

Stefania, Erico. 2011. "The Controversial Issue of Natural Resources: Balancing States' Sovereignty with Indigenous Peoples' Rights." In *Reflections on the UN Declaration on the Rights of Indigenous Peoples*, edited by Stephen Allen and Alejandra Xanthaki, 329–366. Portland, OR: Hart.

Stinson, James. 2013. "Mother Nature's Best Kept Secret? Exploring the Discursive Terrain and Lived Experience of the Ecotourism-Extraction Nexus in Southern Belize." In *The Ecotourism-Extraction Nexus: Political Economies and Rural Realities of (un)Comfortable Bedfellows*, edited by Bram Buscher and Veronica Davidov, 108–129. New York: Routledge.

———. 2017. "The Will to Conserve? Environmentality, Translation, and Politics of Conservation in Southern Belize." PhD diss., University of Toronto.

Takacs, David. 1996. *The Idea of Biodiversity: Philosophies of Paradise*. Baltimore: Johns Hopkins University Press.

Tanner, Lauri R. 2009. "Interview with Judge Antonio A. Cancado Trindade, Inter-American Court of Human Rights." *Human Rights Quarterly* 31, no. 4: 985–1000.

"Ten Points of Agreement between the Government of Belize and the Maya Peoples of Southern Belize." 2000. October 12. Document in author's possession.

Tennant, Chris. 1994. "Indigenous Peoples, International Institutions, and the International Legal Literature from 1945–1993." *Human Rights Quarterly* 16, no. 1: 1–57.

Thompson, J. Eric S. 1930. "Ethnology of the Mayas of Southern and Central British Honduras." Field Museum of Natural History Publication 274, Anthropological Series 17, no. 2. Chicago: Field Museum of Natural History.

———. 1988. *The Maya of Belize: Historical Chapters since Columbus*. Belize: Cubola Productions.

Thornberry, Patrick. 1993. "The Democratic or Internal Aspect of Self-Determination with Some Remarks on Federalism." In *Modern Law of Self-Determination*, edited by Christian Tomuschat, 101–138. Boston: M. Nijhoff Publishers.

Toledo Alcaldes Association and Maya Leaders Alliance. 2014. "Maya Consultation Framework." June 13. Document in author's possession.

Toledo Maya Cultural Council (TMCC). 1995. Proposal for Mapping Maya Land Use in the Toledo District, Belize, Central America. Belize Archives and Records Service, MC-3723.

Toledo Maya Cultural Council (TMCC), and Toledo Alcaldes Association (TAA). 1997. *Maya Atlas*. Berkeley, CA: North Atlantic Books.

Toledo Maya Lands Rights Commission (TMLRC), the Maya Leaders Alliance (MLA), and the Toledo Alcaldes Association (TAA). 2018. Agreement reached between the Toledo Maya Land Rights Commission and the Maya Leaders Alliance and Toledo Alcaldes Association. Punta Gorda, Belize.

Tsing, Anna. 2005. *Friction: An Ethnography of Global Connection*. Princeton, NJ: Princeton University Press.

Tsing, Anna, J. Peter Brosius, and Charles Zerner. 2005. "Introduction." In *Communities and Conservation*, edited by J. Peter Brosius, Anna Lowenhaupt Tsing, and Charles Zerner, 1–34. Walnut Creek, CA: Altamira.

Tully, James. 2000. "The Struggles of Indigenous Peoples for and of Freedom." In *Political Theory and the Rights of Indigenous Peoples*, edited by Duncan Ivison, Paul Patton, and Will Sanders, 36–59. Cambridge: Cambridge University Press.

United Nations Committee on the Elimination of All Forms of Discrimination (UN CERD). 1997. *General Recommendation 23: Indigenous Peoples*. U.N. Doc. A/52/18, Annex V. https://www.eods.eu/library/UN_International%20Convention%20on%20the%20Elimination%20of%20Racial%20Discrimination_General%20recommendation%2023_1997_EN.pdf.

United Nations Declaration on the Rights of Indigenous Peoples (UNDRIP). 2007. https://www.un.org/esa/socdev/unpfii/documents/DRIPS_en.pdf, accessed July 13, 2023.

United Nations Human Rights Committee (UN HRC). 1994. *General Comment 23: The Rights of Minorities (Article 27)*. U.N. Doc. CCPR/C/21/Rev. 1/Add. 5.

Urry, John. 1990. *The Tourist Gaze: Leisure and Travel in Contemporary Societies*. London: SAGE Publications.

Van Ausdal, Shawn K. 2000. "Development and Discourse among the Maya of Southern Belize." MA thesis, University of California, Berkeley.

———. 2001. "Development and Discourse among the Maya of Southern Belize." *Development and Change* 32, no. 3: 577–606.

Van Banning, Theo R. G. 2002. *The Human Right to Property*. New York: Intersentia.

Van Cott, Donna. 2000. *The Friendly Liquidation of the Past: The Politics of Diversity in Latin America*. Pittsburgh: University of Pittsburgh Press.

van den Berghe, Pierre L. 1995. "Marketing Mayas: Ethnic Tourism Promotion in Mexico." *Annals of Tourism Research* 22, no. 3: 568–588.

Vernon, Dylan. 2022. *Political Clientelism and Democracy in Belize: From My Hand to Yours*. Kingston: University of the West Indies Press.

Vivanco, Luis. 2006. *Green Encounters: Shaping and Contesting Environmentalism in Rural Costa Rica*. New York: Berghahn Books.

Wagner, Roy. 1975. *The Invention of Culture*. Chicago: University of Chicago Press.

Waight, Lydia, and Judy Lumb. 1999. *Belize Audubon Society: The First Thirty Years*. Caye Caulker, Belize: Producciones de la Hamaca.

Wainwright, Joel. 2007. *Decolonizing Development: Colonial Power and the Maya*. Oxford: Blackwell Publishing.

———. 2015. "The Colonial Origins of the State in Southern Belize." *Historical Geography* 43: 122–138.

Wainwright, Joel, and Joe Bryan. 2009. "Cartography, Territory, Property: Postcolonial Reflections on Indigenous Counter-mapping in Nicaragua and Belize." *Cultural Geographies* 16, no. 2: 153–178.

Warren, Kay. 1998. *Indigenous Movements and Their Critics: Pan-Maya Activism in Guatemala*. Princeton, NJ: Princeton University Press.

Watt, Melanie. 1989. *Jaguar Woman: One Woman's Struggle to Preserve the Jaguars of Belize*. Toronto: Key Porter Books.

Webber, Jeremy. 2000. "Beyond Regret: Mabo's Implications for Australian Constitutionalism." In *Political Theory and the Rights of Indigenous Peoples*, edited by Duncan Ivison, Paul Patton, and Will Sanders, 60–88. Cambridge: Cambridge University Press.

West, Paige. 2005. *Conservation Is Our Government Now: The Politics of Ecology in Papua New Guinea*. Durham, NC: Duke University Press.

West, Paige, James Igoe, and Dan Brockington. 2006. "Parks and Peoples: The Social Impact of Protected Areas." *Annual Review of Anthropology* 35: 251–277.

Western, David. 1993. "Defining Ecotourism." In *Ecotourism: A Guide for Planners and Managers*, edited by K. Lindberg and D. Hawkins, 7–11. North Bennington, VT: Ecotourism Society.

Wight, Pam. 2001. "Ecotourists: Not a Homogenous Market Segment." In *The Encyclopedia of Ecotourism*, edited by D. B. Weaver, 37–62. New York: CABI.
Wilk, Richard. 1986. "Mayan Ethnicity in Belize." *Cultural Survival Quarterly* 10: 73–77.
———. 1991. *Household Ecology: Economic Change and Domestic Life among the Kekchi Maya of Belize.* Tucson: University of Arizona Press.
———. 1997. *Household Ecology: Economic Change and Domestic Life among the Kekchi Maya of Belize.* [reprint] DeKalb: Northern Illinois University Press.
———. 2006. *Home Cooking in the Global Village: Caribbean Food from Buccaneers to Ecotourists.* New York: Berg.
Wilson, Richard. 1995. *Maya Resurgence in Guatemala: Q'eqchi' Experiences.* Norman: University of Oklahoma Press.
World Bank. 1984. *Belize Economic Report.* Washington, DC: World Bank.
Yashar, Deborah. 1998. "Contesting Citizenship: Indigenous Movements and Democracy in Latin America." *Comparative Politics* 31, no. 1: 23–42.
———. 1999. "Democracy, Indigenous Movements, and the Postliberal Challenge in Latin America." *World Politics* 52: 76–104.
Zarger, Rebecca. 2002. "Acquisition and Transmission of Subsistence Knowledge by Q'eqchi'Maya in Belize." In *Ethnobiology and Biocultural Diversity: Proceedings of the Seventh International Congress of Ethnobiology*, edited by J. R. Stepp, Felice Wyndham, and Rebecca Zarger, 593–603. Athens: University of Georgia Press.
———. 2009. "Mosaics of Maya Livelihoods." *NAPA Bulletin* 32: 130–151.

## NEWSPAPERS/NEWSLETTERS CITED

*Amandala*
*The Beacon*
*Belize Audubon Society Newsletter*
*Belize Times*

## TELEVISION PROGRAMS CITED

Channel 5 News, Belize
Channel 7 News, Belize
*Wake Up Belize!* Channel 5, Belize

## CASES CITED

*Attorney General of Belize et al. v. Maya Leaders Alliance et al.* [Civil Appeal No. 27 of 2010], Belize Court of Appeal Judgment of July 25, 2013.
*Awas Tingni v. Nicaragua*, Inter-A. Ct. H.R. (Ser. C) No. 79 [2001].
*Cal et al. v. Attorney General* (Claims Nos. 171 and 172 of 2007), Belize S. Ct. Judgment of October 18, 2007.
CCJ Appeal No BACV2014/002.
*Delgamuukw v. British Columbia* [1997] 3 S.C.R. 1010.
*Mabo v. Queensland*, (1992) 175 C.L.R. 1.
*Maya Indigenous Communities of Toledo District v. Belize*, Case No. 12.053 (Belize), Inter-Am C.H.R. Report No. 40/04, October 12, 2004, OAS Doc. OEA/Ser. L/V/II.122, Doc. 5 rev. 1 (2005).
*Maya Leaders Alliance et al. v. Attorney General et al.* [Claim No. 366 of 2008], Belize S. Ct. Judgment of June 28, 2010.

# Index

Note: Page numbers in italics refer to illustrations

aboriginal title. *See* common law: and native title
agency: and resistance, 81; and subjection, 68, 77, 81
Alcalde System, 89; colonial use of, 123, 138; incorporation into Belizean law, 123; institutions of, 86, 145, 148; as Maya customary tenure, 98, 123–124, 158; practice of, 85–86, 123, 143–147; regulation of access to community lands, 85–86, 123; regulation of village membership, 86, 123; state attacks on, 90–92, 147–150, 152–156
American Convention on Human Rights, 108–109, 110, 115
American Declaration on the Rights and Duties of Man, 111, 115, 122, 124, 128, 171nn10,11
American Declaration on the Rights of Indigenous Peoples, 104, 108, 112
Anaya, S. James: and Awas Tingni litigation, 109–110; and Belizean Maya litigation, 98, 111, 116, 122, 129, 172nn1,3; and turn to human rights, 103, 106
Awas Tingni, 109–110, 111, 114, 115–116

Belizean history: as contested, 22; dominant narrative of, 26, 35, 92, 113, 124, 125, 168n5; scholarly narrative of, 125–127
Belize Audubon Society (BAS): and devolution of protected areas management, 1–3, 56–58, 169n6; engagement with the market for ecotourism, 62–63, 69, 82, 159–160, 169n2; history of, 44–46; international alliances, 44–54; and NGO government of state officials, 56–58, 62. *See also* education campaign, BAS
Belize constitution: guarantee of nondiscrimination, 135; protections for property, 111, 122, 124, 128, 131, 134–135, 137, 153; reference to Indigenous peoples, 98, 122
Belize Court of Appeal: engagement with the common law, 134–136; Maya lands case decision, 134–137
Belize Supreme Court, 98–99; Jalacte decision, 153; 2007 Maya lands case, 121–127; 2007 Maya lands judgment, 127–129; 2008 Maya lands case, 130–132; 2010 Maya lands judgment, 134; 2019 Santa Cruz case, 152–153
Belize Territorial Volunteers, 150–151; conflicts with Belizean government, 151, 157; confrontations with Guatemalan military, 151, 157; performance of Belizean sovereignty, 150–151
Belize Tourism Board: marketing of Belizean tourism products, 16, 43, 51–52, 58–60, 74; and tourism policy, 43, 51, 58–60
Belize Tourism Industry Association, 51, 59, 74
biodiversity crisis, 43–44

cacao farmers, 131–132
Caribbean Court of Justice: compliance hearings, 152–154; 2015 consent order, 137; 2015 judgment, 137–138
Caste War, 31; conflict between Maya groups, 31–32; and migration, 32–33; role of British merchants, 31, 33

193

Cho, Julian, 93–94, 95, 99
Ch'oc, Greg: as Commissioner of Indigenous Peoples Affairs, 155, 156; as NGO leader, 155; as spokesperson for Maya Leaders Alliance, 132, 172n13
Chols, 23; forced removal of, 26; in government argument in Maya lands cases, 125, 134–136; integration into Q'eqchi communities, 126; in Maya argument in Maya lands cases, 126; relations with Itzajs, 25; Spanish efforts to evangelize and concentrate, 25–26
citizens' rights, 9, 139
clientelism, political, 89, 92
Coc, Cristina, 132, *142*, 145, 149, 150, 154, 155
Cockscomb Basin Wildlife Sanctuary: creation of, 46–55, 65–66; management of, 50, 61–62, 69, 77–82. *See also* Rabinowitz, Alan
Committee on the Elimination of Racial Discrimination (CERD), 106–107, 118; general recommendation, 107
commodification: of Maya culture, 60–61, 114, 169n12; of Maya lands, 89, 94, 157, 160, 162; of nature, 2–3, 17, 42, 51–53, 57–62, 67, 75–78, 82
common law, the: criteria for indigeneity, 13, 124, 127, 132, 135–136; and customary tenure, 29–30, 111, 112, 123; and native title, 112, 123, 128, 135; relation to state legal system, 139–140; use in Maya legal argument, 127
consent order, CCJ. *See under* Caribbean Court of Justice
conservation: and biodiversity crisis, 43–44; and ecotourism, 52–58; and protected areas creation, 52–58
Conteh, Abdulai, 125–126; and general principles, 129; and international customary law, 129; and 2007 Maya lands decision, 127–129; and 2010 Maya lands decision, 134
cosmovision: Indigenous, 18; Mopan, 69, 84–85; Q'eqchi', 85
critical conduct of rights, 15–16, 118–119, 138–139, 160–161. *See also* paradox of rights
culture: anthropological debates over definition, 14–15; as constructed, 14–15; definition in international Indigenous rights standards, 18, 105–107, 112, 116–117; right to, 5, 103, 106–107, 117, 162; as source of property, 5, 18, 117; state definition of, ethnic, 37–39, 136; state definition of, national, 39–40. *See also under* commodification; Indigenous rights: collective subject of

customary law, international: definition of, 112; Indigenous rights as, 112, 122, 129
customary tenure: and the common law, 29, 112, 123, 127; interface with Belizean legal system, 19, 138–141, 161–163; as practice of freedom, 146; as source of Baymen's property, 29; as source of Indigenous collective property, 5, 15, 19, 112–117, 122–124, 128, 134, 138–139. *See also* Alcalde System; common law, the

debt crisis, 6–7, 16, 42–43, 44, 48–50, 52
deforestation, 43, 48
devolution of state responsibilities: to BAS, 50, 57, 62, 67–82, 133, 159; to the market, 3, 52, 63, 72–82

ecosystem, Western concept of, 69–71
ecotourism: and conservation, 58–60; definition of, 58; as mechanism for neoliberal environmental government, 3, 63, 67, 160; resorts, coastal, 59, 74–75, 79–81, 170
education campaign, BAS, 68; and aesthetic value of nature, 71–72; and ecological value of nature, 17, 69–71
environmental subject: content of, 76–77; exercise of agency by, 77–81; formation of, 67–77; neoliberal, 76–77. *See also* education campaign, BAS
ethnolinguistic categories: assumptions regarding, 37–39, 125; shift from racial classification to, 37, 39. *See also* language ideology, Belizean
evolutionary method of interpretation, 109, 110, 114, 115, 117

Forestry Department: and forest management, 36, 47, 49–50, 53–54, 84, 87, 94, 130; downsizing of, 36, 94; performance of state sovereignty, 2, 53, 78, 160
forests: as endangered, 48, 70; as idle lands, 40, 42; as potential agricultural lands, 40, 43, 44, 48; as potential ecotourism attractions, 57, 71; as source of food and housing materials, 47, 66, 69, 86, 96; as source of timber, 3, 5, 17, 29–33, 36, 40, 48, 58; as watersheds, 48, 70
Foucault, Michel: on governmentality, 10–13; on intersections of sovereignty and government, 13, 168n9; on liberalism, 11; on neoliberalism, 8, 12, 14, 168n8; on rights, 8–9; on sovereignty, 9–10; on the state, 3–4, 8–9; on subjects and subjection, 68
free, prior, and informed consent, 143–144, 153, 155. *See also* Maya Consultation Framework

## INDEX

gender: circumscription of women's movement, 72; and income, 72, 74, 77–78, 79, 81; and intra-household conflict, 73–74; and women's activism, 2, 77–79
general principles of international law: in Indigenous legal arguments, 112–113, 122; in judicial decisions, 129, 135. *See also* nondiscrimination, general principle of
govern for the market. *See under* market, the
government: neoliberal, 8, 12–13, 42, 119, 159, 161–164; rationality of, 10
governmentality. *See under* Foucault, Michel
govern through the market. *See under* market, the
Grandia, Liza, 123, 126, 131, 172n13
Guatemalan claim, 32, 35; and International Court of Justice, 109, 133, 150; and Maya lands cases, 125; and 1859 treaty, 8, 37, 41, 133, 151, 168. *See also* Guatemalan incursions
Guatemalan incursions: by civilians, 133, 149; by military, 3, 133, 150; in southern Belize, 133, 150; in western Belize, 133, 149

homo economicus: liberal conceptualization, 11; neoliberal conceptualization, 12, 13, 158. *See also* market subject
human rights: production of, 8–9, 101; use in production of Indigenous rights, 18, 102, 106–107. *See also* International Convention on Civil and Political Rights (ICCPR); International Convention on Economic, Social, and Cultural Rights (ICESCR); International Convention on the Elimination of Racial Discrimination (ICERD); paradox of rights; Universal Declaration of Human Rights (UDHR); *under* culture; *under* property
Human Rights Committee. *See* UN Human Rights Committee

Indian Law Resource Center, 90, 91, 92, 95, 98, 107, 109, 111
Indigeneity, criteria for: defined by attorneys for Belizean state, 113; defined by Belize Court of Appeal, 136, 161; defined by IACHR, 114; defined by ILO 169, 114; in Maya legal argument, 127
Indigenous rights: collective subject of, 18–19, 77, 107, 113, 116–118; culture-bearing subject of, 102, 116, 124, 129, 131–132, 158, 160, 163; Inter-American jurisprudence on, 5, 18, 20, 101, 107–108, 109–119; production of, 5–6, 18, 92, 101–119. *See also* self-determination

indirect rule, 84. *See also* Alcalde System
Inter-American Commission on Human Rights (IACHR): authority of, 108; decisions by, 109–110, 114–116; and development of jurisprudence on Indigenous rights, 109–110, 114–116; and drafting of American Declaration on the Rights of Indigenous Peoples, 104
Inter-American Court of Human Rights (IACtHR): authority of, 108; decisions by, 109–110; and development of jurisprudence on Indigenous rights, 109–110, 115–116
Inter-American Human Rights System, 108; jurisprudence of, 114–116
International Convention on Civil and Political Rights (ICCPR), 9, 135, 138, 106; right to culture, 106–107, 109, 110, 112, 115, 117, 122; right to self-determination, 102, 103; and UN Human Rights Committee, 106–107, 171n8
International Convention on Economic, Social, and Cultural Rights (ICESCR), 9, 102, 103
International Convention on the Elimination of Racial Discrimination (ICERD): and CERD general recommendation, 107; protections for culture, 106–107; protections for minorities, 106; use in Indigenous rights litigation, 107, 109–110, 115, 117. *See also* Committee on the Elimination of Racial Discrimination; nondiscrimination, general principle of
International Labor Organization (ILO): criteria for indigeneity, 114; Convention 107 of 1957, 104; Convention 169 of 1989, 104–105; use of ILO 169 in Indigenous rights litigation, 107, 110, 112, 114, 115, 161
Itzaj kingdom, 23; and challenges to Spanish colonial rule, 25; conquest of, 26

Jalacte, 152–153, 157
Jones, Grant: affidavits, 123, 126, 131; citations to published works, 23–26
Julian Cho Society, 143, 144, 154

language ideology, Belizean: assumptions regarding descent, 37–39, 125; and ethnic classification, 37–39, 125. *See also* ethnolinguistic categories
legal pluralism, 6–7, 16, 19, 138–140, 152–158, 160–161
liberalism. *See under* Foucault, Michel
locations: as property, 29, 123; incorporation into colonial property system, 30
logging concessions: in Cockscomb, 49, 52; in Toledo District, 93–94, 96, 98–99, 111

market, the: conjuring of, 51–52, 57–60; governing for, 12, 17, 78, 81, 89, 99, 159–160; governing through, 3, 12, 52–60, 61–63, 75–82, 159–160; and the invisible hand, 11–12, 167nn6, 7; for land in Toledo District, 89, 99, 157, 160; 'natural processes' of, 11–12; research on, 58, 62, 63. *See also* commodification; Foucault, Michel; market rationality

market rationality, 1, 12–13, 61–63, 75–76, 81–82, 146, 159–160, 163; and agency, 77, 81–82, 146, 159, 160; production of, 75; in relation to non-market values, 29, 120, 162–163

market subject: calculations by, 12, 76, 78–82; mobilization of, 72–82; production of, 12, 66–67, 72–75, 163. *See also* homo economicus; market rationality

Maya Atlas: maps, 96, 97; narratives, 96–98; production of, 95–96; use as evidence in legal cases, 96, 113, 123, 126

Maya Centre: engagement with BAS, 72–82; engagement with tourism, 71–87; establishment of, 64–65; incomes from tourism, 74–75, 76, 80–81; and residents' indigenous ecological knowledge, 66, 69; lands, 65–67

Maya Centre Women's Group: confrontation with BAS, 77–81; creation of, 72–75; and gendered impact of tourism revenues, 73–75

Maya Consultation Framework, 144, 153, 155

Maya homeland, 91–92, 93, 95

Maya Land Rights Commission, 152–154

Maya Leaders Alliance, 23, 130; and implementation of judicial decisions, 143–152, 144–145, 157; involvement in legal cases, 123, 130, 132, 137, *142*, 143; statements by, 132, 148

Maya Mapping Project. *See* Maya Atlas: production of

milpa, 165; annual cycle, 35, 86, 89; denigration of, 70, 87; practice of, 35, 85, 86, *96*; rituals related to, 85; social networks required for, 85

Minister of Natural Resources, 1, 13, 16, 45–46, 48–49, 53–54, 62, 94

Ministry of Indigenous Peoples Affairs, 155, 177n38

Ministry of Natural Resources, 44, 47; involvement in conservation, 45, 46, 49, 50, 52, 62, 159; responsibilities of, 46. *See also* Forestry Department; Minister of Natural Resources

Ministry of Tourism and the Environment: adoption of ecotourism strategy, 57–58; and early development of tourism, 43, 45; and economic value of environment, 57

Moore, Antoinette, 122, 126, 131, 135, *142*

Mundo Maya, 60–61, 119, 169n12

Myles, Rupert: and Belizean antiquities law, 148, 150, 152–153; claims of racial discrimination, 147; conflict with Santa Cruz village, 147–148, 153; destruction of Maya site, 147–148, 150; state failure to prosecute, 150, 152–153, 160

naleb', 85

native title. *See under* common law, the

neoliberalism: dominant approaches to, 3, 12–13; and nature, 3; and environmental government, 3, 75–82. *See also under* Foucault, Michel

nondiscrimination: constitutional right to, 129, 131, 135; general principle of, 112, 116

nongovernmental organizations (NGOs): and conservation, 1, 16, 43–44, 45, 46–55, 67–82, 133; devolution of power from state to, 3, 57, 67–82, 133, 159; government by, 45, 46–61, 67–82, 159; and Indigenous rights, 90–91, 95, 98; relationships with state actors, 45–46; transnational alliances of, 45–61, 90–91, 95–98

oil exploration concessions, 5, 17, 83, 94–95, 99, 111, 115, 149

Organization of American States (OAS), 18; and Guatemalan claim, 133; and Inter-American Human Rights System, 99, 101, 104, 108, 128. *See also* American Convention on Human Rights; American Declaration on the Rights and Duties of Man; American Declaration on the Rights of Indigenous Peoples

paradox of rights, 9, 15–16, 118–119, 138–139, 141–157, 160–161

Peoples United Party, 155; production of Belizean nation, 37; pursuit of independence, 36; and ten points of agreement, 111. *See also* clientelism, political

property: collective, 5, 6, 117, 139; as foundational to capitalism, 13–14, 119; individual, 4, 13–15, 18–19, 22, 29–30, 40, 99, 112–128; production of, 104, 108, 110, 112–115, 122, 128; right to, 5, 18

Quam Bank: eviction, 65–67; lands request, 65; settlement, 65

INDEX

raal cho'och, 145
Rabinowitz, Alan: jaguar research, 44, 46–47; lobbying for protected area, 44, 47–49, 52–53
rationality of government. *See under* Foucault, Michel; government
Reservation Lands Committee, 93, 95
reservations: and Belizean law, 84, 92; privatization of, 89; state creation of, 84; state efforts to abolish, 87–88; state mapping of, 84
resistance, 68, 81, 146
respect: offering, 69, 84–85; relations of, 19, 84–85, 146, 163. *See also* naleb'; tzik
rights. *See* citizens' rights; culture: right to; human rights; Indigenous rights; paradox of rights; property: right to

Santa Cruz Village, 96; arrest of alcalde system leaders, 148–150; conflict with Rupert Myles, 147–150; demarcation of lands, 121; and 2007 Maya lands case, 121–130; and 2019 Supreme Court case, 152–153
seeing. *See* tourist gaze
self-determination: definitions of, 10, 19, 103, 146; Indigenous demands for, 9–10, 18, 102–104, 116, 162–163; right to, 10, 102; state opposition to, 18, 103–105, 116, 119, 170nn4, 5, 173n48
southern highway, construction of, 64, 87, 94
sovereignty: competing claims to, 22–37; failure of state to perform, 75, 94, 134, 150–151; impact of legal pluralism on practice of, 118–119, 139, 161; Maya collective land ownership cast as threat to, 125, 132, 149–150; as performance, 4; performed by non-state actors, 67, 150–157; performed by state actors, 13, 40–41, 78, 81, 99, 121, 148–149, 159; privatization of, 67, 75; selective, 151
state, the: as guarantor of rights, 9, 15, 118, 141; and lack of mastery over rights, 119, 138, 160–161; performative nature of, 3–4, 5, 8. *See also* sovereignty; territory
strategic litigation, 18, 101, 107, 110, 115, 117, 119
subject of rights, 13. *See also* Indigenous rights: collective subject of
subsistence security, 35, 66–67, 78–79

Ten Points of Agreement, 111, 115, 125, 128, 135
territory: Belize as uninhabited, 26, 113, 125, 150; performance of, 4, 8; in relation to lands, 106, 110, 153; in relation to property, 4, 22, 40–41, 106, 127–128, 135, 153, 162; and sovereignty, 3–4, 8, 10, 22–41, 83, 97, 149–150, 162
Toledo Alcaldes Association (TAA): creation of, 92; leadership in land struggles, 93, 95, 130, 132, 143–144, 153, 155–156; membership in, 92; relation to village alcaldes, 92, 143
Toledo Cacao Growers Association, 131
Toledo Indian Movement, 90
Toledo Maya Cultural Council (TMCC), 90–91, 95, 111, 156
tourism: Belizean brand, 43, 50–52, 58–61; growth of, 61; marketing, 50–52, 58–61. *See also* ecotourism; Mundo Maya
tourist gaze, 72, 76
tzik: definition, 84–85; relations, 69, 84–85
Tzuultaq'a, 85, 170n1

UN Declaration on the Granting of Independence to Colonial Countries and Peoples, 9, 102
UN Declaration on the Rights of Indigenous Peoples (UNDRIP): cited in Indigenous rights cases, 112; cited in Indigenous rights judgments, 110, 114, 129; drafting of, 102–104; and land rights, 103, 129; state opposition to, 103–104; UN General Assembly vote on, 129, 170n5
UN Human Rights Committee (HRC), 106–107, 171; general comment, 106–107, 171n8
United Democratic Party, 50, 89, 94, 99, 154; and conservation, 53, 55, 169n6; response to Maya lands decisions, 130; and Santa Cruz incident, 132, 147, 149, 150, 154. *See also* clientelism, political
Universal Declaration of Human Rights (UDHR), 9, 102
UN Working Group on Indigenous Populations. *See* Working Group on Indigenous Populations

Village Council System: collaboration with Alcalde System, 152, 155; as conduit for political party patronage, 89, 92; imposition on Maya communities by state, 89, 92, 99–100; state prioritization of, 152, 155
Village Meeting: as Alcalde System institution, 86, 92, 144, 148; as practice that brings community into being, 145

Wildlife Conservation Society (WCS), 40–48, 52–54, 65
Wilk, Richard: affidavits and testimony, 123, 126, 131, 172nn13, 14, 25; citations to published work, 23, 30–36 passim, 40, 43, 84–87 passim, 92, 147, 170n1
Witz-hok, 69, 84–85

Working Group on Indigenous Populations (WGIP), 91, 95, 102–104. *See also* UN Declaration on the Rights of Indigenous Peoples
World Wildlife Foundation (WWF), 45, 50, 52–54, 62

zone of refuge, Belize as, 26, 126